Between
RELIGION and
POLITICS

Nathan J. Brown and Amr Hamzawy

CARNEGIE ENDOWMENT

FOR INTERNATIONAL PEACE

WASHINGTON DC ▪ MOSCOW ▪ BEIJING ▪ BEIRUT ▪ BRUSSELS

Carnegie Endowment for International Peace
1779 Massachusetts Avenue, N.W., Washington, D.C. 20036
202-483-7600, Fax 202-483-1840
www.CarnegieEndowment.org

The Carnegie Endowment does not take institutional positions on public policy issues;
the views represented here are the authors' own and do not necessarily reflect the
views of the Endowment, its staff, or its trustees.

To order, contact:
Hopkins Fulfillment Service
P.O. Box 50370, Baltimore, MD 21211-4370
1-800-537-5487 or 1-410-516-6956
Fax 1-410-516-6998

The Carnegie Endowment for International Peace gratefully acknowledges the
United States Institute of Peace for its generous support for this research initiative
and the publication of this study.

Library of Congress Cataloging-in-Publication Data

Brown, Nathan J.
Between religion and politics / Nathan J. Brown and Amr Hamzawy.
    p. cm.

    Includes bibliographical references and index.

    ISBN 978-0-87003-255-4 (pbk.) — ISBN 978-0-87003-256-1 (cloth)
1. Islam and politics—Middle East. 2. Islam and politics—Islamic countries.
3. Islamic fundamentalism—Middle East. 4. Muslims—Political activity—Middle East.
5. Political participation—Middle East. 6. Middle East—Politics and government—
21st century. I. Hamzawy, Amr. II. Title.

    BP63.A35B48 2010
    324.20917'67—dc22

                                                                        2010016117

Mixed Sources
Product group from well-managed
forests, controlled sources and
recycled wood or fiber
www.fsc.org Cert no. BV-COC-070702
© 1996 Forest Stewardship Council
FSC

Contents

Foreword

Over the past decade, Islamists have been thrust by events and by their own efforts into the center of the political stage in a number of Arab countries. The parties and movements that Nathan J. Brown and Amr Hamzawy consider in this volume are not ones that form small cells for violent actions. Rather, they are large, diverse organizations that seek (among other things) to participate in the established political process.

The various parties and movements considered here—in Egypt, Morocco, Yemen, Jordan, Palestine, and Kuwait—are hardly new. Most go back decades. But in recent years, all have taken a much stronger interest in electoral competition and parliamentary politics. It is the initial success of these efforts that has earned them so much attention in the Arab world and abroad. In Egypt, the Muslim Brotherhood won one-fifth of the seats in the 2005 parliamentary elections. In Morocco, the Party for Justice and Development earned more votes than any other party in the 2007 parliamentary elections (though because of the electoral system it finished second). The Palestinian Hamas movement won the first parliamentary elections it entered in 2006. In Yemen, Jordan, and Kuwait, Islamist parties and movements have been slower but steadier players; in each country they have also experimented with sitting in the government and trying to form opposition coalitions.

In *Between Religion and Politics,* Brown and Hamzawy delve into the parliamentary experience of Islamists: What made them decide to step up their involvement in parliamentary politics? What did they do with the seats they won? How has the Islamists' embrace of parliamentary elections affected their relations with the regime? Have they managed to build coalitions with other political actors, especially liberal and leftist parties? And how are they likely to react to the ebbing tide of democratization in the region?

The essays in this book explore a kind of "in between" politics—regimes playing with democratic procedures without being fully committed to them and Islamists investing in political participation without sacrificing their broad focus on religious and social activism. And although the long-term impacts of this political "gray zone" remain to be seen, it has already injected elements of dynamism and competition into what was otherwise a persistently stagnant polity in the Arab world.

Jessica T. Mathews
President, Carnegie Endowment for International Peace

Preface

This book represents a collaboration in two senses.

First, it is a collaboration between the two authors—one in which each of us has contributed our own interests and expertise individually but also enriched each other's understanding of the role of Islamists in Arab politics. The resulting work is therefore more than the sum of each of our individual parts. While we both share responsibility for the final product, we should note that Amr Hamzawy contributed the chapters on Morocco and Yemen; Nathan J. Brown wrote those on Kuwait, Jordan, and Palestine. The introduction, conclusion, and Egypt chapter are joint efforts.

Second, the book signifies a different kind of collaboration—that between its authors and a collection of institutions and individuals who contributed their own efforts and support to the project.

In that regard, we wish to acknowledge two institutions: the Carnegie Endowment for International Peace, where we both serve as senior associates; and the United States Institute of Peace (USIP), which contributed vital funding to the project. Carnegie has provided both material support and a very genial research environment. USIP grant support made possible a good portion of the research and writing of the country studies. Of course, the conclusions in this book are only our own and do not represent the institutional positions of Carnegie or USIP.

On an individual basis, three officials at Carnegie deserve special mention: Tom Carothers (for reading drafts and editorial suggestions), Marina Ottaway (for research cooperation and endless discussions on the topic), and Ilonka Oszvald for gracefully combining patience with speed in dealing with all the editorial and publishing issues. At USIP, Steve Riskin has been extremely supportive, especially on matters requiring cooperation between USIP and Carnegie.

Conversations with many colleagues have helped sharpen our thinking on the subject of this book. At the risk of omitting many names of those whose own insights shaped our understanding, we make special mention of Janine Clark, Michele Dunne, Shadi Hamid, Marc Lynch, Michael McFaul, Samer Shehata, Amr al-Shubaki, Josh Stacher, Hussam Tamam, and Carrie Rosefsky Wickham.

And we have incurred more debts as well. We have received invaluable assistance in our research from Dina Bishara, Russ Burns, Andrew Clark, Sarah Grebowski, Jessica Guiney, Mohammed Herzallah, Bassam Moussa, Khaled Waleed, and Diane Zoghivian.

We would be remiss not to mention activists in the movements themselves, who gave very generously of their time in order to provide us with their views on their own political experience.

Finally, we dedicate this book to Luay, Nuh, Ariel, and Eran in the wish that the world in which they live as adults can make greater strides than the one they now inhabit in discovering ways that faith and politics in all their myriad forms may enrich each other.

CHAPTER 1

Islamists in Arab Parliaments

In the last two decades of the twentieth century, Islamist political movements in many Arab countries made a strategic investment in a political process that was stacked against them. They did so in a series of ways, but the most prominent by far was their participation in parliamentary elections. By the first decade of the twenty-first century, their investments appeared to pay off. A series of impressive electoral gains—in Jordan, they have formed the largest opposition bloc; in Kuwait, they have participated both in the cabinet and in opposition coalitions that forced a major electoral reform and sought to bring down the prime minister; in Egypt, in 2005 they won a majority of races they decided to contest; in Morocco, before the 2007 elections they polled the support of almost half the electorate (and ultimately finished a close second to the largest party); in Yemen, they have been a member of a governing coalition and the leading opposition party; and in Palestine, they won a landslide victory and found themselves forced to form the cabinet.

This upsurge sparked different reactions inside and outside the region. Externally, interest in the rise of Islamist movements is inextricably linked to concerns either about terrorism or violence. But the rise of parliamentary Islamism also came at a time when Western interest in promoting democracy and political reform in the Arab world increased, leading to curiosity as well as concern about this apparently potent political force.

Internally, there was also an ambivalent reaction. In some countries, Islamist movements have evolved into cautiously accepted actors in the political arena. While they certainly provoke deep concerns, they are seen as valid players in the limited democratic space that exists in parliament and the press. But in other countries the rise of parliamentary Islamism was regarded by regimes less as a political challenge than as a security threat. Indeed, it is not merely regimes that are unsure of what to make of Islamist participation. The movements themselves are often of two minds. Islamist participation in the political process is not a new phenomenon, but its significance for the movements has recently risen dramatically. When they first entered into politics, the major coordinates of parliamentary Islamism were generally religious purity and moral politics. Islamist platforms generally prescribed a simple solution to the persistent crises of contemporary Arab societies: a return to the fundamentals of Islam or the true spirit of Islam. Slogans such as "Islam is the Solution" and "The Qur'an is our Constitution" have traditionally proved effective in mobilizing enough voters to gain a smattering of seats.

As Islamist movements have gradually integrated liberal and pragmatic notions about politics in rhetoric and practice, this general ideological frame of reference has never vanished. Yet deeper participation in the political process faces Islamist movements today with the challenge of how to manage ideological claims with the pragmatic tussles of politics. On the one hand, Islamists might move toward broader agendas, orienting themselves toward more pragmatic and consensual positions.

But while subordinating ideological claims to the pragmatic concerns of daily political participation may often promote liberal trends within Islamist movements, there are also countervailing trends. Excessive ideological fluidity risks alienating core constituencies, especially in the case of those movements that have not institutionally separated their religious, often missionary, activities from the political role. Further, Islamist movements might find that they could generate broader support not through becoming more liberal but by highlighting issues (such as religious dissidence or controversial cultural expression) where they can mobilize public opinion against other, more liberal opposition forces. The problematic (and sometimes clearly manipulated) nature of Arab elections, coupled with the limited authority of the parliaments that are filled in those elections, discourage Islamist movements from attempting to assemble broad majority coalitions.

In short, as they entered the electoral fray with increasing enthusiasm, Islamist movements were exposed to powerful, but sometimes contradictory, political pressures and attractive, but potentially costly, opportunities.

Islamists' experiences in parliaments have, of course, varied widely. They have adopted different modes of political participation based on the nature of the political environment in which they operate—and accordingly, they have in recent years also devised various strategies to manage the tensions of ideology and pragmatism.

The most stable mode of Islamist participation in formal politics is exemplified by the Moroccan Justice and Development Party (PJD), the Algerian Society for Peace Movement, the Islamic Constitutional Movement in Kuwait, and the Islamic Wifaq (concord) Society, a Shi'i party in Bahrain. These parties and movements have adopted peaceful parliamentary participation as their one and only strategic option. Here there is no alternative to the preservation of the available spheres and mechanisms of political plurality and to gradually solidifying and expanding the pluralistic system through the formulation of a consensus with ruling elites and liberal and leftist opposition groups over the future of the democratization process.

Above all, the PJD and like-minded Islamist movements honor the legitimacy of the nation-state to which they belong, and they respect that state's governing institutions, the principle of equality among all citizens, and the pluralistic, competitive nature of political life. Significantly, some of these movements—notably the PJD and the Islamic Constitutional Movement—have succeeded in separating Islamist *da'wa* (proselytizing) activities and politics, transforming themselves into pure political organizations, guided by an Islamist frame of reference and run by professional politicians, leaving *da'wa* to the broad social movements that gave birth to them.

The embrace of peaceful political participation, which these Islamist groups have generally adopted as much in spirit as in form, has led to a decline in exclusionary rhetoric, whether directed toward the ruling elite or to the liberal and leftist opposition. It has also led to a gradual shift away from ideological diatribes and categorical judgments and toward the formulation of practical political platforms and constructive attempts to influence public policy, whether as minor partners in government or as members of the opposition. For example, in reconciling their religious frame of reference with the imperative of political pragmatism, movements such as the PJD and the Egyptian Wasat Party (a splinter group from the much larger Muslim Brotherhood) have put forward alternative ideological formulas that retain the overall religious character while granting these movements more room for maneuver. In the PJD's platform the application of the Islamic *shari'a* is replaced by a loose reference to general Islamic guidelines (*al-maqasid al-'amma*). The Wasat Party, struggling for public and legal recognition, crafted a call for establishing a democratic political system in Egypt within the framework of the Islamic *marja'iyya* (source or reference). Other Islamist movements have adopted some of this more flexible vocabulary.

A different—though not necessarily contradictory—approach was taken by movements such as the Jordanian Islamic Action Front, the Egyptian Muslim Brotherhood, and Yemen's al-Islah. Representing the second mode of Islamist participation, these Islamists have persisted in the face of a volatile political space and the fragility of their relationship with the ruling elites. If, in Egypt and Jordan, the Muslim Brothers have been given some room to participate in pluralistic mechanisms, in legislative elections, in professional syndicates, and in other areas of civil society, the sword of the security forces is constantly hanging over their heads. On the other hand, Islah in Yemen (as well as the Islamist movement in Sudan) throw into relief the danger of nondemocratic accommodations Islamists have struck with ruling elites and the impact of such paramilitary-technocratic alliances on political life and on the internal dynamics of the Islamists themselves.

The group of movements taking this second approach has worked primarily to establish functional differentiation between two spheres—a general ideological/religious one and a pragmatic political one—rather than recast their identity wholly within the state's political framework. As a result, the conversion to less exclusionary rhetoric and the willingness to adopt more flexible arguments and language occurs far more in some fields than in others. Social and cultural issues, including women's status and intellectual freedoms, can thus sometimes remain embedded in the less flexible ideological framework. But the functional separation allows some within the movement to develop a collection of more flexible political views and practices on other matters ranging from economics to political reform, where positions and language are increasingly driven by pragmatic considerations. In this vein, some movements have deliberately cultivated a group of leaders within the broader movement who focus on the political sphere and develop the skills of appealing to broader audiences, crafting media strategies, running election campaigns, and filing parliamentary inquiries.

Perhaps we might call this category "Islamists who take part until they notify us otherwise." They may have adopted a strategy of peaceful participation within the system, but it is less an irreversible commitment than a strategy that shifts according to the perpetual fluctuation of their role in political life (as in Egypt and Jordan) or the swings in their positions from partners in authoritarian governments to antagonists (as in the case of Yemen). In such movements, leaders and followers continue to hover in the abstract realms of ideology, social narratives, and mega policy (the role of religion, Islamic law, the individual, the group, and the Muslim nation), while ignoring the need to develop a culture that values consensus-making and constructive mechanisms for influencing public policy.

Lastly, the third mode of Islamist participation in politics is exemplified by the Iraqi, Lebanese, and Palestinian cases. Islamist parties and movements operate with relative organizational freedom in the context of political party plurality, but also within a climate of relative chaos. Extraordinary political contexts are shaped by foreign occupation, which has wrought the collapse of the institutions of government and public security, or ongoing, intractable crises of internal discord that so hamper the efficacy of government as to constantly threaten the stability of the political system and encourage the prevalence of monopolistic/exclusivist tendencies, which conflict with the spirit and substance of peaceful participation. Shi'i-Sunni and pro- and antiresistance dichotomies aside, the Islamist movements in Iraq, Lebanon, and Palestine are characterized by regimented internal structures, possession of the means to exercise violence and a tendency to resort to, or to threaten to resort to, violence to resolve their political conflicts. In short, they have dual identities: both political actors and militarized resistance movements.

Contrary to hopes that assimilation would gradually inspire the Islamists of collapsed and failed states to demilitarize their movements and revise their means and methods in a manner that gives priority to peaceful politics, these Islamist groups have failed to develop a full commitment to peaceful participation. It remains that the institution of the state must be revived through a thoroughly civil polity—reinvigorating its neutrality toward the diverse elements of the population and introducing structures and mechanisms to impede religious or nonreligious exclusivist forces from monopolizing public affairs—before political participation can be a truly moderating force upon these Islamists.

There is a rich body of scholarly work on Islamic political thought and Islamic movements. Until quite recently, however, the vast majority of this work has focused on Islamism primarily in intellectual terms; studies of the structure, organization, strategy, and tactics of Islamist movements were rare.[1] When actual movements drew attention, most writers generally focused on fairly abstract attempts to understand the compatibility of prevailing ideologies with liberalism and democracy.[2] This work helped pave the way for a new generation of extremely rich empirical studies that focused on particular Islamic movements, often viewing them as social movements or as proto-political parties.[3] While hardly blind to the political implications of the rise of Islamist movements, however, this scholarship tended to turn attention away from formal political participation in the form of political parties and elections. Only in the very recent past has a body of scholarship begun to emerge that focuses on Islamic movements in the electoral process.[4] This most recent work is generally country specific, though some cross-national studies are beginning to emerge.

This volume seeks to contribute to this emerging body of literature with a broad, cross-national study of Islamist parties in parliamentary elections in the Arab world, focusing on those movements that have opted to cast themselves, at least in part, as electorally oriented political parties.

We have selected six political systems in which Islamist movements have participated in parliamentary elections: Egypt, Jordan, Morocco, Kuwait, Yemen, and Palestine. Each of these countries has an Islamist movement that operates openly, though not always legally. Indeed, each country has a variety of Islamist movements, only some of which seek to participate in the political process.

We will pay particular attention to a series of questions. First, what is the political environment in which the movement operates? None of the political systems examined here are democracies, but all have parliaments and some basis for competitive politics. We will examine the environment to understand how and why the movement has entered parliamentary politics. Second, what relations does the movement have with the regime? Third, what has been the platform of the movement? And what has been its parliamentary agenda? Fourth, has the Islamist movement democratized internally in the course of participation in formal politics? Fifth, what are the relations between the Islamist movement and other political forces—what combination of rivalry and partnerships has been built? Finally, what are the implications for the integration of the Islamist movement as a normal political actor?

In answering this last question, we will pay particular attention to debates within the movement itself; Islamist movements are true political organizations rather than projections of a leading charismatic personality; they are thus often both quarrelsome and reflective regarding their political experience. Moreover, over the last decade, their internal debates have become increasingly accessible to outsiders, as the movements carry out some of their discussions in public and their increased political role has led to greater public interest in their positions.

Each of the country studies contained in this volume addresses these questions, but the diversity in the political systems suggests that we avoid any rigid form. In Egypt, for instance, a large parliamentary bloc of 88 deputies has been able to develop a complex and detailed parliamentary agenda over several years (and one that builds on previous parliamentary experience); in Palestine, the Islamist Hamas movement entered only one parliamentary election, and, while it won a majority of seats, it was able to operate only for a matter of months before the Israelis arrested so many deputies that the movement could no longer obtain a quorum. Some movements (in Yemen, Jordan, and Kuwait) have some experience holding cabinet positions; other movements (most notably Egypt) do not even have a legal status. We will therefore adjust the list of questions and the emphasis given to each according to the circumstances of the case.

But we will return at the end of this book to a more general consideration of the movements' own evaluations of their political experience. After a decade or more of investment in parliamentary politics, what do they think they have achieved? And what are the lessons that the movements themselves draw for the future?

CHAPTER 2

The Egyptian Muslim Brotherhood

Islamist Participation in a Closing Political Environment

I n January 2010, the Egyptian Muslim Brotherhood selected Muhammad Badiʻ as its eighth general guide. While Egypt's leading Islamist movement has sometimes hotly debated the selection of leaders in the past, this time the choice took place under an unprecedented domestic and international spotlight. Muhammad Badiʻ was virtually unknown outside the group. And that itself was a signal about the Brotherhood's future course: there would likely be far more focus on internal organization and less on political work; the movement was positioning itself to focus more on quiet social and educational projects than noisy political struggles. The new direction was not simply a product of internal preferences; the political environment in Egypt had become far less inviting in general. And the Brotherhood was a particular target of growing restrictions on political activity. With these developments, the prospect of a more competitive and pluralistic political system in Egypt was rapidly fading.

Badiʻ himself tried to emphasize continuity with the Brotherhood's political vision and participation in Egyptian politics. He also sent soothing signals in almost all directions: his initial statements upon his selection contained references to the Brotherhood's commitment to peaceful change and its continued dedication to political activity in line with the movement's slogan that it sought "participation, not domination." But if Badiʻ's initial words suggested little change, his actions bespoke a very different style and set of priorities: he declined to take questions; appeared far more reserved than Mahdi 'Akif, his ebullient predecessor, and worked quickly to ensure that the increasingly cacophonous movement recovers its ability to speak with a unified voice. The Brotherhood was not disappearing, but Egyptians watching the movement should have expected it to become more reticent, seek to avoid headlines, and work more gradually, shoring up its own ranks and pursuing less flashy social and organizational work.

The Brotherhood would be likely to preserve its organizational existence in this difficult political environment. And to be fair, it was not totally abandoning the political sphere. However, the contest between the Brotherhood and the regime was about to enter a more muted phase.

The change might be gradual but it would still be significant. Critics have long charged that the Muslim Brotherhood has a vague program, stronger on slogans than substance, and that its political vision cannot answer Egypt's many pressing needs. But that charge held less water in the early 2000s, as the Brotherhood used a variety of venues to spell out its vision for a better governed, public-spirited, prosperous, more just, and increasingly moral and Islamic Egyptian society. Those details emerged as the Brotherhood has become increasingly political. In the first decade of the twenty-first century, the Brotherhood has plunged further into politics, stepping up its electoral participation and developing a more comprehensive and detailed agenda in the process. That effort was waning by the end of the decade. The means through which the Brotherhood had developed its specific set of proposals, such as drafting its political platform and maneuvering in the parliament with the sizable bloc it won in 2005, now seemed less promising. While we hardly endorse the Brotherhood's agenda, we argue that the movement's partial withdrawal as a political force risks returning Egypt to the state of political stagnation that had afflicted it for so long.

In this chapter, we will examine the Brotherhood's engagement in politics—how it came about, what form it took, and the agenda that the movement attempted to develop. Specifically, we will probe:

- The Brotherhood's evolving approaches to politics;
- The environment of shifting red lines and semiauthoritarianism in which the movement has operated;
- The Brotherhood's evolving political positions, especially the mixed results of its experiences exploring the possibilities of forming a political party and writing a platform;

- The movement's experience in forming cross-ideological coalitions to press for further reform;
- The Brotherhood's attempt to sketch out a comprehensive political, social, and economic agenda through parliamentary activity;
- The evolution and costs of that parliamentary effort; and
- The implications of a partial withdrawal from politics.

The Brotherhood and Politics

The Egyptian Muslim Brotherhood, a group that has lacked formal legal existence for six decades, remains one of the most successful social and political movements in modern Arab history. It has sustained its structure and vision through some very difficult periods, adroitly seizing the opportunities that have arisen and squeezing itself into any opening that has emerged in Egypt's generally closed political order.

Many Egyptian and international observers have scrutinized the Brotherhood's words and deeds, sharply debating its commitment to democracy, stance on liberal values, and attitude toward violence.[1] Such debates have occurred within the movement itself, but these issues are not currently—and have only occasionally been in the past—the focal point of internal discussions. Instead, internal debates have centered on a broader, though related, concern with the role of politics: how can and should political efforts advance the Brotherhood's broad agenda in Egypt's shifting political and social environment?

Indeed, the Muslim Brotherhood was founded to pursue a broad reform agenda, which over time has taken on personal, religious, social, and political aspects. The critical debate within the movement in recent decades centers on how much (and in what ways) to stress political participation. Calls for a total withdrawal from politics are heard only on the margins of the movement, and among its critics. But if there is a broad internal consensus that the Brotherhood should remain partially engaged in politics, leaders have nevertheless sharply debated how extensive participation should be, what forms it should take, and how to connect political activity to the Brotherhood's long-term reform goals. And it is very much long-term goals that are at issue. Brotherhood leaders insist—and behave as though—their focus is less on the short-term, even daily tussle of politics and much more on the movement's broad vision of a society in accordance with Islamic principles.

Our concern in this chapter, however, is primarily with Egyptian politics. How has a broadly based, religiously inspired movement been shaped by the Egyptian political system? How has the Brotherhood's political activity affected Egyptian politics, and how is it likely to affect politics in the future? More specifically, what has been the impact of the Brotherhood's growing presence in the Egyptian parliament and what will be the effect of its likely exclusion (partial though it may be) from that body after the elections slated for late 2010?

In the wake of the 2005 parliamentary elections, in which Brotherhood candidates won 88 of 444 elected seats, we described a spectrum of scenarios for Egyptian politics, ranging from accommodation to confrontation between movement and regime. Since that time, it has become clear that the regime has adapted a strategy we described then as a "modified Algerian" scenario.[2] Like the Algerian regime in 1991, Egypt's current leadership has decided to place sharper limits on democratic processes and combat the growing influence of the Brotherhood with a combination of arrests, security measures, legal and constitutional restraints, ideological campaigns, and harassment. The Egyptian regime is more gradual and far gentler than the Algerian one of the 1990s, but it still rejects any attempt to incorporate the Brotherhood as a normal political actor.

Nevertheless, the Brotherhood's leaders have not reacted as though their movement is in crisis. Instead, they have responded slowly, cautiously, almost ploddingly, complaining about the crackdown without actively resisting it. The movement's focus on its long-term vision and its patience and forbearance explains its restraint. However, the effect of its withdrawal is to diminish the movement's interest in the political sphere and the likelihood of integrating the Arab world's oldest and most influential Islamist movement into the Egyptian political scene as a formal party.

Political Environment: Ever Shifting Red Lines

Egypt's current political environment can be characterized as "semiauthoritarian" in that it bars any meaningful contestation over political authority, but still leaves some room for opposition to be expressed and, to a lesser extent, organized.

The basic semiauthoritarian nature of the current Egyptian political order is well-entrenched. Though Egypt was never a constitutional democracy, a real and rising pluralism earlier in the twentieth century gave way to concentration of power with the creation of the current regime in 1952. Since that time, the system has generally displayed three features: it has been highly centralized (with authority concentrated in the presidency); political contestation has been sharply limited; and any attempt by the opposition to recast prevailing political arrangements has generally been regarded by leaders as a security threat rather than a political challenge. Indeed, in the 1950s and 1960s, there was little "semi" about the regime's authoritarianism.

In the early 1970s, however, the authoritarian face of the regime began to soften—unevenly and inconsistently to be sure, but in some significant ways. The three features—centralization, limitation on contestation, and security mentality—remained firmly in place, but were sometimes implemented in less draconian ways. Most notable was the opening of political expression. Beginning in the late 1970s, an opposition press emerged. In the current decade, a host of independent newspapers have proved even more significant in widening the political sphere. State institutions—ranging from the judiciary to the official religious and educational complex known as al-Azhar—have often wrested a greater degree of autonomy from the presidency.

Political pluralism of a limited sort also returned to Egypt when the regime abandoned its practice of designating a single umbrella political party. In the 1970s, some pre-1952 forces (including the Brotherhood) were allowed to reemerge. However, the party environment is hardly free. The governing National Democratic Party dominates the political scene, sometimes merging with the state bureaucracy and parts of the business community and utilizing instruments of the state to maintain its monopoly on power. Opposition parties can be established only under specific conditions, and they have been unable to forge strong links with potential constituents. The Brotherhood itself has never been granted any legal status. It has been discouraged—and in 2007, even constitutionally barred—from forming a political party.

Egyptians often speak of their political system as one that allows dissent within "red lines." Such a description, while accurate, can mislead in one important respect: the "red lines" in question are neither accepted nor consistent. They are not simply unclear, but constantly shifting, pushed and probed by a variety of opposition actors. The "lines" remain far harsher for Islamist political actors than for others, but even for Islamists, they move from month to month.

The constant shifts in the rules of the political game can be seen most clearly in the electoral arena.[3] Egyptian elections are, in a sense, foregone conclusions—there is currently no prospect of political power changing hands based on electoral results. However, all other elements of elections besides results are up for contestation and sometimes violent conflict, with polling routinely accompanied by arrests and clashes among rival groups. The rules governing Egyptian elections have also changed constantly, shaped by a varying combination of regime machinations, court decisions, constitutional provisions, opposition threats, international pressure, and popular apathy.

From the perspective of the Brotherhood, legislative elections afford the opportunity to pursue many different goals—though electoral victory is simply not one of them, at least in the short term. Since its reemergence in the 1970s, the Brotherhood has found ways to field candidates even without legal status by running its nominees under other party labels or as independents. The Brotherhood has responded to each shift in the rules with its own shifts in tactics: it has chosen variously to boycott elections and run ambitious slates of candidates, to forge alliances and to forswear them, and modified its program for electoral purposes while making clear that other principles are unalterable.

But running in elections also carries costs and risks. The Brotherhood's 2005 success in the parliamentary elections, for instance, is said by some within the movement not simply to have vindicated its popular role, but also to have incurred the wrath of an oppressive regime.

How have the shifting rules of Egyptian semiauthoritarianism affected the Brotherhood's positions?

The Evolution of the Brotherhood's Political Stance

The Muslim Brotherhood's broad involvement in Egyptian politics has led to an evolution in its political positions. Participation has led it to stress political reform, develop a conception of a "civil state with an Islamic frame of reference," and craft specific policy proposals (while still leaving significant areas of ambiguity and debate). Before tracing the evolution of its positions, it is helpful to examine the Brotherhood's general attitude toward politics, an equally important but often over-looked evolution.

NEARING THE RUBICON OF A POLITICAL PARTY

The Brotherhood has never rejected participation in parliamentary elections in principle. Its founder, Hasan al-Banna, attempted to run for parliament. But if the Brotherhood did not disavow parliament, it also did not show great interest in electoral politics. In fact, the movement expressed an explicit disdain for party politics, maintaining that the interests of the entire community took precedence over divisive partisanship. Beginning in the 1950s, ideological offshoots from the Brotherhood developed in more radical directions, rejecting any non–*shari'a*-based order as fundamentally illegitimate.[4] The issue of electoral participation was moot, in any case: Egyptian politics took a sharply authoritarian turn in the 1950s, and the Brotherhood became one of the main targets of the regime's repression.

In the 1970s, however, the Egyptian political system began to shift gradually from a fully authoritarian order to the semiauthoritarian one described above, offering the Brotherhood more freedom to maneuver. Older leaders who had been imprisoned or fled the country were reanimating the movement just as Egyptian students were forming a loosely coordinated movement based on greater religious interest and activism.[5] Though the student movement took many forms, some students began to gravitate toward the Brotherhood, which greeted them warmly. The effect was not simply to rejuvenate the movement, but also to infuse it with a variety of new organizational ideas and a greater inclination toward political activism, first through student associations and then, when the new leaders graduated, through professional associations. The Brotherhood harnessed this newfound energy by entering the parliamentary electoral process.

In most elections, the Brotherhood participated in an intentionally non-threatening manner by contesting a limited number of seats. At the previous peak of its electoral success, the Brotherhood participated in a short-lived alliance with the liberal Wafd party that won 58 seats in 1984. Two rounds later, in 1990, the Brotherhood participated in an opposition electoral boycott of parliamentary balloting, demanding a more neutral process for administering elections and a more faithful observance of constitutional guarantees of the integrity of the electoral process. But in most elections, the Brotherhood ran a modest number of candidates, winning a modest number of seats.[6]

In 2005, the Brotherhood leadership decided to step up its involvement in elections by slating 161 candidates. However, the movement still took steps to assure the country's rulers that it was not audacious enough to seek a majority: namely, the number of its candidates was such that even if all had won, the Brotherhood would still have controlled only one-third of the parliament. Further, the group avoided running candidates against the most prominent NDP figures. Brotherhood leaders not only avoided winning a majority in the elections, but they also acknowledged the need to limit their minority work to a level that did not threaten the NDP. Had they won more than one-third of the seats, they would have had a bloc sufficient to obstruct some NDP actions. That would have implied not simply limited participation in parliament, but a direct voice in governance—something the Brotherhood was not yet ready for.

Despite these self-imposed limits, extensive participation brought remarkable achievements. The Brotherhood won 88 seats outright and might have won a score more if there had been no official manipulation and intimidation. In head-to-head contests between Brotherhood-sponsored candidates and National Democratic Party candidates, the Brotherhood won two-thirds of the races. This stunning performance brought the movement face-to-face with the question of forming an electorally oriented political party, a step that carries considerable ideological and organizational significance.

As we have mentioned, the Brotherhood eschewed any move in the direction of forming a party for a long time. Under Hasan al-Banna, its founder, the movement disavowed partisan politics, and even when it did participate, it avoided forming its own party or formally aligning with others. After al-Banna's death in 1949 and until the 1970s, the regime suppressed the movement. When the government allowed it to re-emerge, some younger activists showed interest in forming a party, but the restrictive legal environment and the movement's old guard blocked the move. In 1995, a group of younger activists finally bolted the movement and attempted to form a new "Center Party." The fact that these activists are no longer young but to this day have not succeeded in clearing those legal hurdles has discouraged other members from following in their footsteps.

On an ideological level, formation of an electorally oriented party would force the Brotherhood to leave behind its longstanding if lessening distrust of party politics. Indeed, if the Brotherhood can be accused of having harbored antidemocratic inclinations, these lay not so much in a distrust of democracy in theory as in a distaste for the tussle of daily politics, in which different actors and interest groups struggle to have their preferences translated into policy. On this level, the Brotherhood seems to have changed its objection to forming a party from the realm of principle to that of practice. When asked about their intentions on the question of forming a party, leaders refer only to the political and legal roadblocks, not their ideological hesitations. But the legal obstacles are insurmountable at present and have prevented leaders from grappling with the implications of accepting a pluralist political environment.

At an organizational level, the formation of a political party would have a significant impact in three ways. First, it would create an arm of the movement with a different sense of time. Brotherhood leaders routinely insist—and behave as if—they measure time in decades rather than days. An electoral party, if given full autonomy, is necessarily wedded to an electoral cycle, constantly positioning itself in anticipation of its next performance at the ballot box. In such a context, tactical considerations often begin to trump strategic ones.

This revised time horizon is connected to the second organizational implication of the formation of an electoral party: the inevitable emergence of a new leadership group within the movement, with its own distinct interests and priorities. The establishment of separate electoral arms by similar movements has forced them to grapple with difficult questions: how much autonomy should the party be granted? How much should it be able to draw on the credibility and resources of the broader movement? Does the formation of a party entangle and even sully the broader movement's activities in political struggles?

Third, an electoral party would be far more preoccupied than the Brotherhood has typically been by the necessity of dealing with other political forces, deciding how and when to form coalitions, bargain with other parties, emphasize programmatic distinctiveness, and co-opt supporters from other parties.

In the end, the Egyptian regime has spared the Muslim Brotherhood needing to answer any of these questions. Indeed, it was less the movement's dithering and far more the harsh regime response that blocked the Brotherhood's path toward forming a political party. The movement's leaders explain that Egypt's semiauthoritarian regime has tried to present them—implicitly or even explicitly—with a choice: it can pursue its non-political activities more freely or cling to its political role and face repression. Brotherhood leaders have refused to make that choice, giving up neither politics nor social work. But in refusing to abandon the political field, they have been confronted with a concerted regime effort to force them out. In the future, they will not be allowed to form a party, or even to compete on a non-party basis, as they did in 2005, without facing harsh repression.

DEFINING POSITIONS: MOVING TOWARD THE DRAFT PARTY PLATFORM AND THEN WITHDRAWING FROM IT

While the Brotherhood's path to becoming a political party may be blocked for the foreseeable future, the movement's enhanced political activity has led it to spell out its positions in more substantive terms.

Since it resumed its political activities in the 1970s and 1980s, the Brotherhood has consistently pushed for some measure of political liberalization. The movement's respect for political liberties has not always translated into support for freedom in the social and cultural realms, but its stress on political liberalization has become more marked over the years. By 2004, the Brotherhood was sufficiently advanced in its thinking to produce a comprehensive vision for political reform. The content of that program was remarkable not only for its detail, but also for the way in which it mirrored the demands of opposition groups across the political spectrum. It came at a time when a surge in reform thinking and activism offered a promising sign that Egypt's political stasis might be broken. For a time, the regime seemed not to know how to respond to the onset of an unprecedented degree of internal and external pressure for reform.

In the end, however, the Egyptian regime regained its balance and managed to deflect the challenges fairly easily. As that happened, the Brotherhood came under criticism from its fellow opposition movements on two grounds. First, leaders in some other opposition groups (such as some in the broad coalition known as *Kifaya*) claimed that the Brotherhood's contribution to the opposition movement was cheap talk but little action. Brotherhood members occasionally participated in demonstrations and joint efforts but seemed far too cautious for opposition activists who were determined to break down the "red lines" that had constrained them for so long. When other opposition figures organized street demonstrations or used rhetoric the Brotherhood considered too strong (and even "rude"), Brotherhood leaders held back.

And indeed, the movement's long time horizon and legendary caution suggest that the criticisms levied by other opposition figures were apt: Brotherhood leaders were convinced that this was not an appropriate time to risk everything in a confrontation with the regime.

Critics also charged that the Brotherhood, for all its willingness to embrace aspects of political reform, still saw it as a means of forming an Islamic state. The slogan of "a civil state with an Islamic frame of reference" was too vague to offer much reassurance to the contrary. Accordingly, the Brotherhood set to work spelling out its positions in an extremely lengthy document—eventually reaching 128 pages—that, however provisional, was still explicitly written with a political party in mind. The Brotherhood's purpose in drafting the document was to compel its leaders to settle for themselves—and communicate to those outside the movement—the details of their political vision for Egypt. The document was circulated for comment (originally among a small group, but the document was soon leaked and published) in 2007 but never completed. With the wave of renewed repression that followed the movement's strong electoral performance, Brotherhood leaders kept postponing a final draft, and ultimately made clear that the project is shelved for the time being. But the draft platform still provides a remarkable view of what the Brotherhood's political project looks like on some controversial matters.[7]

SHARI'A

Much of the platform carries forward the Brotherhood's evolving strategy of reassurance regarding the compatibility between its religious agenda and the existing legal environment. The platform shows respect for the country's constitutional institutions, seeking to diminish the presidency but showing genuine comfort with the idea that the people's elected representatives in parliament are generally the ultimate arbiter of which Islamic teachings must be treated as authoritative.

But in a brief passage, the platform seems to take a potentially far-reaching step in a very different direction: it calls for the creation of a council of religious scholars, a body to be elected by the full complement of religious scholars in the country and to advise the legislative and executive branches in matters of religious law. The passage on the council also suggests that the new body might have the authority to comment on a wide variety of legislative and executive acts, and that its word would be binding—not merely advisory—on matters in which it felt the *shari'a* rule at stake was definitive and not subject to divergent interpretations.

The provision for the council seemed to catch some Brotherhood leaders by surprise. On the one hand, the proposed council answered apparent pressure from the movement's more ideologically committed foot soldiers that it not abandon *shari'a* behind anodyne formulas, as well as the insistence of some senior leaders to make *shari'a*-based rules a viable restriction on rulers. And the requirement that the religious council be elected rather than appointed offered to diminish the role of those official actors (like the mufti and the shaykh of al-Azhar) who are seen as co-opted in favor of the entire body of religious scholars, many of whom are sympathetic to the Brotherhood and its program.

On the other hand, by inserting these sentences, the Brotherhood alienated many others both inside and outside the movement and opened itself to the charge of favoring rule by religious scholars. Some members of the Brotherhood criticized the language on both substantive and procedural grounds, claiming that the proposed body of religious scholars was based on an illegitimate privileging of some interpretations of *shari'a* over others, not on any established Brotherhood position. They claimed that the language had not been fully debated within the movement but had been inserted in a set of ill-considered last-minute modifications. Yet the heat of the debate within the movement was exceeded by the firestorm of external criticism. Even intellectuals who had called for acceptance of the Brotherhood as a normal political actor lambasted what they viewed as the movement's lurch in the direction of theocracy.

Not only did the platform force the Brotherhood to pay internal and external costs for its foray into specificity, but it also made a retreat back into generalities more difficult. Brotherhood leaders suggested that if they ever do produce a final draft, it will omit this provision. But while it may be possible to drop the passage from the program or rob it of much of its content, there is no obscuring the fact that some within the leadership have a conception of *shari'a* that strikes many Egyptians as undemocratic. However much the Brotherhood seeks to paper over the differences opened with the platform's language on this topic, it will be dealing with the repercussions of the controversy for some time.

COPTS AND WOMEN

The Muslim Brotherhood's draft political platform forced the movement to pay the price of specificity on one other notable issue: its clear position that women and non-Muslims should be excluded from senior positions in any state governed according to Islamic principles. The argument for this ban was based on a traditional current in Islamic legal and political thought that focused on determining the requirements for a ruler (or, in the terms of the Brotherhood's religion-based discourse, the major positions of governing). Because a ruler in an Islamic society assumes some religious functions, most pre-modern Muslim legal and political authorities held that the ruler himself must be a Muslim. Owing to the public nature of the role, it was also common to insist on the requirement that the ruler be male.

For some within the Brotherhood, this was precisely the sort of clearly established *shariʿa*-based rule that should not be transgressed. But others did not feel so bound: they rejected what they saw as outmoded and unnecessary legal reasoning. And they saw the entire issue as a politically damaging distraction. Opponents of excluding Copts and women argued that standard Islamic legal writings had conceptualized a state based on a patrimonial ruler, not the complex set of institutions that currently exists (or should). They argued that the very different kind of state authority that exists today prevents mechanical application of older understandings. The religion and gender of a ruler matter far less if he (or she) is merely temporarily staffing a high state office in accordance with clear procedures and legal limitations. Further, they argued, there was little benefit to be gained by constitutionally barring non-Muslims from office: in a deeply religious society with an overwhelming majority of Muslims, it was unlikely a non-Muslim would be elected in the first place. (Some went so far as to say that they were fully comfortable with the implications of their more liberal position by stating that they would prefer a qualified and righteous Christian or woman over many members of Egypt's current corrupt and autocratic governing elite.)

The internal debate was only ambiguously resolved. On the one hand, the movement's leaders insisted that their position barring women and Copts was definitive for internal purposes, and that their binding stance would not be withdrawn. However, they also suggested that this was merely a position of the Brotherhood and therefore implied that the exclusion need not be translated into law. Indeed, they even hinted that while they would not change the Brotherhood's position, they could accept a defeat on the matter as long as it came through legitimate democratic procedures.

ECONOMICS

The two short passages on the council of religious scholars and the gender of the head of state drew the greatest attention in the public debate. But the platform focused almost entirely on other issues. Most notable here was a feature that attracted little notice at the time: the great attention to economic matters. Given Egyptians' low standard of living and the Brotherhood's determination to position itself as a serious movement with a political vision, its leaders recognized that they would have to make some attempt to grapple with the country's economic problems to combat the criticism that the movement is focused on marginal issues.

Anxious as they were to show an ability to develop comprehensive and detailed proposals, Brotherhood leaders found that addressing economic issues was more easily said than done. The attempt exposed the Brotherhood to four (often conflicting) pressures. First, its proposals had to be seen as serious and practical. Second, the movement was tremendously suspicious of the Nasserist political experiment, which carried over into a general distaste for socialism and a strong state. Third, the Brotherhood was strongly committed to the vision of a just society governed in accordance with Islamic principles, including protections for the poor and the weak. Private welfare, in the Brotherhood's view, was very much a public concern. Finally, the Brotherhood's commitments to Islamic laws and conservative social values affected its views of a whole host of matters, ranging from banking and finance to tourism.

In the platform, the Brotherhood revealed a preference for a strongly interventionist state that would mitigate the effects of free trade. By contrast, the platform's provisions regarding political and democratic reform focus on a more limited role for the state and a greater role for civil society and nongovernmental organizations. Calling for a state that systematically intervenes in social and economic spheres while simultaneously advocating limits to its political role seems contradictory. Yet the Brotherhood escaped criticism and calls to define the boundaries between a liberal and an interventionist state, owing largely to the distraction of the other controversies.

The draft party platform is an important document testifying to the movement's thinking and its inclinations on many critical areas of Egyptian social and political life. But there are two limitations to relying completely on it to discern the movement's positions. First, the document was explicitly a draft and indeed was never finalized (nor is there any prospect of its being issued any time soon). Second, the platform allowed the movement to address only those issues that concerned it and avoid those that it preferred not to engage.

Relations With Other Opposition Actors

Has the Brotherhood's growing interest in politics—and its evolving vision of reform—allowed it to forge alliances with others working toward some of the same ends? The results of bridge-building among opposition actors in Egypt is mixed at best.

The Muslim Brotherhood's relations with legal opposition parties and protest movements have been largely determined by two political realities. First, in an attempt to capitalize on the limited opening of the Egyptian regime between 2002 and 2005, the Brotherhood made efforts to join forces with other opposition actors to develop a national platform for democratic reform and exert meaningful pressure on the government to accept a greater degree of political competition and pluralism. However, boldness was always tempered by caution. Fearing repression, the Brotherhood was conscious to avoid signaling a determination to challenge the regime's grip on power or to represent itself as an alternative, and thus remained reluctant to commit to formal and electoral alliances with other opposition actors. One of the clearest signs of this understanding was the Brotherhood's self-limited participation in the 2005 parliamentary elections, when it fielded candidates in fewer than one-third of the electoral districts, thus sending the message that it did not seek to challenge the NDP's two-thirds majority in the People's Assembly.[8]

The long-standing mutual mistrust between the Brotherhood and other opposition movements has limited their attempts to harmonize political positions and coordinate activities. Some of these suspicions stem from precisely those areas where the Brotherhood found its draft platform provoking debate. Liberal and leftist parties as well as protest movements have remained deeply concerned by the Brotherhood's ambiguous positions on equal citizenship rights for Muslims and Copts and women's rights and empowerment in society.

The Brotherhood's possible partners further fretted about the negative impacts of *shari'a* provisions on freedom of expression and pluralism and ultimately the contradictions between the group's Islamic frame of reference and the constitutional pillars of Egyptian politics.[9]

The platform discussed above was partially intended to answer suspicions regarding these issues but only deepened them. Some opposition actors also doubt the Brotherhood's willingness to cooperate with them, accusing it of "arrogant behavior" and an "inability to reach compromises" with others.[10] Indeed, in several incidents the Brotherhood has projected the image of a movement too certain of the appeal of its rhetoric, the popularity of its platform, strength of its organization, and the size of its constituencies; it has acted as though it were virtually self-sufficient, needing no cooperation with weaker opposition actors.[11]

The Brotherhood has also had legitimate reason to mistrust the attitudes of other opposition actors. Some legal parties, such as the leftist Unionist Party, al-Tajammu', continue to oppose Islamist participation in politics and thus allied themselves with the regime to limit the Brotherhood's political space. In several incidents, al-Tajammu' leaders even endorsed repressive government measures against the Brotherhood and justified them on the grounds that they were targeting an undemocratic organization. Other parties that fear the Brotherhood's popularity, such as the liberal Wafd, have done very little to protest the manipulation of 2005 parliamentary elections against the movement's candidates or even their de-facto exclusion from local elections in 2008.[12] And although protest movements such as the Egyptian Movement for Change (Kifaya) have in recent years demonstrated a clear commitment to defending the right of the Brotherhood to participate in politics, they have systematically distanced themselves from the group whenever the regime has pursued repression against its leadership.

Even if such suspicions between the Brotherhood and other opposition actors could be overcome, there exists a deep structural difference: while most other opposition parties are focused primarily on politics, the Brotherhood leaders concern themselves with a broad and diverse social movement with many different wings and activities. This tends to make the Islamists cautious, anxious to avoid provoking official repression. When pressed on why they participate only half-heartedly (if at all) in opposition demonstrations, for instance, Brotherhood leaders retort that while Kifaya demonstrators get roughed up, their supporters are hauled in for indefinite periods.

The outcome in recent years of these two political realities—the Brotherhood's determination to participate without evoking the regime's wrath, as well as the mutual mistrust between Islamist and non-Islamist actors—has been the movement's mixed experience of partial cooperation and continued tension in the opposition spectrum. Alliances have been formed on occasion—most notably the 1984 electoral alliance with the Wafd party—but they have generally dissolved after short periods or been limited to short-term tactical coordination.

But even if alliance achievements have been limited, they have left real marks on the Brotherhood's positions. Since 2002, the Brotherhood's partial search for common ground with other opposition actors has resulted in the strengthening of its platform on social, economic, and political reform. In different official pronouncements and programmatic statements, for example the 2004 Reform Initiative and the 2005 electoral program, the Brotherhood's platform has echoed that of liberal and leftist parties calling for constitutional amendments, democratic reforms, government accountability, and freedom safeguards.

The Brotherhood's efforts at coordinating political activities, especially during election campaigns, have also been apparent. Prior to the 2005 parliamentary elections, the group joined the majority of legal opposition parties—including the traditional anti-Brotherhood al-Tajammuʻ and protest movements in forming the United National Front for Change. In spite of the coalition's grand promises, it failed to coordinate opposition activities and harmonize positions toward a national platform for democratic reform. In fairness to the Brotherhood, the only meaningful coordination of action came from its side. The Brotherhood announced at that time that it would refrain from competing against other opposition candidates, revitalizing the slogan "participation without domination," and it honored this commitment during the elections.[13]

In March 2007, the Brotherhood once again joined other opposition actors to form a coalition against the undemocratic constitutional amendments proposed and imposed by the NDP. The coalition threatened to boycott parliamentary debates on the amendments as well as the popular referendum that would endorse them. However, the coalition's members did not see its threats as binding, and several parties such as the leftist al-Tajammuʻ and the liberal al-Wafd defected.[14]

Such cross-ideological fronts and coalitions among Egypt's opposition actors have proved short-lived for several reasons. In most cases, they were not supported by strategic and tactical cooperation on the ground, but on informal agreements between Brotherhood leaders and other opposition actors with limited rapprochement at the grassroots and constituency levels. The Brotherhood's credibility has been greatly

but today

undermined by its inability to harmonize political positions or pressure the regime for common reform policies. Ultimately, the experience of cross-ideological cooperation in recent years has confirmed the limiting impact that mutual mistrust and varying political objectives have on opposition actors.[15]

The Brotherhood in Parliament: Sketching a Comprehensive Agenda[16]

If the Brotherhood can form no party, its platform is withdrawn, and cross-ideological alliances have had extremely limited effects, how can we know what the movement's political agenda is?

A far more specific set of indicators of the Brotherhood's positions is available and quite public: the activities of its deputies in parliament. These records fill in many of the gaps left by the platform and various public statements. While the Brotherhood has never had—and indeed, never sought—a parliamentary majority, its presence in parliament has allowed it the opportunity to sketch out a set of priorities and policy positions on a wide range of questions. This was generally the case before 2005, when the Brotherhood had a small number of deputies who used their parliamentary status and prerogatives to speak forcefully for its agenda. And it was especially and dramatically the case in the wake of the 2005 parliamentary elections, when the Brotherhood assembled an impressive parliamentary bloc, devoted resources to developing an agenda, drafted its own proposals, strategized about priorities, and played the (generally unofficial) role of leading the parliamentary opposition.

The Brotherhood's continued commitment to participate in legislative elections has secured for it a sustained presence in the People's Assembly—the lower chamber of the Egyptian parliament—since the late 1970s.[17] The Brotherhood's presence in parliament has varied greatly in terms of numbers, ranging from a one-seat presence in the 1995–2000 assembly to 88 MPs in the current 2005–2010 assembly. Throughout the last three decades the nature of the movement's parliamentary platform has also shifted: calls for the application of *shari'a* and the promotion of religious and moral values that the bloc prioritized until the 1990s have given way to issues of legal and political reform, socioeconomic policies, and human rights violations in the 2000–2005 and current assemblies. Although religious and *shari'a*-based priorities remain key elements in the Brotherhood's parliamentary activities, their significance in shaping the movement's platform has diminished gradually. Other elements have remained unchanged, such as the preoccupation with government accountability, anti-corruption measures, and the group's vague stance on women's rights and equality between Muslims and Copts.

It is important not to overstate what the Brotherhood's parliamentary deputies can achieve. Though the group's nearly continuous presence in parliament since the late 1970s has enabled its MPs to acquire extensive oversight tools as well as a collective ability to challenge the government, its impact on the legislative process has been minimal. Brotherhood deputies can certainly annoy the government, pepper its ministers with questions, and bring issues to the public sphere for discussion, but they do not have the votes necessary to write laws. In the People's Assembly of 2000–2005, the seventeen Brotherhood MPs made use of parliamentary oversight tools—such as inquiries, interpellations, questions, discussion requests, and the formation of investigative committees—over 6,000 times, far more than any other parliamentary bloc.[18] In the current assembly, with the Brotherhood's 88 MPs, movement deputies resorted to oversight tools over 20,000 times.[19] But in spite of the Brotherhood's increasing parliamentary activity, its platform remains largely unimplemented.

The Muslim Brotherhood bloc's failure to pass platform legislation is ultimately linked to the ruling National Democratic Party's firm grip on parliament, where it has persistently secured a comfortable two-thirds majority in every assembly since 1976. Even in the current assembly, in spite of the Muslim Brotherhood's significant growth in representation to almost one-fifth of the entire body, the NDP holds three-quarters of the seats and is virtually unchallenged in passing its draft legislation and forming the cabinet.

Over time, the Brotherhood has gradually learned to deploy its extensive experience in providing services and charity—both of which have been key elements of its constituency-building activities—to augment its oversight activities. Charity networks and service provision centers have facilitated constant exchange between the Brotherhood's MPs and considerable segments of the Egyptian population, especially in impoverished areas. This, in return, has made it possible for the MPs to detect direct incidents of corruption, to take note of the concrete impacts of social and economic policies, and to shape a narrative that builds political support for their parliamentary activities.

In this context of strong oversight performance and weak legislative impact, the Brotherhood's parliamentary activities in recent years have centered on five pillars: constitutional and legal amendments, political reform, social and economic legislation, religious and moral legislation, and women's rights. The following section examines the Brotherhood MPs' parliamentary platform in relation to these five pillars, in both the 2000–2005 and the current 2005–2010 assemblies.

CONSTITUTIONAL AMENDMENTS

In general, the Brotherhood's parliamentary bloc has developed its own set of proposals for reforming Egypt's constitutional order, while also advancing a critique of the constitutional amendments proposed by the regime. Indeed, the issue of constitutional amendments has occupied a prominent position in the debates and platforms of various political actors in Egypt since 2002. The Muslim Brotherhood's particular position took shape in 2004, when it released its "Initiative for Reform," and it was further developed in its 2005 electoral platform. Although these documents made no explicit references to amending the national constitution, they implied that intention by proposing reforms to empower legislative and judicial authorities vis-à-vis the executive branch of government, refashion the roles of several state institutions in the political and cultural spheres, and nullify various laws enshrined in the constitution that limit political rights and freedoms.[20]

In the run-up to the 2005 presidential and parliamentary elections, President Hosni Mubarak proposed an amendment to Article 76 of the constitution allowing multi-candidate presidential elections. In so doing, he appeared to yield to opposition demands to abandon the decades-old system of popular referenda designed merely to confirm the regime's candidate for the presidency. The Brotherhood, however, rejected the proposed amendment as insufficient. In May 2005, it called for a boycott of the referendum to confirm the amendment, although it did not boycott the presidential elections in September of that year.[21] The Brotherhood objected to the president's proposal because it restricted the ability of independents and opposition parties to field presidential candidates. Specifically, the proposal required political parties who wished to put forth a presidential candidate to have at least five percent of the assembly's seats. Independents in particular were required to have the support of 250 elected members of the People's Assembly, Shura Council (the upper house of the Egyptian parliament), and local councils.

According to the Brotherhood, these stipulations clearly favored the NDP, which has always held a majority of the 620 seats in the People's Assembly and the Shura Council. At the time Mubarak proposed the amendment, the seats of the opposition and the independents combined formed only 6.4 percent, still less than the quorum specified by the amended Article 76. The NDP used its majority to pass the president's original proposal despite the opposition of the Brotherhood, independents, and others. And the regime simply ignored calls to amend Article 77 of the constitution in order to specify a term limit for the presidency.[22]

The Muslim Brotherhood opposed another set of presidential election laws proposed by the NDP and designed to benefit the regime later in 2005. This time the Brotherhood proposed alternative legislation on the issue, including a provision to hold the presidential elections in several stages, because there are not enough judges to supervise national polling when it is held on a single day—and the lack of judicial oversight provides ample opportunity for vote rigging. In addition, the Brotherhood bloc called for complete judicial supervision over the elections and rejected the proposed inclusion of nonjudicial figures in the oversight committee.[23]

The Muslim Brotherhood persisted in its opposition to the constitutional amendments proposed by the president and the NDP throughout the 2005–2010 People's Assembly. The largest battle took place over a large set of presidentially proposed amendments in 2006 and 2007: on December 26, 2006, President Mubarak called for the amendment of 34 constitutional articles to prohibit the establishment of religious parties and introduce more changes to presidential and legislative election laws, without setting a term limit for the presidency. After an initial attempt to take part in the ensuing discussions, the Brotherhood's deputies pulled out of the March 18, 2007, parliamentary session on these amendments, claiming that the NDP had failed to take their views into account.[24] Soon after, the Brotherhood called for a boycott of the referendum on the constitutional amendments.[25]

Opposition actors and independent observers criticized the package of amendments as offering the appearance of political reform while actually moving in the opposite direction.[26] Of the 34 amendments introduced and eventually approved, the Brotherhood bloc focused its critique on the following elements, which it interpreted as limiting political freedoms and impeding its political activism:

- Amendments banning religiously based political parties and activities, which clearly obstruct the Muslim Brotherhood's transformation into a legal party and limit its participation in politics. The Brotherhood views the ban as completely inconsistent with Article 2 of the constitution, which stipulates Islam as the religion of the state in Egypt and *shari'a* as its major source of legislation.

- Further amendments to Article 76 regarding presidential elections that upheld the requirement of independent candidates to gain the support of 250 elected members in the NDP-dominated People's Assembly, Shura Council, and local councils. (Though the amendments did reduce the number of seats in parliament required for a legal political party to field a presidential candidate from five percent to three percent.)[27]

- An amendment laying the groundwork for a proportional system of legislative elections, which suggested that Egyptians would no longer vote for individuals but instead for party lists. In the Brotherhood's view, this amendment cemented its exclusion from regular electoral politics, since it is not allowed to form a political party.[28]

- An amendment to Article 88 that reduced judicial oversight of elections by forming special oversight committees composed of both judges and former government officials. The Brotherhood charged that the new system would increase opportunities for election rigging and manipulation.

- Amendments to Article 179, which would allow the enactment of a terrorism law. The constitutional amendments asserted the right of the Ministry of Interior to curb political and civic rights by restricting the press, subjecting journalists to potential imprisonment, and allowing governmental bodies to observe and control the activities of political parties.[29] The Brotherhood joined other opposition critics to charge that the effect would be to allow the regime to replace the long-standing state of emergency with a new set of permanent legal tools designed to restrict political life.

- The Brotherhood MPs criticized the fact that, yet again, the proposed amendments did not include Article 77, thus leaving the number of presidential terms unlimited.[30]

POLITICAL FREEDOMS, PUBLIC FREEDOMS, RULE OF LAW, AND HUMAN RIGHTS

The Muslim Brotherhood's stances on constitutional amendments were specific expressions of its more general pursuit of greater political freedoms. Much of its ordinary parliamentary activity in both the 2000–2005 and 2005–2010 People's Assemblies followed this line. Brotherhood MPs opposed NDP-sponsored amendments designed to stifle the political freedom of religiously based parties and consolidate the regime's executive power. The Brotherhood bloc also took legislative initiative by actively participating in discussions pertaining to these issues (political freedoms, public freedoms, checks and balances between branches of government, and elections) and proposed a few meaningful amendments and draft laws to open Egypt's political sphere and protect it from abuses of power. However, the NDP promptly dismissed this legislation.

In 2000, the Brotherhood bloc explicitly called for an end to the state of emergency, which has been in continuous effect since 1981. Indeed, with a few short respites, Egyptian governments have invoked a state of emergency for the last seven decades, providing legal justification to compromise the rights of Egyptian citizens.[31] But the Brotherhood's efforts came to naught; the NDP used its crushing majority to extend the state of emergency for three years in 2003, two years in 2006, and then again in 2008 until May 2010.[32] Since 2003 the Brotherhood bloc has repeatedly warned that the perpetual extension of the emergency law indicates the regime's intention to restrict already limited political freedom.

Throughout the parliamentary sessions of the last ten years, Brotherhood deputies have questioned the prime minister, minister of justice, and minister of interior on the issues of prison torture, interrogation of citizens, and actions taken by intelligence officers. MPs have stressed that Egypt's violations of human rights provide an important pretext for international intervention in the country's internal affairs. The Brotherhood's inquiries pressured the parliamentary committee on Defense and National Security to organize a number of field visits to prisons in the summer of 2004, and Brotherhood deputies contributed to the written report of the committee's findings.[33] In June 2005, the parliament bloc addressed the issue of poor prison conditions and insisted that supervision be entrusted to the Ministry of Justice, rather than the Ministry of Interior.[34] Also during the 2000–2005 period, the Brotherhood bloc proposed the inclusion of an additional clause in the Law of Criminal Procedures to forbid the preventive detention of journalists and doctors based on mistakes that occur during professional practice.[35] Like most of the Brotherhood's initiatives, this legislation was decisively blocked by the NDP parliamentary majority.

From 2005–2010, the Muslim Brotherhood's platform and activities in parliament have been extended to encompass judicial independence. The Brotherhood entered the field with enthusiasm in the middle of the decade following a contest between the executive branch and dissident judges. As the government moved to bring some independent judicial voices to heel, the Brotherhood tried to push in the opposite direction, developing and endorsing proposals to remove tools of executive domination over the judiciary. Thus, in addition to rejecting NDP-proposed amendments that aimed to subject the judiciary to greater executive authority,[36] the Muslim Brotherhood submitted an alternative draft law. The draft, presented on March 7, 2006, by MP Subhi Salih, sought to separate judicial and executive authorities and ensure judges' neutrality and independence by holding them accountable only to the Judges Club. The NDP law was passed in its original form in 2006.[37]

In 2006, the Brotherhood bloc also developed its own alternative draft law for forming and organizing political parties. Its sought to ease the formation of parties—which currently must be legalized by the quasi-governmental Political Parties Committee—and safeguard their freedoms, which have been violated through confiscation of their documents, restricting their activities, and eavesdropping on their communications. The proposal would have also freed party publications and newspapers from the restrictions of the Law of Press and Publications.[38] As with most Brotherhood initiatives, the alternative articulated the group's vision but had no legal effect; the government's 2005 Political Parties Law stands.

The Brotherhood's effort to guard civil rights has extended to proposed legislation on the Law of Criminal Procedures. On April 4, 2006, the Proposals and Complaints Parliamentary Committee approved the Muslim Brotherhood's legislation limiting preventive detention to a period of less than three months in the case that the accused person is not notified of the date of his/her tribunal session. The clause is intended to protect the accused from interrogation and distinguish between preventative detention, which the Brotherhood considers a violation of civil rights and actual imprisonment.[39] The Brotherhood bloc also proposed an amendment to the Penal Law calling for life imprisonment of interrogators and jailers who torture prisoners. However, the NDP majority rejected this amendment.[40]

In an effort to strengthen civil society, MP Yusri Bayumi announced in December 2008 that he was preparing a draft law to ensure the freedom to establish NGOs, labor unions, and professional associations.[41] Bayumi called for the simplification of the procedures necessary to form these bodies and demanded that the Ministry of Social Solidarity's systematic intervention in their administration be curbed. Parliament did not approve the draft law.

Regarding citizens' freedom of expression and association, the Muslim Brotherhood bloc earlier rejected a draft law proposed by the Ministry of Religious Affairs on April 2, 2008, forbidding demonstrations inside mosques. According to Brotherhood MPs, the real aim of the proposal was to further reduce spaces available for free expression under the pretext of protecting places of worship.[42] During the discussion of the draft law, MP Husayn Ibrahim proposed adding a clause to allow demonstrations for important national and religious causes, as well as all peaceful demonstrations during the daytime, as long as they do not risk damaging mosques or politicizing places of worship. The parliament ignored Ibrahim's suggestion.

Finally, on freedom of the press, in 2009 MP Muhsin Radi proposed a draft law to cancel Article 190 of Law 58/1937, which forbids journalists from publishing the procedures and decisions of tribunals deemed destructive to the public order and citizens' morality. According to the Brotherhood bloc, the current article not only restricts the freedom of the press,[43] but also violates the constitution, which states that all tribunals are public.[44]

SOCIAL AND ECONOMIC LEGISLATION

In general, the Muslim Brotherhood has used its parliamentary presence to call attention to the government's socioeconomic shortcomings, including its allegedly exclusive representation of the interests of the business elite, negligence of the needs of lower-income classes, and failure to address the country's serious developmental problems. The Brotherhood has pursued these themes through inquiries, more formal interpellations, assessments of national budget proposals, and related media activities. Brotherhood deputies have repeatedly blamed the government for inflation, unemployment, rising prices, corruption, and the decline in wages. In the same regard, they have also stressed that the government's economic failures have aggravated phenomena of social instability, such as crime, sexual harassment, and the illegal migration of Egyptians.[45]

For a variety of reasons, between 2000 and 2005, the Brotherhood bloc voted against all annual budgets submitted by the government to the People's Assembly. Most significantly, the seventeen deputies cited asserted that despite the government's increased social expenditures,[46] the quality of health and education services had not actually improved, and that economic burdens continued to afflict lower-income households. According to the Brotherhood bloc, each budget should have allocated greater public funding for long-term investments in an attempt to create jobs and increase economic growth. The Brotherhood also repeatedly criticized the government for failing to increase the country's tax revenues and decrease its budget deficit, as well as its allocation of subsidies for Egyptian exports, a decision the Brotherhood claimed would benefit few. Lastly, the Brotherhood rejected government taxation policies that it saw as unduly burdensome to lower-income households.[47]

With regard to the national debt, MP Hamdi Hasan directed an interpellation to the Prime Minister and the Minister of Finance in January 2004 concerning its ballooning size, which had reached the equivalent of 90 percent of GDP.[48] Hasan accused the government of failing to contain the debt increase and claimed that it had not been transparent regarding the size of the increase, which has negative ramifications for the public debt and social spending.[49] In 2004, MP Sabir 'Abd al-Sadiq also addressed the government with an interpellation on the gap between its annual expenditure rate and revenues[50] and criticized it for failing to facilitate economic liberalization as well as its channeling of foreign direct investment to sectors with limited productivity, such as oil.

Throughout this period, the Brotherhood bloc also pursued issues of administrative corruption, bribes, and private exploitation of public property by way of inquiries and interpellations, as well as evidence gathered in the Central Auditing Organization's (CAO) annual reports.[51] In 2002 the CAO report revealed 72,000 cases of financial government corruption,[52] and Brotherhood MPs claimed in 2004 that corruption was costing Egypt more than 100 billion Egyptian pounds per year.[53]

The Brotherhood also focused on the government's lack of economic transparency and provision of false information. In February 2004, Brotherhood deputies accused the government of providing incorrect economic indicators that contradicted those found in the reports of international organizations; statistics released by the regime claimed that economic growth for Egypt (4 percent) was higher than international assessments (2 percent).[54]

In 2004, movement deputies severely criticized the government's privatization and trade liberalization policies, on the grounds that they had negative impacts on livelihoods and the public debt. They argued that these policies were leading to sharp price increases in basic goods such as food, steel, and construction materials, while wages and salaries failed to rise commensurately. They held the liberalization policy and the floating exchange rate responsible for the devaluation of the Egyptian pound by 50 percent. Furthermore, the privatization of public establishments resulted in unemployment because private entrepreneurs refused to retain former public employees,[55] and the government spent available social security funds in a vain attempt to pay off the internal public debt.[56]

In March 2004, the Brotherhood bloc waged an intense public campaign to pressure the government to discuss the enforcement of a monopoly law, which it reasoned would revive the Egyptian industrial sector, improve the quality of Egyptian manufactured goods, and stabilize prices.[57] The Brotherhood claimed a rare legislative success in this regard with the passing of the Law of Protecting Competition and Forbidding Monopoly in February 2005, which forbids deals and mergers between companies that hinder competition and oust smaller competitors from the market.[58]

With its increased representation in the 2005–2010 parliament, the Brotherhood has continued with similar efforts. Its deputies have again voted against the annual budget. Further, they have criticized the Plan and Budget Committee for its lack of transparency and proposed reallocating public funds from various sectors—such as subsidies on exports and energy, and media budgets—to education and public health. Brotherhood MPs reiterated their proposals to cut the budget deficit, improve the quality of health and education services, increase public investment in order to create jobs, and monitor privatization projects.[59] In response to the 2008/2009 budget, the bloc proposed revisiting the country's taxation and tax collection policies. In 2009/2010, several of the eighty-eight Brotherhood deputies refrained from criticizing the government for its attempts to stimulate investment and reduce subsidies, but they pushed it to reprioritize the social agenda and demanded tax reform.

In recent years the Brotherhood bloc has continued its anticorruption campaign, claiming that successful curbs on corruption would improve the country's investment climate and alleviate some of the negative impacts of privatization on the lower and middle classes. In 2007, Brotherhood deputies accused the government of allowing some companies to gain monopolies over food staples by failing to control prices.[60] On January 13, 2008, MP Sa'd al-Husayni proposed a draft law to amend the Competition and Monopoly Law of 2005 in order to apply stricter penalties to monopolies. The draft law proposed exacting a penalty of 1 billion Egyptian pounds on monopolists, canceling their business permits, fining the managers of their companies, and possibly sentencing them to prison.[61] The NDP majority rejected the measure.

In 2007 and 2008, the Brotherhood parliamentary bloc questioned the minister of finance on the government's mismanagement of social security funds, and its use of the 270 billion Egyptian pounds from the Indemnities and Salaries Fund to cover the public debt. In 2008, the bloc directed 104 inquiries and twelve interpellations to the government on the import of expired foods, especially wheat, which had been allegedly carried out by businessmen close to the regime.[62] In December 2008, MP Muhsin Radi accused the government of wasting several billion Egyptian pounds' worth of grant money provided by international donors to develop education, local governance, agriculture, microcredit, and women's empowerment.[63]

Thus, in areas intertwined with questions of political reform and economic policy, the Brotherhood has used its parliamentary bloc to develop its general policy inclintions into a sustained series of initiatives and detailed proposals to demonstrate that it can offer a comprehensive alternative vision for Egyptian politics. But what of the more traditional areas of concern for the movement? The Brotherhood has worked to pursue this new comprehensive agenda without abandoning its long-standing emphasis on religion, morality, and the family. A close examination of its record in parliament reveals only partial success in pursuing the new, broad agenda alongside the older, narrower one.

RELIGIOUS AND MORAL LEGISLATION

Throughout the 2000–2005 and 2005–2010 parliamentary assemblies, the Muslim Brotherhood has pursued its traditional religious and moral platform based on calls for the application of *shari'a*.

Most interestingly, the Brotherhood has worked hard to portray its religious agenda as compatible with—and even a full expression of—its comprehensive reform program. Some of the religious issues it has raised, such as the right of veiled women to be hired for government-funded television channels, have been linked to the freedom of expression and belief. On other issues, such as torture and the rights of the press, the Brotherhood has used its religious and moral priorities to defend political freedoms and human rights.

But even as it has worked to integrate its various agendas, the Brotherhood has made an unmistakable shift in emphasis. The movement's religious and moral platform in parliament has clearly declined in salience over the last ten years. Brotherhood deputies have been preoccupied with parliamentary debates on constitutional amendments, political freedoms, and socioeconomic legislation, often at the expense of *shari'a*-based legislation. But the change of emphasis is relative; Brotherhood deputies have not been silent on religious issues.

In a few rare instances throughout the 2000–2005 People's Assembly, Brotherhood deputies addressed moral and cultural issues closely related to the application of *shari'a*. For example, they presented the following inquiries:

- To the Ministry of Culture in 2001 concerning the government-funded publication of three novels containing direct "sexual references" that the Brotherhood considered offensive to Islamic and public morals. The inquiry led to the suspension of several officials in the Ministry of Culture, which henceforth sought the judgment of al-Azhar on the content of government-funded books and publications.
- In June 2002, Brotherhood deputies questioned the government in relation to what it perceived as official attempts to limit al-Azhar's role in the educational sector and de-emphasize religion and Arabic language in school curriculum.
- To the government regarding the "Miss Egypt" beauty competition in April 2004, which the Brotherhood rejected as an insult to Islam and an act of defiance to *shari'a*.[64] The Brotherhood also called for the resignation of the Grand Shaykh of al-Azhar in 2003 due to his mild reaction to the French government's decision to ban the veil in schools and universities and criticized the decision of the Egyptian Ministry of Information to forbid female TV anchors from wearing veils.[65]

In terms of legislative proposals, Brotherhood deputies presented legislation in 2002 to adjust laws to the framework of *shari'a*.[66] and to forbid critics of Islam and the Prophet Muhammad from entering Egypt. In 2003, the Brotherhood pursued similar legislative initiatives, including measures to forbid alcohol in Egypt and ban art that makes obvious references to sexuality, such as movies that have intimate scenes and concerts featuring female singers. The Brotherhood bloc also proposed draft legislation aiming to strengthen articles of criminal law that punish acts of adultery, the consumption and purchase of alcohol, and gambling. The proposed articles, which were not passed in the assembly, would have subjected certain perpetrators of these crimes to monetary fines, imprisonment, and even whipping.

The Brotherhood bloc also proposed amendments and laws to preserve the institution of al-Azhar and its independence. Brotherhood MPs proposed laws to reform al-Azhar's institutional framework, decision-making process, and the management of its endowments. Several times during the 2000–2005 assembly, MP 'Ali Laban presented his draft of a proposed amendment to Law 103/1961 stipulating that the Grand Shaykh of al-Azhar and the associated Board of Religious Scholars should be popularly elected rather than appointed by the government, as has been the case since the 1950s.[67] Also during this period, MP Husayn Ibrahim proposed a draft law to restore al-Azhar endowments that had been confiscated by the government.[68]

During the People's Assembly of 2005–2010, the Brotherhood continued its efforts to secure al-Azhar's independence by rejecting a December 2006 draft law sanctioning the appointment of high al-Azhar officials, which was nevertheless passed by the NDP majority.[69] In 2008, the Brotherhood bloc questioned several figures—including the prime minister, the minister of religious affairs and endowments, and the minister of development—accusing the government of weakening al-Azhar University by cancelling its branches in some governorates and neglecting the development of its curriculum.[70]

Brotherhood deputies continued to raise issues similar to those it had raised in the 2000–2005 assembly pertaining to the application of shari'a and morality. In 2007 MP Muhsin Radi questioned the minister of religious affairs and endowments on his policy of allowing the security services to control mosques and limit the preachers' proselytizing activities.[71] In the plenary debate related to Radi's question, several movement deputies raised other objections to the Ministry, criticizing it for publishing a document condemning female circumcision, forcing preachers to attend lectures organized by the Egyptian Anglican Church in Alexandria, and asking Friday preachers not to curse Israel.[72]

Just as it has tried to connect its religious agenda to political reforms, the Brotherhood has tried to introduce Islamic principles into its economic program in order to demonstrate their relevance to citizens' needs and Egypt's developmental challenges. Thus, Islamic banking and economics have become an element of the Brotherhood's parliamentary activities to promote *shari'a* and Islamic morals. In 2008, MP Ibrahim al-Ja'fari proposed a draft law to amend the Law of the Central Bank,[73] entreating it to create Islamic banking supervision units and run Islamic banks in a manner different from commercial banks. However, parliament rejected the draft law. Later in the 2005–2010 assembly, Brotherhood deputies attempted to present Islamic banking as a solution to the global financial crisis. Elaborating on the concept, MP 'Alam al-Din al-Sikhawi proposed in 2008 the introduction of an alms law (*zakat*) that would oblige Egyptian Muslims to give their regular Islamic tax payments to special banks, which then would distribute them among poor households and unemployed citizens.[74]

In terms of other legislative efforts related to the Brotherhood bloc's religious and moral platform, in 2008 and 2009 several MPs proposed amendments to the Law of the Child, a government initiative designed to bring Egypt in line with international human rights standards. Brotherhood deputies entered the debate by citing legal components they considered contradictory to *shari'a*[75] and sought to change three issues in particular. First, the bloc objected to the application of legal penalties for marriage under the age of eighteen years, which the Brotherhood considered a violation of the *shari'a*-based legal age of sixteen years. Second, it claimed the government's power to interfere in family affairs in order to protect children ran contrary to the Islamic principle of household privacy.[76] Finally, the Brotherhood protested vehemently against the stipulation of the law that enables mothers—including single mothers—to pass their family names to their children, claiming that the clause is a sign of aggressive de-Islamization and Westernization in Egypt. The Brotherhood may have scored rhetorical points, but its efforts left no legal impact, as the NDP's draft law passed without modification.[77]

WOMEN'S ISSUES

The Brotherhood's attempt to combine a broad reform agenda with a specifically religious vision has caused confusion and ambivalence on issues relating to gender and the family. Throughout the 2000–2005 and 2005–2010 assemblies, Brotherhood parliamentarians failed to develop a clear, policy-oriented platform regarding women's rights and political participation. Movement deputies have to a great extent viewed women's issues through their usual religious and moral lenses and thus treated them exclusively based on their "compatibility with *shari'a* provisions." As a result, the Brotherhood bloc has been preoccupied primarily with defending the religious rights of Muslim women—such as the right to veil and protesting against government-introduced legislation "incompatible" with *shari'a* provisions. Brotherhood leaders have generally resisted calls for a greater role for women in public life, but they have grounded their opposition in fairly cautions terms. Despite the failure to present a fully alternative vision, the Brotherhood bloc has also made some initial forays into developing a more positive (and not merely defensive) agenda on social issues, in an attempt to address the needs of women, albeit in a manner that might strike some intended beneficiaries as paternalistic.

On various occasions throughout the People's Assembly of 2000–2005, the Brotherhood bloc defended the right of women to veil and criticized government voices that pushed for a ban of the full face veil (the *niqab*) in public spaces.[78] It has continued these attempts in the 2005–2010 Assembly.

In the current assembly, the Brotherhood bloc has actively participated in parliamentary debates on the aforementioned Law of the Child, several aspects of which touch on women's rights.[79] The draft, which sought to reinforce the ban on female circumcision and place even harsher restrictions on the practice, faced severe criticism from movement deputies who maintained that it violates Islamic teachings and attempts to impose Western values and morality on Egyptians.[80] Muhammad Sa'd al-Katatni, the head of the Brotherhood parliamentary bloc, said in 2008 that the abolition of female circumcision runs "counter to the norms, customs, and nature of the Egyptian people."[81] The law passed in June 2008, banning female circumcision as the NDP had intended, with a clause stipulating that the practice is permitted only in cases of "medical necessity." [82]

Throughout the 2005–2010 People's Assembly, the Brotherhood bloc has also dealt with legislation on the representation of women in politics. Most notably, the Muslim Brotherhood rejected the Law of Women's Quota, which passed the Assembly in June 2009. Among other changes, the law added 64 new seats specifically for women to the People's Assembly, thus increasing the total number of Assembly seats from 454 to 518.

The Brotherhood deputies considered the amendment a response to external pressures and warned that the change would open the door for other "social groups" to make similar demands, hinting at Egypt's Christian community.[83] The Women's Quota Law, they said, serves the interests of the NDP and ultimately contradicts the constitutional article[84] that proclaims all Egyptian citizens as equal.

While the Women's Quota Law will expand women's political participation in Egypt, its actual application stands to benefit the ruling National Democratic Party and consolidate its power in the People's Assembly, at least in the short run. Because the NDP controls the state resources and institutions vital to winning women's seats, these new slots will be difficult for the Brotherhood and other opposition parties to win with independent MPs. And the Muslim Brotherhood is an especially unlikely recipient of these seats, due to its enduringly ambivalent position toward women in politics.

Has the Brotherhood in Parliament Articulated a Reform Vision for Egypt?

Although the remarkably active Muslim Brotherhood bloc has dealt with a wide range of issues in parliament over the past decade, social, economic, and political legislation have been at the core of its platform and activities, both in terms of oversight and legislative attempts.

Social and economic concerns such as monopolies, corruption, privatization, tax systems, and public debt have occupied the Brotherhood bloc's agenda, culminating in an extensive use of oversight powers to address failed government policies at these levels. Brotherhood deputies have also made extensive use of their—limited—legislative tools to address Egypt's lack of freedom and political reform, although to no avail. They have protested and attempted to block government-proposed constitutional and legal amendments that are interpreted as attempts to consolidate Egypt's semiauthoritarianism. But the prioritization of these issues has often come at the cost of the Brotherhood's religious and moral platform, which enjoyed a formative role in the movement's parliamentary participation before 2000. Indeed, the Brotherhood's religious and moral platform has been reduced to illiberal stances on women's issues and scattered calls for the application of shari'a provisions.

Several factors can account for these shifts in parliamentary priorities and activities of the Brotherhood. First of all, broad public debates in Egypt since 2002 and 2003 have focused increasingly on the issue of political reform and the need to hold the government accountable for its performance in social and economic fields. Freedom and governance deficits have become integral components of regular press coverage, opinion writing, and television talk shows. Therefore, it comes as no surprise that a significant part of the Brotherhood's parliamentary platform has reflected the growing discourse on reform, freedom, and governance in Egypt. The 2004 Reform Initiative, the 2005 electoral program, and the 2007 draft party platform have represented milestones in this regard.

Secondly, the "reform drive" of the Brotherhood has been bolstered by systematic efforts from other political forces in Egypt to reach out to the movement and join it in developing a grand opposition platform. However ambivalent these efforts seem at times, both liberal and leftist forces have cooperated in this effort, yielding a nationwide debate on social, economic, and political reform that became especially animated from 2003 to 2005.

Lastly, the diverse composition of the Brotherhood bloc helps explain its changing priorities and activities in parliament. In the current assembly especially, the 88 Brotherhood MPs come from many different professional and scientific backgrounds are thus qualified to address a wide range of parliamentary issues, as demonstrated by the level of detail with which they have discussed annual budgets and legislation pertaining to political freedoms.

Yet the relative marginalization of the Brotherhood's religious and moral platform in parliament has posed a serious challenge for the movement: how can it pursue social, economic, and political reforms in parliament while preserving its Islamic credentials? While the Brotherhood has been blocked from forming a political party, one strategy for dealing with the tension between its specific religious and broad political agendas is to formalize political operations in organizational terms. And indeed, in recent years, one can observe a functional separation between the parliamentary bloc, which addresses reform issues, and the leadership of the movement—the General Guide and the Guidance Office—that prioritizes religious and moral concerns in official pronouncements, media statements, and other activities. The themes of the Brotherhood General Guide's Weekly Address between 2005 and 2009 generally followed very much in line with this trend.

Yet a second and equally serious challenge has resulted from the limited outcome of the Brotherhood's participation in parliament, especially in terms of legislative output. In the eyes of many Brotherhood constituents and activists, the movement's pursuit of reform issues in parliament has simply not paid off; its de-emphasis of religious and moral issues has proven vain and fruitless. Nor has the Brotherhood's participation in parliament, they argue, opened Egypt's political sphere. The Brotherhood's leadership has increasingly felt the need to account for this negative balance and offer explanations for its priorities to the rank and file. Discussion and debate surrounding this issue has called into question the priority of political participation as a strategy, especially in comparison to the success of wider social and religious activities. One outcome of this growing issue has been a changing balance of power within the movement's leadership between advocates of political participation and those concerned with the Brotherhood's social and religious role.

Future Prospects: Preservation and Stagnation

Viewing the events of the first decade of the twenty-first century year by year from the perspective of the Muslim Brotherhood, one would be struck by the rapid, almost heady ascent of the organization in relation to the Egyptian regime followed by a sometimes gradual but definite decline.

In the first half of the current decade, the Brotherhood managed to overcome many of the effects of the harsh repression of the 1990s, select a new leader on two occasions, place itself at the center of Egyptian political debates, reach out to other opposition forces, develop a clear reform agenda, attract and foster the public role of a new generation of movement activists, and show that it was the most viable opposition political movement in the country.

However, in the second half of the decade, the Brotherhood felt the brunt of repressive measures, with its activists harassed and some leaders arrested, its space for political opposition constricted, and clear preparations under way in government to exclude its candidates from the next round of parliamentary elections. While the movement did manage to select a new leader in 2010 (for the first time replacing a head who retired rather than dying in office), the process provoked bitter public arguments among leaders, a very unpleasant experience for a movement with a marked aversion to airing dirty laundry.

But again, movement leaders insist that they measure their success only in the long term, and if that is the case, they had room for satisfaction. They navigated the ever-shifting rules of Egypt's semiauthoritarian order and showed not just resilience, but also deeply rooted support and occasionally even an ability to seize the initiative. They entered politics with enthusiasm without being co-opted or corrupted; became more sophisticated, and showed the ability to articulate not only appealing slogans, but detailed proposals. The Brotherhood also weathered a difficult post-September 11 international environment, convincing some international observers that it is not linked to al-Qaeda, and that it may even be the sort of Islamist movement that the West can safely engage.

Yet any further progress would seem to require a renewed political opening in Egypt. It is difficult to see the Brotherhood continuing to play such a public role absent some political reform. Here the Brotherhood may have learned a hard lesson over the past decade: the better their leaders play the political game, the more likely they are to be shoved out of the political arena (or, to maintain the metaphor, the more the rules of that game are rewritten to exclude them). In short, the Brotherhood has encountered a paradox: the more it presents itself as a credible force for political reform, the less reform is likely.

And the Brotherhood's slightly improved level of international respectability proved of limited utility. It is true that the Brotherhood no longer frightens most Western governments, and that foreign diplomats, academic specialists, and journalists came to have a far greater knowledge and sophistication about its ideology and programs. However, the Egyptian regime has also demonstrated its own importance to several regional diplomatic processes that the United States in particular holds dear, and the Brotherhood is aligned with a set of political forces (such as Hamas) deemed inimical to Western interests. Thus, despite the Brotherhood's increased respectability, the international community would likely place few roadblocks to continued repression of the movement.

Facing the challenges of operating in Egypt's semiauthoritarian political sphere, making more noise than tangible progress in parliament, and eyed with mistrust by other opposition actors, the Muslim Brotherhood moved to scale back its political ambitions to mere self-preservation.

The organization was forced to prioritize the management of its own internal affairs over its political role and opposition activities. Furthermore, the Brotherhood's ability to clarify the ambiguities regarding important political and societal issues was compromised by the strong and sometimes contradictory pulls of its diverse constituencies and critics. And the most comprehensive attempt to address all "gray zones"—the draft party platform—was effectively withdrawn by a movement that increasingly considers shyness a virtue.

The first major impact of the regime's continued repression of the Brotherhood and restrictions on its participation has been a gradual closing-off of the formal political sphere for the movement. In spite of the Brotherhood's significant representation in the 2005–2010 People's Assembly and the solid appearance of its parliamentary bloc, it has become an isolated movement with little influence on the outcome of the legislative process and on Egyptian politics in general. Prospects for the future do not look any different.

The second major impact has been a growing recognition by many Brotherhood leaders that the movement is under siege and will remain so for the foreseeable future. The dominant view within the movement is that the Brotherhood should focus its energies on sustaining organizational solidarity in the face of regime repression rather than expend efforts in a futile bid for political participation. In other words, the closed environment in which the Brotherhood has been operating—which has worsened following the 2005 parliamentary elections and was manifested as recently as February 2010 in another wave of arrests of Brotherhood leaders, including a vice general guide and three members of the Guidance Office—offers no incentive for continued prioritization of political participation, prompting the movement to turn either inward or toward the social and religious aspects of its activism.

Under these conditions, it comes as no surprise that the Brotherhood's internal dynamics have been shaped by a series of debates on the strategic value of political participation. Brotherhood leaders who argued earlier for more participation have either changed their minds or lost ground in these internal debates. And in the current environment, it becomes far more convincing to argue for relative isolation, a focus on internal organizational solidarity, and the prioritization of social and religious activism.

The general guide, Muhammad Badi', is known for his interest in the movement's internal solidarity and its activities in the social and religious spheres. In regard to political participation, Badi' acknowledged in his January 2010 acceptance speech that the Muslim Brotherhood represents itself in parliament and community work as a peaceful and legitimate force to bring about reform in Egypt.[85] However, Badi' also asserted that the Brotherhood's traditional formula that true reform begins at the level of individual souls, spreading through families and society in order eventually to affect the country's political situation— a clear indication of his inclination to re-prioritize social and religious activism.[86]

The Brotherhood's retreat will not be total. None of its leaders argue for complete withdrawal and isolation, and Egypt's increasingly closed political system still leaves a few doors ajar for opposition voices. The Brotherhood is likely to secure a smattering of seats in the new parliament if it decides to run. It, along with the regime, will survive. But the contest between them is entering a new phase, and preservation of both parties may imply political stagnation for the country. With the Brotherhood's retreat, a fleeting opportunity that seemed to arise in the middle of the decade for building a more pluralistic political system and for an open political contest between competing visions for Egypt's future appears to have been lost.

Appendix A

Election year	Seats contested	Seats won
1976	1 (as independents)	0
1979	2 (as independents)	0
1984	18 (under New Wafd party list)	8
1987	40 (as part of the Islamic Alliance, with the Socialist Labour Party and Socialist Liberal Party)	38
1990	0	0
1995	160 (as independents)	1
2000	70 (as independents)	17
2005	150 (as independents)	88

CHAPTER 3

Jordan and Its Islamic Movement

The Limits of Inclusion?

I n the Arab world, Jordan has the longest history of an Islamic movement competing regularly, legally, and openly in elections. Members of the Jordanian Muslim Brotherhood have even joined the government. And although the relationship between rulers and Islamists in Jordan has often been tense, both sides have tried to avoid provoking the other into outright confrontation. In that sense, Jordan's rulers have worked to test the proposition that inclusion breeds moderation—or, more modestly, that limited inclusion coupled with periodic warnings will discourage extremism. For their part, Islamist leaders have worked to test the proposition that it is better to participate in the system than to work toward overthrowing it—or, more modestly, that more can be gained by testing red lines and pushing them outward than by crossing them brazenly. They have gone so far as to establish their own party, the Islamic Action Front (IAF), to focus on political activity. In short, both groups have come to regard the other as a rival to be dealt with politically, rather than an implacable adversary to be crushed.

But the tense relationship is now being tested. The Brotherhood and the IAF have become deeply divided within themselves, and more radical voices have gained increasing support in recent years. The Jordanian regime also shows growing signs that it regards the Islamist movement as a security threat.

Yet past patterns have not been erased, however, even if they have been strained. In the past, Jordan's general approach to independent and oppositional political movements—whether Islamist, nationalist, or leftist—oscillated between co-optation and repression. At present, however, Jordan appears to be pursuing both strategies at the same time.

The Jordanian Islamist movement—represented by the IAF and its parent movement, the Jordanian Muslim Brotherhood—is no stranger to political anomalies. In fact, its existence reflects a whole series of paradoxes. Like some of its sister movements in other Arab countries, the IAF competes in elections but deliberately avoids winning them. Even though it is unusually diverse in its ideological currents—even by the standards of its sister movements—it has suffered schisms and divisive internal debates only on short-term tactical questions. Operating in a political context in which parties and movements are organized around dominant individuals, neither the Muslim Brotherhood nor the IAF has produced a charismatic figure. Even more unusually, neither has seen any of its leaders die in office; instead they retire, complete their terms, or are forced out. The party constantly finds its critics questioning the sincerity of its democratic commitments—yet it has stressed issues of political freedoms and democratic institutions for half a century. Indeed, the IAF may be the most democratic party in the region in terms of its internal operations. Long reputed to be aligned with the government, it is now the only viable opposition party in the country. Long the adversary of leftist and nationalist forces, the IAF now keeps those movements relevant through an alliance with them (since a joint front of opposition elements adds credibility to the IAF's positions and the other opposition forces' deteriorating base makes them very much junior partners).

Yet for all these anomalies, Jordan's Islamist movement finds itself poised on the brink of deeper conflict with the government because it has not been able to escape overriding regional realities. In recent years, the Israeli-Palestinian conflict, the war in Iraq, and the U.S. war on terrorism have dominated the movement's agenda and deeply colored its relations with the Jordanian regime.

This analysis of the IAF and its role in Jordan's politics examines:

- how the Islamist movement has historically remained within the Jordanian legal and constitutional framework but also used that framework to form organizations with a broad and deep reach in Jordanian society;
- what the IAF stands for—and how much its members argue about its aims;

- how participation in parliament has led its leaders to conclude—despite ongoing and sometimes bitter debate—that accepting the sharp restrictions on their activities has generally been worth the benefits of legality and official recognition;
- how both the regime and the Islamic movement are now debating whether or not a serious confrontation is unavoidable;
- how the Islamist movement has tried to build alliances with other opposition actors—and how it has succeeded in those efforts only because of the weakness of its new partners; and
- how international pressures have aggravated the tensions between regime and opposition without making an unbridled confrontation inevitable.

Working Within—and Stretching—the Rules

The Jordanian political system has always placed sharp limits on political opposition, but by using a set of tools that stops short of harsh authoritarianism, it has left some openings for resourceful and cautious movements. The Islamist movement has largely accepted the limitations and worked around them to build an impressive set of social and political organizations.

The IAF operates as the political wing of Jordan's Muslim Brotherhood. Formed in 1945 and loosely affiliated with the Egyptian Muslim Brotherhood, the Jordanian Muslim Brotherhood is broad-based and dedicated to pursuing an Islamic society and way of life through a variety of social, charitable, educational, and political activities. This wide focus helped the Brotherhood develop a deep reach in Jordanian society. Its relationship with the regime has been uneasy, punctuated by occasional periods of open conflict, but enjoying long periods in which the Jordanian regime has favored an approach of accommodation and even co-optation. The Jordanian government has never opted for the "Egyptian solution" of banning and suppressing the Brotherhood.

The relationship between the government and the Islamist opposition has been so much less antagonistic in Jordan than in other countries that some specialists have spoken of a tacit alliance between the Brotherhood and the regime. But such a characterization clearly goes too far. Even in the protracted period of friendlier relations (from the 1950s through the 1970s), the regime kept a close eye on the movement and arrested its leaders several times for political offenses. One prominent member of the Muslim Brotherhood has even gone so far as to attempt to write a history of the movement stressing its stubbornly oppositional nature.[1]

It would be most accurate to avoid extremes and describe the regime's historical relationship with the Brotherhood as wary and guarded but not overtly hostile. When the Jordanian regime confronted its most severe challenges—from nationalist movements in the 1950s and Palestinian movements after 1967—the Brotherhood stood aloof, earning a reputation as being less threatening. It was therefore allowed to operate in many social spheres and even run candidates for the parliament, often criticizing government policy (especially on cultural and Islamic issues) but not posing a direct challenge to the regime.

Historically, Jordan's Muslim Brotherhood has faithfully operated within the framework of Jordanian law. The government has shifted that framework to contain the Brotherhood, but often merely steered it into new fields of activity. For a long time, for instance, the movement was steered into social and charitable activity by the legal environment in which it operated. When a new, more liberal political party law was issued in 1992, the Brotherhood seized the opportunity to create a new political wing, the IAF.

Like its parent organization in Egypt, the Jordanian Muslim Brotherhood began with a general social focus, but moved quickly into international affairs with a heavy interest in the emerging conflict in Palestine. It stayed clear of becoming overtly critical toward the government, but it never eschewed political activity. The movement ran candidates in Jordanian parliamentary elections in the 1950s and 1960s, but won less than a handful of races in each cycle. However, when parliamentary elections were resumed in 1989 after a hiatus that lasted over two decades, the Brotherhood leapt beyond its past performance, winning 22 of 80 seats.

Over the years, movement deputies used their parliamentary seats to call for implementation of Islamic law and to condemn cultural practices deemed non-Islamic (such as the visit of an ice-skating troupe that wore costumes considered excessively revealing). The movement's positions on many issues—ranging from Palestine to *shari'a*—were strong and uncompromising and its language sometimes shrill. It denounced a U.S. aid offer in 1957 with the slogan "No reconciliation [with Israel], no dollar, no atheism, and no imperialism." But the Brotherhood stayed within the boundaries of peaceful opposition. In the two most serious political crises the country faced (between the palace and the leftist/

nationalist opposition in the 1950s and between the regime and Palestinian movements in the late 1960s), the Brotherhood stayed neutral. Thus, when both crises resulted in a sharp political crackdown, the Brotherhood was exempted. Although its members and even leaders were sometimes arrested for brief periods, the Brotherhood as a whole was allowed to continue operating.

In this way, the Brotherhood gradually extended its reach into new social and political fields. It began to expand first into a range of charitable activities, founding the Islamic Center Society in 1965 and a web of other organizations and societies in the decades since. Some of these nongovernmental organizations (NGOs) such as the Islamic Center—the Brotherhood's largest operation—are very closely associated with the Brotherhood and are virtual wings of the movement, while others are run by leading Brotherhood activists, but less strongly linked with the movement.

Over time, the Muslim Brotherhood took advantage of the prevailing legal and political environment to move into other fields as well: It attracted some figures in the religious establishment; ran candidates in professional association elections (such as the bar and the medical syndicate); and began to publish its own periodicals. In each of these fields, however, it encountered significant legal obstacles. Its NGOs, for example, were kept under close watch. In July 2006, the Jordanian cabinet replaced the board of the Islamic Center, charging that it had engaged in financial improprieties. The move came in the midst of a confrontation between the Islamist movement and the government and was widely perceived as heavy-handed. The Jordanian government has also restricted movement supporters from giving sermons and it attempts to regulate the content of those sermons it does allow. The government has also shut down newspapers associated with the movement, and in 1993 it issued a decree enacting a restrictive press law to provide itself with new legal tools. More recently, the government passed legislation restricting the issuance of fatwas that do not have official sanction. The government also contemplated moves to restrict the political activities of professional associations. While it ultimately took only mild steps in that regard, it resisted Islamist movement demands to allow the formation of a teachers' union and continued to hint at legal changes for professional associations.

These measures did not suppress the Islamist organizations but created a set of obstructions and shifting red lines that hampered their operations without closing them down altogether. In one important sense, the measures did have a real institutional effect by creating a movement of closely associated organizations rather than a single, centralized organization. The movement's various arms, however much they resented the legal restrictions, complied with them, establishing separate bodies in each field to ensure that each activity was based on independent and solid legal foundations. The various organizations were linked and identified themselves as part of a single movement, but they remained legally distinct, each with its own administrative and governing structure.

Thus it should be no surprise that when parliament passed the new, liberalized political party law in 1992, the Islamic movement did not attempt to repackage the entire organization as a political party. Despite a long history of competing in elections, the movement decided to form an entirely new political party, the Islamic Action Front. The decision was not an easy one. More radical members suspected that the new party might become so anxious to succeed that it would temper opposition to (or even acquiesce in) non-Islamic laws and practices or negotiations with Israel. But others argued that the prospect of political participation was simply too attractive to turn down. Not only did it offer a secure legal vehicle for the movement's political activities and mobilization, but formation of a separate party also offered the opportunity of appealing to independent Islamists outside the Muslim Brotherhood and thus broadening the movement's reach and influence.

In the end, the party's supporters won the day. But the issue of political participation was far from resolved. Those who were suspicious could have remained on the sidelines but instead most joined the new party—preventing a split between it and the broader movement, but also ensuring that the conflicting orientations over political participation would be replicated within the party itself. The newly created IAF satisfied its supporters from the beginning: In the first election in 1993, it won 16 seats (raising its parliamentary total to eighteen, with closely allied independents), in spite of the creation (by dubious legal means) of an electoral system specifically designed to minimize the party's influence.

The IAF has built an impressive set of internal democratic structures. Its leaders are elected by the membership, with regular turnover in top positions. At key points, it has polled its members for guidance on important decisions, most notably on two occasions to decide whether or not the IAF would boycott elections. The party also selects its candidates in a process that begins with branches holding primaries before forwarding names to the party leadership.

But if it follows the letter of democratic procedure in its internal operations, the IAF shows some problems with the spirit. Leaders battle over decisions and positions but not with a completely free hand—the mother Brotherhood movement plays a strong role in shaping the party's program and leadership. The IAF has yet to establish a separate identity from its parent movement, the Muslim Brotherhood. While the IAF and the Muslim Brotherhood have fully separate legal identities, the IAF has made some critical decisions after consulting and deferring to Brotherhood leaders. In addition, the Muslim Brotherhood selects the head of the IAF (or, more accurately described, makes a suggestion that is always accepted). Since 2007, the Brotherhood has been deeply divided by its own internal disputes, leading mother movement and political party to intervene directly and forcefully in each other's affairs and (as will be explored below) barely papering over their differences.

The IAF is also haunted by charges that it is deferential not merely to the Jordanian Muslim Brotherhood but to its sister Brotherhood organizations, particularly in Egypt and Palestine. Although the Jordanian Muslim Brotherhood was formed—and continues to identify itself—as a branch of the international organization founded in Egypt, its association with the Egyptian movement has clearly grown merely collegial. The Jordanian movement did request guidance from the Egyptian movement in 1989 about whether or not to accept ministerial positions, but the Egyptians' response was tardy and ambiguous, hardly resolving the matter before the IAF made a decision.

IAF's association with Hamas is deeper and, in recent years, has been extremely controversial—both inside and outside the movement. The relationship with Hamas is not simply close but also complicated, due partly to geographical proximity and the prominence of the Palestinian cause in Jordanian politics, but also because the movements share common roots (in the period when Jordan ruled the Palestinian West Bank, the Muslim Brotherhood on both banks of the Jordan was a single organization) and Palestinians participate heavily in the IAF. In fact, some Jordanians view the IAF as a surrogate for a Palestinian political party—an identification that has deepened in recent years. A number of Jordanians of Palestinian origin have risen to leadership positions within the movement, though movement activists insist that internal discussions never raise an individual's status as either an East

Bank Jordanian or a Jordanian of Palestinian ancestry. But even if that is true, the primacy of the Palestinian issue and the IAF's relationship with Hamas has grown increasingly divisive within the movement, and most advocates of a more distant relationship have East Bank roots. As Hamas has risen in Palestinian politics, it too has sought to take its place as a separate chapter in the international confederation of Muslim Brotherhood movements, and that has necessitated disentangling the Jordanian Muslim Brotherhood from its historical institutional linkages with Hamas. In 2009, this process set off a bitter dispute within the Jordanian organization over how to divide the unified branches of the Jordanian-Palestinian Muslim Brotherhood operations in the Gulf states, sparking accusations from some East Bank Muslim Brotherhood activists that Hamas sought to subordinate the Jordanian movement to its informal control.

Yet despite these complicated international relationships, the IAF has had an impressive electoral record in Jordanian politics, with its achievements limited primarily by the nature of the country's legal framework (which has actually become more restrictive since the organization first ran), the party's self-restraint, and (at least in 2007) its internal squabbles. Although the IAF's success over the years has largely left the proponents of a distinct Islamist party feeling vindicated, the controversy over its creation has carried over into its operations. Each round of parliamentary elections has set off divisive debates over whether or not the IAF should participate in a skewed process. While each debate ended in a decision—to participate in 1993, 2003, and 2007, and to boycott in 1997—the general terms of the IAF's participation in the electoral process have not been resolved, and members have continued to rehearse the arguments long after elections were held.

The formation of the IAF has exposed the Islamic movement to external challenges as well as internal divisions. Jordan's rulers have come to see the formation of a network of Islamist NGOs, the activities of Islamists in professional associations, and the electoral performance of the IAF as a significant challenge. Indeed, over the past two decades, the Jordanian regime has gradually come to regard the Islamic movement as its most significant domestic rival, taking the place occupied by Arab nationalists, leftists, and Palestinian nationalists in earlier generations.

As a result, the main debate among Jordan's ruling elite seems to be whether to treat the Islamist movement as a security challenge to be dealt with by repression, or a political one to be contained, co-opted, harassed, and managed rather than vanquished.

Wrestling With a Political Platform

The IAF has developed a series of political platforms that stand little chance of implementation over the short term, but provide an accurate barometer of the state of consensus and disagreement within the party as well as its willingness to test the limits of loyal opposition.

AREAS OF DIVISION

While the IAF maintains a semblance of unity, and most schisms do not lead to serious splinter groups, the party and the Islamic movement in general remain diverse ideological coalitions. Those who follow the movement often refer to "hawks" and "doves," while others talk of a more complex picture with a "centrist" and "Hamas" wing. Indeed, there are rival camps within the party, and unlike most sister Islamist groups in the region, these opposing camps have increasingly criticized each other in public.

Three significant issues divide the IAF membership: attitudes toward the Jordanian political system; the role of Islam; and Palestine. Each of these issues is characterized by a "hawkish" and a "dovish" position, and there is some overlap among the three issues. But movement insiders and close observers agree that the factionalization of the IAF and the broader Islamist movement is more complex than a simple set of two or even four camps; there are a variety of intermediate positions and significant differences among even like-minded groups about how salient each issue is. The tendencies come into clearer view on two occasions. First, the forces come into sharper focus when the IAF and the Muslim Brotherhood elect their leaders; at these times, the majority generally reveals itself as a coalition of smaller groups rather than a single unified camp within the movement. Because of the complex nature of such coalitions, analysts often debate what the election results indicate about the strength of various camps, but neither hawks nor doves have succeeded in wresting control of the movement. Second, the factions line up fairly clearly when the issue of participation in Jordanian parliamentary elections arises. In 1997 and 2007, the battling became so intense, the movement came close to fracturing.

The first issue dividing IAF activists is their attitude toward the Jordanian political system. Those on the dovish end of the spectrum think and act very much as members of a loyal opposition, affirming their fealty to the throne and making clear their interest in participating in the political process rather than overthrowing it. Others criticize such figures for being too quick to curry favor with officials; one leading hawk, for example, proclaimed that "pragmatism means conceding principles and fixed positions, and this is something we cannot do," admonishing that "parliamentary elections are a means," not an end. More directly and severely, another IAF leader has written that opposition should come naturally to the movement since "the Muslim Brotherhood and any regime that does not apply Islam should not be in the same trench." In one sense, the internal dispute has narrowed in recent years: earlier generations of leaders argued about the legitimacy of participation in Jordanian politics. That debate has been almost completely resolved; there is little principled objection left to running in elections, for instance, and the remaining debates, as intense as they are, concern how to do so in practice. But in another sense, the internal division about attitude toward the Jordanian political system may have deepened: some see the movement as essentially a Jordanian one, confined to the boundaries of the Jordanian state and political system. Others see the movement as part of a regional resistance front against Zionism and American domination. And that trend may have grown, drawing on the alienation of many Jordanians—especially, but not exclusively, those of Palestinian origin—from the country's political system.

The second source of disagreement is Islam. While all movement members are Islamist in the sense that they push for a greater role for Islam in public life, some speak of fostering the evolution of Jordanian society in an Islamic direction, while others stress the application of the Islamic *shari'a* over the short term. Indeed, some members of the latter camp stress the need to implement *shari'a* to such an extent that their arguments echo those of prominent radical leaders and movements, such as Sayyid Qutb or the Hizb al-Tahrir.

Palestine is the final issue dividing the movement. All leading members of the movement share a basic support for the Palestinian cause and opposition to the Jordanian-Israeli peace treaty and normalization of relations with Israel. But that unity cannot mask divisions over emphasis as well as willingness to identify with Hamas. Some IAF members show greater interest in other subjects and often phrase their criticism of Jordanian policy toward Israel in comparatively understated terms. Others back the most extreme forms of Palestinian resistance and speak of liberating all of Palestine. Some movement leaders are very closely identified with Hamas—and indeed with a specific wing of Hamas, the political bureau, led by Khalid Mish'al, who lived and worked in Jordan for some time.

FORMING A PLATFORM

Since the IAF encompasses a range of ideological orientations and positions, it should be no surprise that its members present different faces to various actors outside the movement. As the party's critics often point out, this has led to some ambiguity in its positions. King Abdullah has spoken of the Muslim Brotherhood operating in a "gray area," positioning itself differently in accordance with the demands of the situation. Indeed, the variations in IAF's position reflect not simply differences within the movement but—as is natural for any political movement—the specific context. When mobilizing constituents among the general population, the IAF and the Brotherhood tend to emphasize broad issues with wide appeal, especially those related to Palestine and, more recently, Iraq. When working to reach more religious or socially conservative parts of the population, they speak more often of social issues. And in election campaigns, the party emphasizes its lack of corruptibility and demands a more responsive and less authoritarian political system.

It is precisely in election campaigns—when the party is compelled to put together a platform—that the IAF might be expected to hone a specific message, reconcile contradictions, and contain internal divisions. But because the party has no chance of winning an election and is thus never faced with the possibility that its electoral commitments might have to be transformed into a set of governing guidelines, its electoral program can still contain a considerable amount of ambiguity and grandstanding. Still, in elections, various factions of the party come together to hammer out a more specific set of positions than they are normally required to articulate.

In recent years, the IAF's electoral platforms have resembled those of its sister Islamist movements, placing great emphasis on political reform. But its evolution on reform issues has been unusual. In earlier years, the Jordanian Islamist movement was something of a trendsetter among its Arab counterparts, since the Jordanian Muslim Brotherhood (when it was the body running candidates, before the formation of the IAF) always stressed political freedoms. But despite a long and nearly continuous history of calling for political reforms, the Jordanian movement has begun to lag behind other regional Islamist movements in focusing on internal issues. Just as other Islamist movements from Morocco to Palestine began echoing the Jordanian Muslim Brotherhood's electoral appeals for political reform, the IAF balked at placing a primary emphasis on the issue. Political reforms are still a very significant and even central theme in the party's electoral platform, but their relative role is smaller than might be expected given its long history of involvement in the issue. In October 2005, the IAF issued its most detailed reform program, a document so full of liberal and democratic ideas and language that a leader of a secular opposition party was forced to confess that it differed little from the programs of other reformist parties. In 2009, some movement leaders attempted to revive and advance their political reform agenda by developing a new theme: Jordan should move toward a constitutional monarchy. But the initiative soon fell victim to internal divisions, with intense wrangling over whether the leaders were legitimately speaking for the movement as a whole.

More generally, the emphasis on political reform has not obscured the greater passion many movement activists feel for a variety of international causes, especially Palestine and Iraq. Indeed, regional conflicts have figured in IAF campaigns, although the movement has sometimes had to tread carefully in its rhetoric. The IAF is deeply opposed to normal relations with Israel and has taken a leading role in resisting normalization. But since the 1994 Jordanian-Israeli peace treaty, the country has been clearly committed to a peaceful relationship with Israel. The treaty was a royal initiative, making it more difficult for reformers to criticize, at least during the 1990s. Indeed, IAF deputies absented themselves from the vote on the treaty rather than vote against it. The treaty was also hard to assail on legal grounds, because it was ratified by the Jordanian parliament, but the cooling Jordanian-Israeli peace and renewal of Israeli-Palestinian violence in 2000 have made less polite opposition safer. In the 2003 elections, for instance, the IAF issued a strident platform referring repeatedly to the "Zionist enemy," and leaving little to the imagination:

> Palestine is Arab and Muslim and its liberation is a duty for all Arabs and
> Muslims. In all cases, working to liberate Palestine is a central concern

in relation to all Muslims. No entity has the right to concede any part of Palestine or give legitimacy to the occupation on any part of its holy land. Our struggle with the Jews is creedal and civilizational. It cannot be ended by a peace treaty. It is a struggle over existence, not borders.[2]

And the most enthusiastic supporters of the Palestinian cause have not only adopted strident prose but also insisted that there is no separation between Jordanian and Palestinian issues, questioning the separation that has been official Jordanian policy for close to one quarter century. Less severe voices within the IAF have called for a popular referendum on the peace treaty as a way of seizing the democratic high ground and preserving the movement's strong opposition credentials without directly criticizing a core policy of the regime. And they have also suggested that the Palestinian cause is important but that internal Jordanian issues are distinct and also a primary focus for the group's work.

In recent years the IAF has branched into other international areas as well, most notably Iraq. While the Jordanian government maintained quiet cooperation with the U.S.-led occupation of the country, the IAF assailed the war and occupation in very strong terms and made clear that the insurgency was legitimate resistance similar to the Palestinian resistance to Israeli occupation. Jordanian government policy itself drew less direct IAF criticism, but the movement's stance was clear. Some of the more extreme IAF members went so far as to praise some of the actions of Abu al-Musab al-Zarqawi in Iraq. Given al-Zarqawi's involvement in attacks in Jordan itself, such a position could easily be portrayed as treasonous, and indeed, the regime seized the visit by four IAF MPs to the funeral tent erected by al-Zarqawi's family in 2006 to act against the movement's radicals. The parliamentarians were arrested and charged with inciting violence. Less extreme members of the IAF were caught in the middle: clearly embarrassed by some of the radical language of their colleagues, they felt compelled to criticize the arrests as an illegal and unacceptable infringement on freedom of speech and parliamentary prerogatives.

Finally, the IAF has emphasized Islamic issues in its election platforms, although here its positions have sometimes been restrained for an Islamist organization. The IAF's 2003 platform called for the application of Islamic *shari'a*, identifying it as a religious obligation and basic goal of the party, but it offered remarkably few details to that end. Where it did cite examples, it used very gentle terminology, such as suggesting that certain parts of commercial law be modified in ways that were consistent with *shari'a*. The platform refers to the "supreme goals" of *shari'a*, proposing a common strategy for Islamist movements to emphasize ways in which pursuit of *shari'a* is consistent with public welfare and not an imposition or set of burdensome restrictions. The IAF's overall approach is one of firm dedication to Islam and Islamic legal principles but also an inclination toward gradualism and persuasion rather than radical and imposed change. But, as will be seen below, the IAF's formulation has not eliminated all suspicions of the movement among its opponents.

Participating in Parliament

The IAF is forced to operate within an electoral framework deliberately designed to keep it a parliamentary minority, and this has necessarily had deep effects on the group's decisions and strategy. Although the matter remains a subject of continuous debate within the movement, IAF leaders from most factions have become convinced that the benefits of participation in parliament—open and legal operations and a fairly free voice—are enough to outweigh the costs and severe limitations placed on them.

The IAF was formed to take advantage of a liberalizing political atmosphere in Jordan, but it discovered the limits of liberalization even before it had contested its first election. The deck was already stacked against Islamists because districts with a greater proportion of Palestinians—not coincidentally, IAF strongholds—have been historically underrepresented in Parliament. But in August 1993, shortly before the November polling date, King Hussein issued a decree that tilted the playing field against the Islamists still further: Voters in each multi-member district were allowed to vote for only one candidate. In the previous election, voters had as many votes as there were seats in the district, so that they could select three candidates in a three-member district, with the top three vote-getters winning seats. With voters only selecting a single candidate from a long list, many inclined toward familiar family or tribal names, thus diminishing the effects of party and ideological orientations on the outcome. (For an overview of IAF performance in parliamentary elections, see table 1.)

The king and the cabinet issued these amendments to the electoral law as provisional measures under a constitutional authorization allowing

Table 1. Muslim Brotherhood and Islamic Action Front Parliamentary Performance

Year	Number of Candidates Running	Number of Winners	Number of Seats Being Contested
1954		4	40
1957		4	40
1963		2	40
1967		2	60
1984 by-elections		3	8
1989	29	22	80
1993	36	16	80
1997	Boycotted		80
2003	30	17	110
2007	22	6	110

Note: In some elections (especially early ones), candidates ran as individuals not formally nominated by the movement so that the number of movement candidates is difficult to measure. In later elections, the size of the parliamentary bloc was enhanced by independents closely allied with the movement.

them to act when parliament is not in session to address "matters which admit no delay." Since the motivation for this law had nothing to do with any emergency but only a desire to circumvent parliament and diminish the IAF's representation, its constitutionality was quite dubious. But when Jordan's High Court struck down a press law issued under similar circumstances, it earned a public rebuke from the king and its chief justice was retired.

Thus the IAF was presented with an electoral law it could not contest, but after some hesitation it decided to run candidates anyway. The decision rankled, however, and in 1997 the IAF managed to assemble a coalition of opposition parties that threatened to boycott the elections if the law were not changed. They followed through, and the IAF remained absent from parliament until the 2003 elections. The decision was a difficult one for the movement and many leaders were clearly frustrated by it (some even left to run as independents). While the boycott was popular with much of the movement's rank-and-file, the party leaders eventually reached the conclusion that they had erred in withdrawing from parliament, which is the least restricted political sphere in which they can operate. By 2003, they had persuaded the party to re-enter elections.

Remarkably, the IAF's successes in 1993 and 2003 were limited not only by the electoral law, but also by the party's own self-restraint. In 1993, only 36 candidates ran, competing in a parliament of 80 seats. In 2003, 30 candidates competed in a parliament of 110 seats. The IAF's decision not to run a full slate of candidates was motivated partly by the law: Leaders concluded after the 1989 elections that they had won fewer seats because they had run too many candidates, leading their supporters to split their votes. But the decision had deeper roots, which stem from a political calculation that the regime will not allow the party to win a parliamentary majority and will use any means necessary to prevent that outcome. Thus, running only a limited number of candidates appears to be an optimal strategy: It guarantees the victory of some candidates, avoids splitting the party's vote, communicates the IAF's popularity, and guarantees seats in parliament.

But if principled objection to participating in politics had lessened by 2003, the movement has been increasingly divided over tactical decisions about whether to run, how many seats should be contested, and who the candidates should be. In 2007, elections led to a deterioration in relations between the movement and the regime, and set off squabbling within the movement that brought it to the brink of a fissure.

The problems may not have begun in Jordan, but in Palestine, when Hamas won the parliamentary elections in January 2006. Immediately after Hamas' victory, some IAF figures began thinking about attaining a similar result. Within a few days, the leader of the IAF's parliamentary bloc startled Jordanians by going beyond the very general traditional claim that under a fair law "Islamists in Jordan would obtain a majority" to asserting that they might actually govern. He described his movement as "prepared to assume control over the executive branch to realize the hopes of the people."[3] For an opposition movement to contemplate winning and governing might be normal in a democracy, but in Jordan such daydreaming was treated as nearly seditious. While movement leaders continue to insist that they would win about half the seats in a fair election, they tried to dampen speculation that they were reaching for victory any time soon. In the summer of 2006, when I asked a prominent Muslim Brotherhood leader whether the IAF would run a full slate of candidates in the next parliamentary elections, he responded, "We will not repeat the disaster of Hamas."[4] Since that time, the prospect of governing has receded even further.

But heightened tensions with the regime nonetheless set off a dispute within the movement. In local elections in 2007, the party pulled out the morning balloting began, charging that the regime was working to fix the vote. The move caught some leaders by surprise and set off a prolonged battle over the parliamentary elections a few months later. The IAF leadership split over the issue. In the end, a less confrontational group took control of the campaign, but in the process they sidelined the party's fiery leader, Zaki Bani Arshid. The party also ran a smaller number of candidates than it had in the past, a slate consisting of prominent senior leaders who generally eschewed confrontational rhetoric and strategies. (In 2003, the movement had tried to present a fresh face and minimize jockeying among top leaders by favoring younger candidates.) This strategy—putting forward a smaller, experienced, and more moderate set of candidates—seemed to offer the regime the sort of Islamic opposition it would prefer.

The result was little short of a disaster. Only six candidates won, the worst showing in the party's history. IAF leaders charged that severe government interference and electoral irregularities had occurred. But even if all their accusations had been correct, it was clear that more than the regime was to blame: sidelined IAF Secretary-General Bani Arshid had communicated his disdain for the ticket and stated that the movement should have pulled out of the elections. He—and some leaders aligned with him—had simply sat out the campaign. The split movement was unable to mobilize all of its supporters or generate any enthusiasm.

After the election, a series of conflicts erupted in full public view. Divisions between party and movement dissolved as the various camps used whatever organizational tools they had to settle scores. The angry leaders of the 2007 campaign hauled Bani Arshid before a Muslim Brotherhood tribunal, eventually securing his resignation. A harder-line group secured a bare majority in the IAF leadership, and its opponents quickly charged it with departing from the traditionally consensus-driven decision making style. For the next three years, the movement seemed paralyzed by a welter of disciplinary measures, public squabbles, resignations, suspensions, walkouts, and tenuous compromises and truces.

At the end of 2009, King Abdullah dissolved the parliament that had been elected in 2007. Rather than calling for new elections immediately, however, he directed the cabinet to draft a new election law to be issued by decree—using the same highly questionable procedure that had been employed in 1993. (Actually, using the prerogative of issuing emergency legislation was an even more dubious step in early 2010 than it had been thirteen years earlier. The reason parliament could not pass legislation was that the king had dismissed it, claiming that the country urgently needed a new election, which he then postponed for an extended and indefinite period until a new law could be written by decree.) The IAF did try to unify behind a demand for a fairer electoral system, but its internal divisions inhibited it from taking a forceful stance.

USING PARLIAMENTARY SEATS

Securing representation in parliament has thus involved the movement in a variety of internal and external struggles. What has it won them?

Current political circumstances guarantee the IAF a voice in the parliament, but also virtually ensure that it can be outvoted on any issue. Even when the IAF reaches out to other opposition movements to form a coalition (as it has increasingly done), the party gains a few votes at most because the opposition parties have been singularly unsuccessful in creating strong electoral bases.

How then does the IAF use its seats in parliament? As with many regional Islamist movements, it works to be careful, disciplined, and strategic. Just as the Muslim Brotherhood exercises a supervisory role over the IAF, the IAF keeps a close watch on its deputies, beginning with the nomination process. It allows local units to hold primaries, ensuring both a measure of party democracy and a slate of candidates who are popular in their districts. But the national organization does not simply approve the list of local primary winners; it seeks to create a balanced national ticket that reflects ideological currents within the party. It also makes its own assessment of the electoral attractiveness of various candidates, favoring those who are effective speakers. In 2007, the national party leadership was especially heavy-handed, insisting that only experienced and moderate candidates should be placed on the ballot.

And party oversight does not stop with candidate selection. The party is responsible for composing the platform, a document the IAF takes quite seriously and views as something of a binding contract with voters. Once candidates reach parliament, the party retains the authority to make major strategic decisions, such as whether to vote for or against the government in a vote of confidence, although day-to-day parliamentary affairs are entrusted to the parliamentary caucus.

Mindful of their limited ability to affect the composition of the government or pass legislation, IAF parliamentary deputies are still extremely active in using the parliament as a platform to raise specific kinds of issues. In recent years, they have focused on several key concerns:

- *Palestine:* While the peace treaty between Israel and Jordan is in full effect, there are many opportunities for the IAF to raise issues related to Palestinian affairs—whether calling for the Jordanian government to resolve its differences with Hamas or issuing a *fatwa* (a ruling on a point of Islamic law given by a recognized authority) that it is a religious obligation to support Hizbollah in its conflict with Israel.

- *Economic issues:* IAF members of parliament use their positions to highlight the material concerns of Jordanian citizens. In early 2006, for instance, they took the lead in denouncing fuel price increases, even leading public marches calling for a rollback. They focus on local concerns as well, such as complaints from members about problems in their individual districts.

- *Corruption and waste:* Although the party may lack the parliamentary weight to push through legislation, it can use parliamentary questioning to raise specific issues, and has forced the government to respond on issues of wasteful government expenditures and favoritism in awarding contracts.

- *Political reform:* Long a focus of Islamist demands, IAF deputies continue to call for an end to restrictions on the political process—whether the subject is demonstrations, arrests of political activists, prisoner rights, appointment (rather than election) of some local officials, press restrictions, election law, or government moves against professional associations.

- *Social, cultural, and religious issues:* The IAF has traditionally focused on perceived infringements on Jordanian and Islamic values. While the party's rhetoric on *shari'a* has grown fairly general, deputies still raise specific questions, especially when they are likely to have some popular resonance. For instance, in 2006, IAF deputies complained about the sale of alcohol to minors and the use of English in higher education.

These various spheres seem fairly disparate, but the Jordanian political environment—and the approach of the IAF—ensure that they have become deeply intertwined. All issues are seen as related. For example, the IAF's interest in undermining normalization with Israel and dedication to issues of daily life lead it to charge Israel with exporting spoiled meat. The focus on material and moral corruption are often implicitly linked in the righteousness of the party's rhetoric on such issues. As one observer of Jordanian politics puts it: "In Jordan, if you talk about corruption, you are talking about the circle around the king. If you talk about democracy, you are talking about the Palestinian issue [because of the Palestinian majority]." Fundamental political disputes underlie daily disputes, and underlying all fundamental political disputes is the issue of Palestine. When IAF deputies representing a Palestinian refugee camp call for provision of services to their constituents, their audience hears a demand for Palestinian rights. When they press for a more equitable distribution of parliamentary seats, they hear a call for an end to the lopsided districts that prevent a Palestinian majority in parliament.

With its close identification with the Palestinian issue, its support base in the Palestinian population, and its close links to Hamas, the IAF cannot (and does not seek) to disassociate itself from the Palestinian cause. Some observers go so far as to describe the IAF as a surrogate for a Palestinian political movement in Jordan. To be sure, the identification is not complete: Some IAF leaders wish to develop a more broad-based agenda, and many native Jordanians support the IAF. But even when the IAF tries to move beyond the Palestine issue, it finds that it is not alone in connecting Palestine to other major political disputes. For instance, when government officials call for professional associations to concentrate on issues of professional concern, their clear intention is to minimize public criticism of policies regarding normalization and the peace treaty with Israel.

The IAF's effectiveness in influencing Jordanian policy has been limited not only by the interlinking nature of the issues but also by the small number of its deputies and the constitutional limitations of the parliament (coexisting with a palace that is willing to use its constitutional tools with no trace of bashfulness or self-restraint). The IAF is thus unable to bring down the government or pass legislation.

On occasion, its parliamentary role has allowed the IAF to obstruct or delay government action, though not because of any parliamentary vote. On some occasions, the movement has wrested concessions through direct bargaining or confrontation (rather than parliamentary procedures) from a government not anxious to court controversy. Generally, in order to obtain concessions, the IAF must speak for a unified opposition (and not merely its own interests) against an uncertain or divided government—such as when parliament delayed consideration of an amended law of professional associations in 2005. Sometimes extraparliamentary forums provide similar opportunities, such as the National Charter of 1991 or the National Agenda of 2005, in which some members of the Islamic movement participated and were able to press issues. In short, the IAF can exercise a veto when Jordan's rulers agree—in the interests of national unity—to grant it veto power, but it cannot force policy to reflect its preferences in any other circumstances.

Thus, the chief reward of parliamentary participation has been the ability to operate openly as a political party and to raise issues and visibility. The IAF's steady participation in parliament has given it considerable experience in using the body as a platform, and in recent years its abilities have been enhanced by its increased attention to forging opposition alliances, chiefly with nationalist and leftist parties. While those parties have very little to contribute in terms of a popular base, the opposition front (which the IAF can dominate) allows the movement to speak as something more than a narrow political party. The opposition generally presents itself implicitly as the nation's conscience, raising awkward issues, nationalist complaints, and reform demands with all the uncompromising dedication that comes from being deprived of any power to make decisions.

Forming a Political Party: At What Cost to Islamist–Regime Relations?

The relationship between the IAF and the Jordanian regime has become steadily more adversarial since the party's founding at the height of Jordan's experiment with political liberalization in the early 1990s. Starting in early 2005, the two sides sparred over a series of legislative initiatives the regime generally packaged as reforms but which sometimes amounted to subtle restrictions on various areas of political life. These related most notably to professional associations, but also to political parties, terrorism, and other subjects. By 2006—in the wake of the Amman hotel bombings and the Hamas electoral victory—the two sides were engaged in open confrontation, bounded only by the IAF's determination to protect its gains and the regime's desire to keep the center of gravity of the Islamic movement from passing from loyal to disloyal opposition. There is also some sign of debate on both sides on how much to contain the current confrontation.

Although the Islamic movement has always criticized the regime's failure to follow Islamic principles as well as its alignment with Western powers, its refusal to make common cause with other regime opponents from the 1950s through the 1970s limited the extent to which it was regarded as a threat. However, a series of developments in recent years has increased the regime's concern. First, since leftist, Arab national-ist, and Palestinian opposition movements have virtually collapsed, only Islamic movements represent an internal challenge. Yet this in it-self would not necessarily lead to confrontation, since the regime has shown strong signs that it prefers to keep the Islamic opposition pub-lic and legal rather than encourage underground movements operating outside of legal channels (such as the jihadist and Salafi movements).

Two major international developments have conspired to sharp-en the contest between regime and Islamic opposition, transforming a source of domestic tension into a potential crisis. First, the rise of Hamas had already proved a source of contention because of the IAF's close support for—and identification with—the Palestinian resistance movement and the regime's attempt to distance itself from the Israeli–Palestinian dispute and maintain a working relationship with the Israeli government. More than a policy dispute divides the two sides, however. The Jordanian regime is clearly concerned that Hamas may draw on its sympathizers in the country for material and moral support, actively pulling the country back into conflict with its very powerful neighbor, much as Palestinian movements did in the aftermath of the 1967 war. For that reason, the regime has restricted Hamas operations inside Jordan, refusing to allow some of its prominent leaders to reside in (or even visit) Jordan. The Palestinian elections in 2006 brought Hamas to power in the Palestinian Authority, sharpening the potential for a new round of Israeli–Palestinian violence that would place Jordan in a very awkward position. With Hamas in power and Jordan a main route for Palestinian travel and finance, pressure from the IAF to support Hamas threatens to damage the regime's ties not only with Israel but also with the United States.

Second, the U.S. invasion of Iraq similarly heightened the sense of con-frontation between regime and Islamist opposition. Throughout the 1990s, popular sentiment against Iraqi sanctions ran deep in Jordan, and the IAF made Iraq central to its appeal. When the United States invaded

Iraq in 2003, the existence of U.S.–Jordanian security cooperation was widely known but not widely discussed, nor was the extent and precise nature of Jordan's support revealed. While U.S.–Jordanian cooperation on Iraq thus became a taboo issue in public debates, the Islamist opposition's rhetorical support for the Iraqi insurgency constituted no crime, and the IAF embraced the cause with enthusiasm. This continued even when a Jordanian citizen, Abu al-Musab al-Zarqawi, emerged out of a fairly faceless insurgency to become its most recognized figure. Al-Zarqawi himself was deeply controversial because of the astonishing brutality of his methods as well as an enmity toward Shi'a that verged at times on a genocidal fixation. The bombing of three Amman hotels in November 2005 transformed him from an embarrassment into a threat, and the IAF swiftly condemned the action. IAF leaders pointed out that al-Zarqawi had bitterly denounced mainstream Jordanian Islamists for their willingness to participate in the system. But it proved far more difficult for the IAF to disentangle itself from all that al-Zarqawi represented in Iraq, and significant portions of the party (as well as some of the leaders) retained a degree of admiration for him.

Thus, in the aftermath of the U.S. invasion of Iraq and the election of Hamas, the IAF's foreign policy positions came to be seen by some more security-minded officials as moving outside the boundaries of loyal opposition. IAF leaders protested loudly that they had consistently refrained from violent political action in Jordan and remained committed to nonviolent change. Yet such assurances could only go so far toward assuaging the fears of a regime concerned that turmoil in Iraq and Palestine could spill into Jordan and perhaps return the country to the political atmosphere of earlier decades, when domestic politics seemed not merely boisterous but also unstable, and constantly threatened to disrupt the regime's alignment with Great Britain and the United States.

In the spring and summer of 2006, the regime seized on a series events to press the confrontation with the IAF and Muslim Brotherhood. First, it claimed to have uncovered preparations by Hamas to launch attacks within Jordan. The charge was implausible, because while Hamas has never shied away from violence, it has studiously avoided undertaking any attacks outside of Palestine, and its electoral triumph—when it was desperate for diplomatic and financial support—would have been a curious moment to begin a terrorism campaign in Jordan. (Far more credible would have been a charge that Hamas was smuggling weapons through Jordan, though such a move would probably have provoked too much sympathy among some Jordanians to have been politically useful for the regime.) Whether concocted or not, the effect was to place the IAF on the defensive at a time when its sister Palestinian movement had just realized its most significant triumph. Shortly afterward four members of the IAF were arrested while visiting the funeral tent erected by al-Zarqawi's family. They were charged with incitement not simply for the visit but for offering comments that implied support for Al-Zarqawi's actions in Iraq. It was no surprise that the regime seized the opportunity to portray the deputies as offending the memory of the victims of the Amman bombing. But the step it took—arresting sitting parliamentarians for their statements, holding them in a remote location, and then trying them in a special state security court—was unusually aggressive by Jordanian standards.

In July 2006, the cabinet took an additional step, acting on a report by the public prosecutor alleging irregularities in the management of the Islamic Center, the largest NGO associated with the Islamist movement, to replace the organization's board. Other moves followed—such as the dismissal of some movement leaders from faculty positions at a private university traditionally friendly to Islamists.

The leadership of the Islamist movement was uncertain about how to respond to the onslaught, particularly because the regime sent conflicting signals. Some measures targeted the movement as a whole (one of the dismissed faculty members, for instance, was a leader of the dovish stream within the movement). But at other times, there were indications that the regime was seeking only to move against certain tendencies within the Brotherhood. In a June 2006 interview with *Der Spiegel,* King Abdullah, in responding to whether he was going to redefine his relationship with the Muslim Brotherhood, claimed that the Brotherhood confronted a choice:

> They have to redefine their relationship with us. They have been working in a gray area in recent decades. I think society throughout the world now has to decide what is good and what is evil. I believe that the majority of the Brotherhood wants a good future for this country, and a good future for their children. I think that we can all work as a team. But there are some principles. *Takfir* [declaring proclaimed Muslims to be apostates] is not one of them.[5]

In an effort to ease tensions, mediators arranged meetings between the Islamist leadership and key regime figures, including the king himself (although as the confrontation escalated, his personal participation ended). Significantly, the figure then heading intelligence, Muhammad Dhahabi, was among the key participants, underscoring that the regime had come to see the Islamist movement as a security rather than political challenge. Although Islamist leaders refused one of the central regime demands—an apology for the Al-Zarqawi funeral tent visit—they did issue two statements clarifying their positions on a variety of controversial matters. The content of the statements provoked little controversy within the movement, but the act of issuing them under strong regime pressure provoked deep division. Many leaders resented the defensive tone the movement had struck; their resentment only deepened when the expected payoff for the statements failed to materialize.

Deeply divided internally, the IAF finally resorted to a poll of its members before its leaders decided against withdrawing from parliament, although they admitted that the decision was far from unanimous. The IAF's leader explained the calculation of the winners of the internal debate in terms that seemed designed to mirror and mimic the king's statement. He spoke of divisions within the country's leadership and explained that the IAF wanted to encourage moderate voices within the government who were seeking to avoid confrontation.

The sense of brewing confrontation in 2006 and 2007 ebbed slightly in subsequent years, but it hardly disappeared. The Islamic Center remained under sequestration and the regime ultimately put some of its leaders—pillars of the Muslim Brotherhood, including its strident leader—on trial for financial improprieties. But in a sense the internal battles within the Islamist movement—some of them actually provoked by disagreements on how to react to regime threats and warnings—may have made further regime action seem unnecessary.

Building Alliances With Other Opposition Actors

The IAF has historically had a tense relationship with other political actors in the country. In the 1950s it stood largely aloof from the Arab nationalists and leftists who promised fundamental political change. In the 1960s it regarded the Palestinian national movement warily, supporting its goals but criticizing its nonreligious rhetoric and the flirtation with leftist ideologies by its most confrontational leaders.

In the conflict between the regime and its opponents, the Islamic movement refused to make a clear choice, which left it without clear allies. In the past two decades it has made serious efforts to break free of this isolation, the success of which is due in large part to the decline in non-Islamist political actors. The result has been to leave the IAF as the only effective political opposition movement in the country.[6]

Despite its uneasy relations with government and opposition actors, the Muslim Brotherhood and its political arm, the IAF, have long been accepted, however grudgingly, as legitimate movements. Nonetheless, the movement still provokes suspicions—and not only in regime circles. Critics of the Islamist movement feel that they have not yet been fully assured in three key areas of concern:

- *Jordanian integrity:* Especially given the heavy IAF focus on Palestinian issues, some Jordanians suspect that the party does not fully accept that its first loyalty is to Jordan. Sometimes this charge may be an indirect way of pointing to the heavy participation of Palestinians in the IAF. In 2002, the palace launched a "Jordan first" campaign, pressing the issue of the integrity of Jordan and playing down the Palestinian cause through use of a seemingly innocuous slogan. But precisely because the slogan was so innocuous and lacked clear content, the IAF easily responded that they had always put Jordanian interests first—an answer that its critics found as evasive as the slogan itself. In addition, the IAF claimed, not without justification, that parts of the campaign were subtly aimed against the IAF and its charitable and political activities.

- *Violence and terrorism:* Jordan has been fairly free of political violence, and the Muslim Brotherhood prides itself for having consistently rejected violence since its founding. Yet its critics are not assured even by this long-standing record, fearing that the movement houses trends that flirt with jihadist ideologies and come close to engaging in *takfir*. Furthermore, the IAF lends strong support to movements such as Hizbollah, Hamas, and the Iraqi insurgency that do use violence. In all these cases, the IAF insists that the critical difference is that such movements are living under some form of occupation and that violent resistance is a natural right under such conditions. Few Jordanians would find fault with this position, but some still worry that should elements of the Islamic movement ever decide that the Jordanian government is complicit in supporting anti-Islamic regimes, it will turn to less peaceful methods of pursuing its objectives.

- *Religion:* Islamist movements in the Arab world routinely confront the charge that they seek to impose their particular understanding of Islam on the entire population. The IAF has become familiar with this criticism, despite the heterogeneous nature of the movement. Its intense internal debates do not serve to reassure skeptics that the IAF disavows any monopoly on truth.

These criticisms are not surprising coming from Jordanians sympathetic to the regime or those with leftist and more secular leanings. What is more unexpected is the tendency in recent years for members of the Islamist movement to show some sympathy with these critical views. Some former Muslim Brotherhood and IAF members have left the movement precisely because they felt it had not gone far enough to resolve ambiguities in its positions on these very issues. A few have continued to serve as independents; and a small group also formed a new political party, the Hizb al-Wasat (Center Party), which deliberately presents itself as a more moderate and less oppositional Islamic alternative. The protracted debate over boycotting the 1997 election occasioned some of these departures from the movement, but not all of those who subscribe to these criticisms have left the movement. In fact, IAF members identified as doves are often the ones who wish to push the party further toward definitive positions on these issues.

There is certainly a limit to what the IAF can do to reassure its internal and external critics on these points. The movement does not exercise any political power, and many of the suspicions stem not from its proclaimed positions but from expectations of what it might actually do if it became more powerful or more estranged from the regime. So there is a limit to how far reassuring statements can go in quelling suspicions. The movement has nevertheless tried to do so, but its efforts often provoke new questions.

Perhaps the most comprehensive effort to answer critics came in the midst of the movement's confrontation with the regime in July 2006. On July 6, the IAF and Muslim Brotherhood issued a lengthy joint statement with thirteen points proclaiming the movement's:

- Rejection of extremism and terrorism;
- Acceptance of Jordanian and Arab societies (thus affirming their loyalty to the state and downplaying their opposition to nationalism) and of Muslims (thus disavowing any attempts to engage in *takfir*);
- Disavowal of any monopoly on truth;
- Support for national security;
- Support for national causes (such as combating poverty);
- Acceptance of political and intellectual pluralism and dedication to participating in the political process;
- Rejection of foreign interference;
- Acceptance of national fixed principles (*thawabit*) and insistence that no individual or group has a monopoly on defining these;
- Insistence that opposition to some government policies did not suggest rejection of the Jordanian state;
- Desire to strengthen Jordan's ability to face foreign challenges;
- Support for Hamas and insistence that success for Hamas did not threaten Jordan;
- Concern with charitable work; and
- Embrace of moderation.

Movement leaders clearly hoped that this statement would express their strong convictions in a manner that was both unapologetic and reassuring to its critics. But they did not pull all their punches, however. They accused their critics of jealousy of their success in charitable work. And the statement hardly resolved all ambiguities. While it rejected *takfir* of Jordanian society, the statement was more equivocal concerning *takfir* of individuals; it also could not deny that those with more radical views on the matter remained within the movement. Five days later, the movement's leaders added an additional statement that affirmed their acceptance of the "Amman declaration," a conciliatory statement issued by Muslim religious leaders in 2005 at the end of an international conference, operating under royal patronage, to combat religious extremism. (It was this second statement that appeared too obsequious to some movement members, as mentioned above.)

Yet while the movement has not, and probably cannot, reassure all its critics, it has scored some significant success in recent years in forming opposition coalitions. Given the strong distrust between the Islamist and leftist and nationalist opposition, rooted in events in the 1950s, the formation of an opposition front is a significant accomplishment. As discussed above, the coalition is explained partly by the decline of the left (and its consequent interest in forming alliances), but also due to a strong coincidence of interest and ideology in support of political reform.

It is also critical to bear in mind that the mainstream Islamist movement cannot concentrate solely on assuaging regime and leftist critics; it must also fend off more radical Islamist activists who suspect that the Muslim Brotherhood and IAF have allowed themselves to be co-opted. Some of the more radical activists (particularly some Salafis) have eschewed politics altogether, and regard the mainstream movement as overly engaged in a society that is not completely Islamic; others (particularly jihadists) regard it as too willing to compromise with a non-Islamic regime. What is remarkable about the mainstream movement is that it has managed to retain support from some more radical leaders and individuals within its ranks. The distance between Muhammad Abu Faris—one of the most extreme leaders in the IAF—and the jihadists sometimes seems short indeed (the chief difference is that Abu Faris counsels patience rather than violence in order to combat the forces he sees as hostile to Islam in Jordan). This has caused embarrassment to others within the movement and rendered the Brotherhood and the IAF more suspect in the eyes of the regime.

But movement leaders—and in more charitable moments, some regime figures—argue that containing such radicals within the framework of the mainstream movement has benefits for social and political stability. Some within the movement do incline toward more radical ideas, but as long as they remain within the movement they do not act upon them. They may harbor feelings of admiration for al-Zarqawi, but they do not seek to emulate him within Jordan.

In recent years, more confrontational voices have been gaining ground in the movement. More radical elements have increasingly aligned with those who favor prioritizing the Palestinian issues to tilt the balance in relations inside the movement and the IAF itself. More conciliatory leaders along with those who view their primary political horizon as domestic continue to hold some influential positions. Because they have a stronger presence in intellectual circles and can sometimes present a gentler face to the outside in general and the regime in particular, they may be indispensible. But they may have lost some of their influence with the rank-and-file membership. These internal shifts as well as an increasingly wary regime have raised the possibility of a more sustained confrontation between government and Islamist opposition.

Staving Off an Egyptian Solution

By forming a political party to participate in elections and parliamentary life, the Islamic movement in Jordan has realized concrete gains. It has built an organization that is still largely accepted as a legitimate political player; it has obtained regular and legally protected access to various public fora where it can present its views; it has developed a wide-ranging and comprehensive political vision; and it has deepened the organizational capacity of the Islamist movement, producing a political party that is reasonably democratic in its internal operations and far more than the sum of the activities of a few prominent leaders.

But while the IAF can present the Islamist movement with many accomplishments, in the current Jordanian political environment, it may have trouble moving beyond what it has already achieved. The electoral system is designed to allow the IAF to participate, but only as a minority bloc in parliament. Many fundamental issues in Jordan, especially those involving foreign and security policy, are placed beyond democratic contestation, and the regime and even the IAF's fellow opposition political actors continue to view the Islamist movement with deep ambivalence and suspicions.

This frustrating position does offer some elements of stability. The IAF's freedom to maneuver continues to be circumscribed by its institutional links to the Muslim Brotherhood. Despite its technical independence, it remains very much the arm of a broader movement that has a long-term set of ideological, social, charitable, and educational goals and refuses to act primarily with the next election in mind. And the movement as a whole has restrained the party in moving either toward a more ambitious electoral strategy or withdrawal from the political process. The gains offered by the IAF, while real, remain limited and sometimes shaky and fail to convince the broader movement to set the IAF completely free.

Participating in a fully functioning democratic political system may indeed have a moderating effect on Islamist movements over the long term, but that opportunity is hardly likely to be offered in most Arab states. The most that will be available will be constrained competition in a partially liberalized system. The long history of the Islamic movement in Jordan suggests that many activists and leaders will take such an opportunity seriously, but they will still constantly chafe at—and challenge—the restrictions placed on them. Continued tension between regime and Islamic opposition will thus be inevitable, and if each remains strong, they will continue to oscillate between confrontation and détente.

If the IAF is most likely to remain in its current form—a coalition of groups struggling over the Islamist movement's direction—then the regime will probably hold back from a more repressive approach, which some Jordanian analysts refer to as "an Egyptian solution." To be sure, the IAF is viewed as threatening because it effectively transforms issues involving Jordan's external security—most obviously Palestine, but also Iraq and the relationship with the United States—into domestic political challenges. And the regime will probably have difficulty resisting the temptation to play on divisions within the movement. But the alternative to a unified, legitimate Islamist opposition might be the emergence of a splintered but much less restrained set of movements. Movement leaders recognize that the threat of radicalism not only worries the regime but also places limits on its willingness to use purely repressive tools. A member of the IAF's executive committee publicly explained that a confrontation "will increase the level of extremism in Jordanian society and promote the fashion of excess and inclination to violence among the youth."[7]

Ultimately, then, until fundamental change occurs either in the Jordanian political system or its external environment, the uneasy tension between the IAF and the regime is unlikely to evolve into partnership, but there will still be powerful voices on both sides working to avoid degeneration into unbridled hostility.

CHAPTER 4

Party for Justice and Development in Morocco

Participation and Its Discontents

Introduction

I n Morocco, the Islamist Party for Justice and Development (PJD) has adopted peaceful participation in politics as its only strategic option. In Iraq, Lebanon, and Palestine, Islamist movements have dual identities, as both political actors and militarized resistance movements. In Egypt and Jordan, ongoing confrontations between the ruling establishments and the Muslim Brotherhood have precluded stable Islamist participation in politics, but in Morocco, the PJD participates openly, and is gradually introducing more openness.

The PJD and similar "participation-comes-first" Islamist movements in Algeria, Kuwait, and Bahrain resolve to respect and play by the rules of the political game, and to seek consensual agreements on the conduct of public affairs. This characteristic is partly a result of the ruling establishments in these countries, which manage Islamists' participation in politics without systematically repressing or excluding them.

The PJD and like-minded Islamist movements have never questioned the legitimacy of the nation-states in which they operate and have always recognized the state's political framework as the only legitimate space for their actions. They have also never expressed doubts that politics should be competitive and pluralistic by nature. This attitude among Islamists has led to the decline of religion-based exclusionary rhetoric, whether directed toward ruling establishments or liberal and leftist opposition actors. It has also gradually shifted Islamists away from ideological diatribes and categorical judgments toward formulation of practical political platforms and constructive attempts to influence public policy.

Most significantly, some of these movements—notably the PJD—have succeeded in separating Islamist *da'wa* (proselytizing) activities and politics, transforming themselves into pure political organizations guided by an Islamist frame of reference and run by professional politicians, leaving *da'wa* to the broad social movements that gave birth to them.

But the PJD and other similar Islamist movements also face serious challenges. For one, political participation has so far fallen short of the Islamists' minimum expectations and in turn has failed to fulfill the hopes and aspirations of their constituencies. With only limited success, the participation-comes-first Islamists have opted to transcend the restrained pluralism of the political systems in which they operate and achieve meaningful reform that redistributes power between the ruling establishments and the opposition.

One major demand of Islamist platforms is to push for legal and constitutional reforms to expand the prerogatives and oversight powers of legislative and judicial institutions in the face of overly powerful executive bodies. Yet Islamists have not succeeded in creating a healthier balance between the various branches of government. Most have failed in their attempts to overcome their historical rivalries with the ruling establishments and to create pragmatic alliances with nonreligious opposition forces. More troubling, still, is that the meager fruits of Islamists' participation have led their constituencies to question key choices. The separation between *da'wa* and political activities has come under attack, as has the pragmatic focus on social and economic concerns rather than issues of morality. Indeed, Islamists in these movements have been accused of watering down religious commitments to advance in the political process.

Such is the environment in which the PJD has been operating since its establishment in 1997. At a time when mainstream Islamist movements across the Arab world have chosen to participate in politics, questions have arisen over the nature of their participation and its repercussions on the wider political environment as well as on the movements themselves. Because of the diversity of Islamists' approaches to political participation, any analysis of these questions must steer clear of generalities stemming from ideological prejudices or selective citations of past Islamist experiences, which are insufficient to grasp the complexities and constantly unfolding developments in this part of the world. Similarly, the reductionist view of Islamists as groups of ideological zealots whose rhetoric alone is a sufficient guide to their political actions is overly simplistic.

In this chapter, we seek to answer four questions concerning the PJD's participation in Moroccan politics:

1. What are the institutional and political conditions that have shaped the participation of the PJD?

2. What are the issues that the PJD has prioritized in its participation, especially in legislative institutions?

3. What is the impact of the PJD's participation internally on the party and externally on the wider political environment?

4. Finally, how has the PJD responded and adapted to the challenges of its participation in the semiauthoritarian political system of Morocco?

The Institutional and Political Context

The PJD participates in politics under several distinct conditions, some of which are imposed by the powerful monarchy and its allies—known in Morocco as the *makhzan* (ruling establishment)—while others are shaped by the PJD's position within the Islamist spectrum and its need to preserve the loyalty of its popular constituencies. The conditions for which the monarchy is responsible are either institutional or arbitrary and are imposed by the ruling establishment to contain the political opposition including the Islamist PJD. In contrast, the conditions shaped by the preferences of the movement's constituencies are the result of the fragmentation in Morocco's Islamist spectrum and the dynamics of competition among different Islamist movements. Unlike the Muslim Brotherhood in Egypt and Jordan, for example, the PJD in Morocco cannot take religiously motivated constituencies for granted. Rather, it has to compete with the more popular al-'Adl wal-Ihsan (Justice and Charity) movement, which boycotts formal politics, as well as other Islamist political parties. Therefore, the PJD has to abide by certain inviolable guidelines to keep and expand popular support.

INSTITUTIONS

Unlike other countries in the Arab world, Morocco has had a long history of a multiparty legislature, which prompted many observers to speculate that Moroccan legislatures are in a better position to make considerable contributions to the reform process. This characteristic facilitated the emergence of a culture of vigorous political debate in which the opposition is an active participant, but its overall impact is often overrated.

Prior to the 1996 constitutional revision, Morocco had a unicameral legislature. The parliament had 333 members serving six-year terms. Two-thirds of the deputies were elected directly (single-member district, winner-take-all system), and one-third (111) were elected indirectly through five electoral colleges (Morocco's 1,544 local councils indirectly elected 69 of the deputies and the government chose the remaining 42). Those representatives elected indirectly were usually close to the ruling establishment and were therefore often used to impede reform initiatives.

The revised 1996 constitution split the legislature into two branches, with direct election for all the members of the lower chamber (the House of Representatives)—a longtime demand of opposition parties—and the indirect election of the upper chamber (the House of Councilors) by professional associations, labor unions, municipal councils, and various interest groups. But to ensure that the king's reform enterprise does not cede too much power to the opposition, the upper chamber was given extensive prerogatives to counterbalance the lower house. In addition, the constitution gives nonelected bodies such as the royal court and the constitutional council the power to promulgate or block laws that they find controversial.

The Moroccan institutional order has other serious problems that impede democratic progress. Article 19 of the Moroccan constitution proclaims the king to be the "supreme representative of the nation," and he is the military's supreme commander and the country's religious leader. The constitution grants the king extensive powers, unmatched by either the executive branch or parliament. The king appoints the prime minister following legislative elections; the ministers of justice, defense, foreign affairs, religious affairs, and interior; and the governors of Morocco's sixteen provinces. He can terminate the tenure of any minister, dismiss the prime minister, dissolve the parliament, call for new elections, rule by decree, declare a state of emergency without explanation, and revise the constitution. The king also appoints all prefects of economic regions, secretaries of state in each ministry, directors of public agencies and enterprises, judges, and half of the members of the High Constitutional Council, including its president. And none of these decisions is subject to review by any other entity.

Furthermore, the country has a weak judiciary. The Moroccan constitution endorses the principle of separation of powers, but the Ministry of Justice still plays a significant role in judicial affairs. The Ministry of Justice oversees administrative matters related to the courts' work, including their budgets.

The Interior Ministry also has a great deal of power over Morocco's internal affairs, as it runs most of the country's security services, is involved in the allocation of local and regional budgets, is responsible for supervising and licensing associations and political parties, and directs local and national elections. It is no surprise then that Idriss Basri, head of the Ministry of the Interior from 1979 to 1999, was viewed as the most powerful man in Morocco after the king.

There are also various laws in place that are seen as too restrictive and fundamentally antithetical to the reform process. One example is the current election law, which keeps the proportional representation system in place but precludes any one party from gaining a meaningful majority of seats in the parliament. The Interior Ministry runs the election process, drawing the electoral districts, registering voters, and examining and announcing the results. The districting in particular is criticized for giving more seats to rural areas and undermining the weight of urban votes, which in turn negatively affects the electoral performance of many of the opposition parties, especially the urban-based PJD.

A new political party law was passed in October 2005 after extensive rounds of deliberations that involved representatives from the executive and judicial branches as well as a number of political parties and civil society organizations. The Interior Ministry originally proposed the law in 2004 to replace the 1958 law for associations in the code for public liberties. The 1958 law prohibited civil society organizations from engaging in political activities and gave the Interior Ministry the authority to deny permits to organizations involved in activities deemed sensitive by the regime. The 2005 law aims at regulating the internal affairs of political parties and associations. It requires parties to submit mission statements, detailed briefs on their leaders and general membership, and declarations of all of their financial assets; prohibits the establishment of parties on racial, tribal, or religious bases; and stipulates that parties allocate quotas for women and young men in representation in the various bodies of their organizations.

Some parties registered their concern that the new law grants too much power to the Interior Ministry and that a party's disqualification procedures should be left entirely to the judiciary. In the final draft of the law, the government responded to this concern by expanding the role of the judiciary and making it the last arbiter in matters related to penalizing political parties. The Interior Ministry, however, still has considerable privileges that enable it to hinder the certification of new political parties. Some leftist parties brought up the issue of the separation between state and religion and urged the government to completely prohibit any reference to religion in political party platforms. The final draft stated that religion cannot be the founding principle of a political party. This provision makes Islamist parties particularly vulnerable to broad interpretations of the law since they typically use religion as a frame of reference in their political programs.

There are other institutional barriers on the local level. Despite the fact that efforts to decentralize governance have shaped the Moroccan regime's recent reform initiatives, the municipal councils' scope of authority remains very restricted. The Law on Municipal Organization includes an extensive list of municipal council actions that need to be verified and approved by the Interior Ministry. This preapproval requirement covers every financial, budgetary, and investment decision and limits the governing capacity of the parties elected to run these local governing bodies.

ARBITRARY DECISIONS

Along with institutional conditions, there are arbitrary measures that also aim to contain, if not stifle, serious opposition. Rigging elections and buying votes, administrative interference, and extensive networks of patronage regularly ensure a favorable outcome for the ruling establishment's allies and surrogates in local and national elections. Although the 2002 and 2007 legislative elections were praised by international observers as relatively free and transparent compared with previous elections, the aforementioned problems, especially in rural areas, were common. In addition, opposition parties complain that access to national media is highly skewed in favor of parties and candidates close to the ruling establishment. Appealing election results on the grounds of violations is a difficult and chaotic process, which more often than not leads nowhere.

Perhaps more significantly, the state's security apparatus remains largely under the control of the Ministry of the Interior and is seldom held accountable for acting against political opponents of the regime. In February 2008, Moroccan authorities banned an opposition Islamist party known as al-Badil al-Hadari (Civilizational Alternative), a centrist Islamist party whose leaders call for the introduction of elements of genuine and effective democracy, like accountability and openness in governance, without compromising the country's legitimate national and religious foundations. The Interior Ministry claimed that leaders of al-Badil were involved in the activities of a "dangerous terrorist" network. Approximately 32 individuals were arrested, including al-Badil's Secretary-General Mustafa al-Mu'tasim and his deputy Muhammad al-Amin, in addition to a journalist, a leftist politician, a PJD official, and others.[1]

The arrests triggered a furious debate in the country. Some commentators and analysts interpreted the incident as signaling a more restrictive "change in the government's attitude towards moderate Islamists."[2] Regardless of whether it signaled a broader policy change or not, it did reveal that Moroccan authorities are willing and able to suppress opposition actors in the name of fighting terrorism.

The Moroccan regime is especially intolerant of any criticism of the royal court. In 2008, al-Jazeera News Network referred to contacts between the late King Hassan II and the Israeli intelligence agency (Mossad), and, a few days later, the network's Morocco bureau was forced to stop broadcasting its Maghreb News Program from Rabat and its chief was put on trial. Moreover, the government has arrested and prosecuted a number of Moroccan journalists over the past few years for similar offenses.

INTERNAL CONSTRAINTS

In addition to the restraints imposed by the political environment in which it operates, the PJD also has to accommodate limitations that emanate from its own base. After all, the party caters to a traditional and devout constituency that highly values moral and ethical issues.

Historically, Islamism has had a relatively limited appeal in Morocco compared with its popularity in other Arab countries. Islamism as a political force has been constrained by the state's control of religious authorities and symbols and the king's claim to be the Commander of the Faithful and a descendant of the prophet. Islamist movements have also been constrained by traditional kinship and village associations. Even so, Islamism has been on the rise in the last decade, in part because of the recent political openings and in part because of the pronounced lack of an effective secular political opposition. Islamists have a comparative political advantage because, unlike most other Moroccan political parties, they are strongly connected to their grassroots organizations and have the ability to mobilize them during elections.

Islamist activism in Morocco started in the 1960s as a result of the perception of inadequate state implementation of basic Islamic doctrines regarding social reforms and economic development policies. Unlike other countries in the Arab world, Morocco's Islamist movement is quite fragmented. It includes two main groups—namely, al-Tawhid wal-Islah (Unity and Reform) and al-'Adl wal-Ihsan—as well as scores of smaller organizations.

Morocco's two main Islamist groups have very different ideological and historical trajectories. Al-Tawhid shares ideological commonalities with the Muslim Brotherhood in Egypt and elsewhere. Most of its senior leaders were former members of the active and militant organization al-Shabiba al-Islamiyya (Islamic Youth), which acquired its weight and importance during the mid-1970s. In contrast, al-'Adl is unique in that it has no organizational or ideological links with older Moroccan or Arab Islamist movements. In fact, it did not gain public attention until the 1980s when, as an organization, it crystallized around the ideas and leadership of a former public school teacher and Sufi activist 'Abd al-Salam Yassin.

Al-Tawhid. With the goal of political participation in mind, al-Tawhid leaders sought to dissociate themselves from militant Islamist elements and present their movement to the ruling establishment as a moderate and responsible actor that renounces violence and accepts the legitimacy of the existing system. Al-Tawhid sprang out of al-Shabiba al-Islamiyya, which started out as a clandestine militant organization in the late 1960s and was implicated in the assassination of 'Umr bin Jallun, a famous Moroccan leftist leader. Tensions and disagreements within al-Shabiba led to the defection of many of its members, especially in Rabat, and some of the defecting members formed a group led by 'Abd al-Ilah bin Kiran called Jam'iyat al-Jama'a al-Islamiyya (Association of the Islamic Group). The leaders of the Jam'iyat attempted to gain official recognition through a number of letters—sent to the king and the Interior Ministry—and petitions for legal status throughout the

1980s. The group changed its name in 1992 to Harakat al-Islah wal-Taj-did (Movement for Reform and Renewal). In 1996, the group formed a new movement and called it al-Tawhid wal-Islah.

Between 1992 and 1997, al-Islah wal-Tajdid—later al-Tawhid wal-Islah–leaders were involved in extensive deliberations with 'Abd al-Karim al-Khatib, leader of the Democratic Constitutional Movement—a political party established in 1967 that had been virtually absent from the political scene for many years—to negotiate a deal that would allow its members to participate in the political process by joining his party. Al-Khatib agreed in 1997. The Islamists gradually joined the party, and in 1998, the party changed its name to the Party for Justice and Development (PJD) and has since been known as the political wing of al-Tawhid wal-Islah and as the largest Islamist party in the country.

Al-'Adl. Al-'Adl has a very different experience from al-Tawhid. It is a very popular movement in Morocco today. The movement's main goal is the establishment of an Islamic Caliphate. On this basis, it refuses to participate in the formal political process. Yassin, the movement's founder, was greatly influenced by the Islamic revolution in Iran and was highly impressed by the way the revolutionaries turned Islamic ideas into practice. Yassin was widely known for his activism and criticism of the monarchy in the 1970s; in 1974, he sent a letter to the late King Hassan II in which he criticized him and called on him to repent of his ways and return to true Islam.

In September 1981, Yassin announced the creation of his movement and attempted to acquire legal status in 1982. The government rejected Yassin's request on the basis that the movement mixes religion and politics. In September 1987, the movement adopted its current name—al-'Adl wal-Ihsan—which coincided with an escalation in tensions between the movement and the regime. Authorities placed Yassin under house arrest in December 1989, banned the movement in January 1990, and detained three members of the guiding bureau shortly after. The three members spent two years in jail, but Yassin, the General Guide, remained under house arrest for almost a decade.

Al-'Adl emphasizes spiritual education on the individual and collective levels. It seeks to present itself as a major actor in Moroccan society but at the same time refuses to acknowledge the legitimacy of the current political system. It regularly calls for boycotting local and parliamentary elections, for a radical overhaul of the current political environment, and for a new social contract between the government and the people based on Islamic precepts.

RELATIONS WITH OTHER OPPOSITION PARTIES

The PJD has not only been challenged by its relations with al-'Adl wal-Ihsan, however. Since its formation in 1998, there has been a great deal of antagonism between the PJD and the secular and traditional parties in parliament as well. In fact, these forces, especially the leftist parties, spearheaded the anti-PJD media campaign following the 2003 terrorist attacks. On August 6, 2007, major secular and traditional parties, including the Union of Popular Socialist Forces (USFP), the al-Istiqlal Party (Independence Party), the People's Movement Party, the National Rally of Independents, and the Party of Progress and Socialism, signed an antiterrorism declaration condemning radicalism and all forms of religious bigotry. The PJD did not take part in the initiative, despite its role as a major political force in the country. This underlined the persistent unease between the PJD and other opposition forces. After all, leaders of these groups have frequently denounced the PJD over the past few years, accusing it of harboring radical sentiments.

This hostility of the opposition forces can be explained by the sudden emergence of the PJD as a dominant force on the Moroccan political scene at the expense of many of these other parties. Regardless of the root causes, however, collaborative legislative work is more difficult when there is a high level of mistrust between major parliamentary actors.

The task is made even more difficult because the Moroccan ruling establishment is suspicious of the PJD. During the parliamentary session (2003–2004) in which the antiterrorism law was approved, then-Prime Minister Idriss Jattu delivered an impassioned speech in which he attacked the "dark forces" in Moroccan society, a term often used by secular politicians to attack Islamists. The PJD had good reason to feel targeted by the state. Former secretary general al-'Uthmani acknowledged this reality in an interview: "Following the events of May 2003, many in the political class showed their leftist inclinations by trying to exploit the opportunity to discredit the PJD, accusing it of having a hand in terrorism." [3]

Following the 2007 parliamentary elections, Fuad 'Ali al-Himma—former state minister in the Interior Ministry, MP, and close ally of the king—announced that he was forming a new political movement. He put together a coalition of MPs who had split from their parties. The new group called itself Movement for All Democrats (MTD). Reportedly, this new group intended to provide another safeguard against the influence of the PJD in parliament. On March 3, 2008, the privately owned Moroccan daily *al-Sabah* reported that the founders of the MTD have pointed out that the Islamists will be left out of this initiative because the latter is a "modern, civilized project."[4] The PJD was upset by the move and saw it as an attempt to further isolate it and fragment the parliament. In 2008, al-Himma's group, promoted by the monarchy, developed into a wider coalition encompassing several small parties and recreated itself as the Party for Authenticity and Modernity (al-Asala wal-Mu'asara).[5] The group was seen as the king's party and after securing significant gains in the partial parliamentary elections of September 2008 and the municipal elections of June 2009, the Party for Authenticity and Modernity has advanced to the forefront of Moroccan politics and continued its aggressive strategy to isolate the PJD.[6]

Only with regard to its relations with the leftist USFP has the PJD succeeded in changing the pattern of hostility and mistrust with which it has been received by secular and traditional parties. After the 2007 elections, the two parties began to partially coordinate their activities in parliament, step up their cooperation at the municipal level, and create ad-hoc electoral alliances in 2008 and 2009.

Clearly, the poor legislative performance of the PJD is in part the product of its troubled relations with other political actors, but there is another more fundamental predicament that, even in the context of good relations with other political actors, will invariably hinder the PJD's various legislative initiatives. A more objective view of the PJD's legislative record has to take into account the fact that these shortcomings are directly correlated with the domination of the ruling establishment over the legislative process. The Moroccan monarchy maintains a comfortable loyal majority in parliament, which in turn prevents the utilization of legislative oversight instruments and a genuine separation and balance between the various branches of government.

The PJD's Priorities in Parliament

Despite the PJD's troubled relations with most other political actors, it has gradually gained members in Morocco's parliament, winning nine out of 325 seats in the 1997 legislative elections, 42 in 2002, and 46 in

2007. And PJD members of parliament have become particularly active in recent years, focusing their legislative efforts on significant social and economic issues such as corruption, poverty, and unemployment.[7] The unimpressive track record of the PJD's parliamentary representatives, however, has caused the party a number of problems. Popular doubts have grown about the ability of the PJD to translate its opposition activism into meaningful policy measures through participation in the political process—a challenge that Islamist opposition movements have been struggling with across the Arab world. Moreover, in spite of its moderate platform, the PJD is still viewed with suspicion by policy makers inside and outside Morocco. Some leftist political parties have occasionally suggested that the PJD's ultimate goal is the promotion of extremism and radicalism in the Moroccan polity. A 2006 report prepared by the U.S. Congressional Research Service questioned the PJD's ambiguity and asserted that

> . . . like many Islamist groups across the globe, it is difficult to discern what the PJD's true goals and objectives are over the long term. Some believe that, although the party has agreed to work within the current system, it remains committed to establishing an Islamic state in Morocco with Islamic law, or Sharia, as the basis for legislation.[8]

PARLIAMENTARY PLATFORM AND EFFECTIVENESS

Certainly, the PJD's activism in parliament has not always been focused on substantive reforms. On occasion, party members put religious issues at the forefront of their legislative debates, for example, protesting the distribution of an unedited movie that included inappropriate (intimate) scenes in 2005, or occasionally bringing up the issue of alcohol distribution to Muslims.

Nevertheless, in fairness to the PJD, since 2002 the party has become less preoccupied with debates on religious and ideological issues than have Islamist political movements in countries such as Egypt and Jordan. Under the leadership of former Secretary General Sa'd al-Din al-'Uthmani and current Secretary-General 'Abd al-Ilah bin Kiran (elected in July 2008), as well as the generation of young activists who joined the party in the late 1990s, the PJD has revamped its image in significant ways. The party has evolved into a venue for serious debates on the public policy measures needed to address Morocco's social and economic problems.

The PJD contributed to a remarkable breakthrough in 2005 with the endorsement of a new, more liberal version of the *mudawwana* (the code regulating marriage and family life in the country). The revision of the *mudawwana* greatly improved women's social status and was opposed by more conservative Islamist elements. Indeed, the PJD participated in the negotiations for the new code and ultimately accepted its provisions, despite the fact that they do not bear a clearly Islamist stamp. The party's leadership defended its position by arguing that the code had been adopted through a democratic process and therefore had to be respected. In an interview conducted in 2006, al-'Uthmani defended his party's decision to support the law, saying that it was approved by religious authorities, was comprehensive, helped families (and women in particular), and was formulated only after extensive deliberations and consultations with many political, religious, and civil society representatives.[9]

Indeed, the PJD has emerged as a pragmatic player committed to political participation and keen on searching for real solutions to the persistent needs of the populace. Ideological assertions, including calls for application of *shari'a* (Islamic Law), have been gradually reduced to low-key objectives. It bears emphasis here that instead of referring to *shari'a*—or to an Islamic frame of reference (*marji'iya islamiyya*)—the 2007 electoral platform of the PJD mentioned the "protection of Morocco's Islamic identity" as its main religious-based priority.

The PJD has also made tremendous efforts to present an exemplary bloc in parliament. The party regularly circulates attendance sheets to make sure that its deputies attend their parliamentary sessions and committee hearings. It also frequently demands that parliament deal seriously with the issue of member absenteeism. PJD members of parliament (MPs) are known for submitting the greatest number of written and oral questions. The party has also worked on training its MPs to draft and propose legislative initiatives. MPs have professional support units made up of experts who can provide specialized advice on technical matters pertaining to various public policy legislation. These efforts have been interpreted as part of the PJD's agenda to empower representative institutions in the country.

What has really defined the PJD's parliamentary experience has been its MPs' emphasis on transparency in the House of Representatives and strong support of anticorruption initiatives, in addition to the constant demand for accountability and better accessibility to the executive. On at least one occasion, the PJD sent a letter complaining to the chair of the Constitutional Council about what its MPs considered unconstitutional behavior by the minister in charge of organizing the executive's affairs with the legislature. The complaint protested the delay tactics used by the minister to circumvent legislative efforts to question officials from the executive on a variety of issues.

The PJD was fierce in its opposition to the election law passed in late 2006 and later had some of its provisions revoked by the Constitutional Council. The PJD rejected the law mainly because it limits participation in the electoral process and opens the doors for more corruption. 'Abdullah Baha, former party whip in parliament, said in an interview that

> The Justice and Development Party demands an independent commission to supervise the elections . . . and guaranteeing independent monitoring for the election processes by civil society institutions. Also, we renew our rejection of the exceptional reviews to the election regulations . . . we want to create healthy conditions for the national campaigning to maintain and defend democracy against the lobbies of personal interests, and political and financial corruption.[10]

The PJD also had reservations about a government-supported political parties law, though it initially supported the measure because it encouraged transparency, democratic procedures, and accountability within political parties. In an interview, former Secretary General al-'Uthmani explained:

> It is a good law, as it stipulates that there be 200 prospective members to create a new party, instead of seven as it had been previously. It also includes provisions that all parties be internally democratic, include a certain percentage of young people and women in leadership structures, and practice transparency in management and finances.[11]

The PJD nonetheless had some reservations, particularly because the political party law was seen as an attempt to shift attention away from the need to achieve comprehensive constitutional reforms in Morocco, and because it used broad language that could be open to many interpretations in the provisions pertaining to the ideological foundations of parties. Nonetheless, these reservations were expressed in a careful and nonconfrontational manner because the ruling establishment strongly supported the law. Eventually, the party abstained from voting on the matter.

There were other laws with which the PJD was uncomfortable but had no choice but to support. The 2003 antiterrorism bill is a case in point. In May 2003, five suicide bombings rocked Morocco and left 45 dead and nearly 100 injured. Thousands of Islamists were arrested, 50 were sentenced to life in prison, and sixteen to death. One of the individuals arrested, Yunis Usalih, a local official in the PJD, was accused of having prior knowledge of the terrorist attacks. A major anti-Islamist backlash orchestrated by the monarchy and a few pro-establishment parties made no effort to discriminate between moderate and militant Islamists. In fact, many public figures were calling for officially dismantling the PJD and banning its members from the political process. The party was politically isolated and smeared in the media by political rivals and opponents. It was this pressure that ultimately forced the PJD to vote in favor of the 2003 antiterrorism bill, which is widely seen as a setback for civil liberties and freedoms in the country. The new bill restricts, among other things, freedom of expression, and penalizes journalists with fines and prison sentences for writing anything that may be interpreted as supporting terrorism or defaming public officials and endangering public order.

PJD MPs have also been active participants in the discussions on a new organizational law for the Supreme Court, which if passed would allow for the investigation and punishment of government officials, in addition to a number of other reforms. Because of its importance and sensitivity, the law has been debated and postponed on and off since the 1997–2002 parliamentary cycle. The PJD is against the provisions that stipulate that two-thirds of the two legislative chambers (that is, the House of Representatives and the House of Councilors) are needed before court procedures can be initiated against officials implicated in any offenses. This condition, the PJD argues, is impossible to achieve given the fragmented makeup of the Moroccan parliament. Being able to hold government officials to account is critical for the PJD because it presents an opportunity to advance some of the constitutional reform elements that the party often emphasizes in its political programs. Indeed, there are three main pillars for the PJD's constitutional reform vision: (1) institute all necessary mechanisms to secure the independence of the judiciary; (2) expand the supervisory and legislative prerogatives of the House of Representatives and review those of the House of Councilors; and (3) ensure that the executive branch is accountable to parliament.

The PJD also had a number of other proposals concerning the Supreme Court law: decrease the number of judges in the agencies of the Supreme Court to ensure efficiency, limit the role of the Ministry of Justice in these types of investigations, and make the employees of the Supreme Court subject to supervision by parliament and not the Ministry of Justice.

This type of parliamentary activism, apparent in the 2002–2007 cycle, stands in contrast to the PJD's emphasis on ethical and religious issues during the 1997–2002 cycle. Some of the issues raised by PJD MPs then included the issue of non-Islamic banking, alcohol consumption, Islamic education, immoral practices in the tourism industry, and reforming the cinema industry to ensure that it complied with Islamic teachings. In an interview, al-'Uthmani addressed this development:

> In the beginning we focused on articulating general principles. Over time we became more experienced and capable of evaluating government policy in a detailed way, as well as making political deals. This is progress, and we are looking to expand this expertise in the future.[12]

Moreover, in placing economic and social issues at the core of its 2007 electoral platform "Together to Build a Just Morocco," the party demonstrated that it was on a unique evolutionary trajectory relative to the rest of the Arab Islamist scene. Indeed, the first aspect that attracts attention in the program is its level of detail, particularly on economic and public policy measures. The program includes development index data comparing Morocco's performance with that of other Arab and developing countries to show how far Morocco lags behind other countries' performance indicators, especially in terms of literacy, poverty reduction, youth employment, and health care.

New ideas for economic reform are explored in depth and evaluated critically in the platform. It begins by outlining the most urgent problems facing the Moroccan economy and follows by prescribing a very specific road map for economic recovery. There are no signs that the PJD intends to demolish the current system or revolutionize the economic model by introducing laws and regulations that make it more Islamic. In fact, shari'a does not appear at all in the economic policy section. Moreover, the platform explicitly states that the party's goal is to establish reliable pillars for a healthy, competitive, open economy that is able to provide job opportunities for more Moroccans.

Interestingly enough, the prescriptions section in the platform starts by outlining concrete policies to lift the state of research and development in the education sector, making it integral to economic development.

Among the proposals are increasing governmental investment in new and technologically advanced research centers, reforming universities, providing incentives for private investments in research, emphasizing science and social studies in school curricula, and improving communication networks among researchers and specialists in similar fields of study. In terms of regulation, the party proposes revamping the rules regulating doctoral degrees and rechanneling the focus of the National Center for Science from supervision to active participation in scientific research.

On the macro level, the PJD's economic plan intends to increase GDP growth from 4.5 to 7 percent between 2008 and 2012, maintain low inflation (below 2 percent), improve the balance of trade, reduce public debt, balance the budget, increase public investments (by 7 percent annually until it reaches 20 percent of the budget in 2012), and privatize government-owned businesses. The only reference to Islam is related to Islamic banking, which the platform mentions in the context of diversifying investment tools and facilitating the participation of Islamic banks in the national economy.

In terms of social welfare policies and taxes, the PJD favors a generous redistribution of wealth to combat poverty, deal with the negative consequences of unemployment, and cover the costs of a universal health care system. The PJD's program endorses a progressive tax code that encourages innovation, does not punish productivity, and is sensitive to international competitiveness needs. The party is in favor of gradually lowering corporate taxes, while raising taxes on profits made in the stock and the real estate markets. The PJD also supports minimum wage laws, subsidizing agricultural ventures, and making public and private loans more accessible.

In terms of lowering unemployment, the PJD's proposed policies focus on investing in training, education, and institutional innovation. There are also sections in the PJD's platform that deal with improving specific economic sectors like fishing and agriculture, transportation, and energy conservation. The policies are very progressive in terms of mandating government intervention to protect and improve these sectors.

The PJD's most recent parliamentary work—in the new 2007–2012 parliamentary cycle—includes opposition to the 2008 budget law. The party had many reservations about the law and ultimately voted against it. In a reversal of frequent government criticisms of Islamist movements, the PJD argued that the law showed the government's lack of concrete strategic plans to resolve the collective exigencies at hand and suggested that the influence of big business over the parliament had pushed the legislation in the wrong direction. PJD MPs also raised a variety of different concerns on the environment, the industrial sector, and energy policy that the law does not adequately address. The PJD tried to insert amendments to the law, but was denied that right. It protested and claimed that the government and its allies in parliament violated the constitution by denying the opposition the opportunity to discuss proposed amendments.

In 2008 and 2009, the PJD raised a number of issues in parliament including accountability issues with the main electricity provider, discrimination against veiled women in the workplace, inflation, and consumer protection. This kind of parliamentary activism is in sync with the nature of the PJD's work during the previous cycle.

But despite the spate of policy activity, the PJD has largely been unsuccessful in strongly shaping or influencing the legislative process. This lack of real progress is in part the result of the mistrust that exists between the PJD and other influential forces in parliament, but primarily the consequence of the virtual powerlessness of the parliament in Morocco's semiauthoritarian environment.

Impacts of PJD Participation in the Political Process

In and of itself, the participation of the PJD in the political process has not led to the realization of a healthy democratic order in Morocco, nor has it brought Morocco closer to that order. An objective assessment reveals that the limited role of Islamists and the trifling consequences of their participation merely reflect the inherent weaknesses of democratic instruments such as electoral regimes and legislative institutions in the Moroccan political setting. But while the PJD's political participation has had only limited impact on Moroccan politics, it has had a significant impact on the PJD internally.

SEPARATION AND OVERLAP WITH AL-TAWHID

As mentioned earlier, al-Tawhid wal-Islah was formed in 1996 and the PJD emerged as its political wing in 1998. The relationship between *da'wa* and political activism was not a major issue at the time, but the May 2003 terrorist attacks in Casablanca expedited the process of reviewing the relationship between the movement and party, especially as secular and traditional parties intensified their attacks on the movement and accused it of being responsible for terrorism. Following the attacks, the movement brought about a rapid division of labor between itself and the party.

The close ties between al-Tawhid and the PJD have frequently come under harsh criticism from Moroccan officials. Critics charge that the party participates in politics according to the dictates of the constitution (which bars the use of religion for political purposes) while at the same time maintaining links with al-Tawhid, a religious and proselytizing movement. Indeed, many PJD cadres still maintain their positions in al-Tawhid's highest decision-making body, the executive bureau, including Muhammad Yatim (member of the PJD's General Secretariat), 'Abdullah Baha (member of the PJD's General Secretariat), and 'Abd al-Ilah bin Kiran (current secretary-general).

Certainly, many al-Tawhid and PJD members see the need to address the question once and for all in order to silence critics and preserve al-Tawhid's religious and social character, which they feel has been compromised by the party's political engagement. Muhammad Yatim has raised this concern in recent years. Considered one of the movement's most important theorists, Yatim argues that conceptually the movement starts from an assumption that Islam is an all-encompassing religion, but that does not mean that separation between some of the movement's specialized and general activities is not necessary. Muhammad al-Hamdawi, the current president of al-Tawhid's executive bureau, often describes the relationship between the movement and the party as one of *shiraka* (cooperation) between two independent institutions. He views both entities as having a common goal but functioning as independent organizations. Ahmad al-Rayssuni, former president of al-Tawhid's executive bureau and a current member, frequently contends that there is some overlap between the movement and the party's activities, but that overall the party responsibilities lie in reforming state institutions and policies, whereas the movement's responsibilities lie in education and *da'wa*.[13]

Other members of the movement were even more concerned. Farid al-Ansari, a former member of al-Tawhid, resigned from the movement in 2000 because of this very issue. In 2007, he authored a book titled *The Six*

Mistakes of the Islamist Movement in Morocco, in which he argued that involvement in politics is one the biggest mistakes committed by the movement's leadership.[14] In 2008, even al-'Uthmani, former secretary-general, recently argued that "the best relationship between religion and politics according to Islam is not complete severance but is also not perfect union. It is rather connection but with distinction and differentiation."[15]

There is indeed plenty of evidence that confirms that the movement and the party are institutionally independent. The conditions for membership in the movement rely on religious and moral considerations. Membership for the party, however, only requires that its members share the party's political orientation and general frame of reference. Moreover, the rules for advancement within the movement are not based on political considerations. Punitive measures also differ from the movement to the party; a member expelled from the party for political reasons may not necessarily be expelled from the movement and vice versa. All in all, al-Tawhid's activities are tailored for *da'wa* purposes, whereas the political component of the movement's agenda is entirely handled by the PJD. It bears special notice that the manner with which the movement reaches out to other Islamist groups, such as al-'Adl wal-Ihsan, is also different from the party's approach. For instance, al-Tawhid often voices public support of al-'Adl when the government cracks down on it. The party, in contrast, is typically more careful in its response to such confrontations in order to avoid provoking tensions with the regime. So when Nadia Yassin—'Abd al-Salam Yassin's daughter and the unofficial spokeswoman of al-'Adl—said in a 2005 interview that the monarchical regime is inadequate for Morocco, the PJD's leadership hastened to condemn her remarks.[16]

While there is an institutional separation between al-Tawhid and the PJD, separation between the movement and the party on the level of membership remains a major issue. The movement's members constitute the vast majority of the party's overall membership and leadership. There are a number of regulations, however, that prevent the movement's executive bureau president and his deputy from occupying any positions in the party. In fact, al-Hamdawi resigned from the PJD upon his election as president of al-Tawhid's executive bureau. The substantial overlap in membership can be explained by the fact that the PJD is a relatively young political party; it is likely to grow more independent with time. To a great extent, the party's ability to attract constituencies that do not necessarily share al-Tawhid's religious predispositions will depend on its electoral and parliamentary performance. Sustained success in the elections and effectiveness in parliament may enable the PJD to reach out to new constituencies. Yet exactly in relation to these two benchmarks, the PJD's experience in recent years has indicated some stagnation.

Elections and the Post-Participation Debate

As mentioned earlier, despite much effort expended in parliamentary challenges, the PJD has remained an inconsequential force in terms of shaping government policy. It can credit no major pieces of legislation to its name and has continued to struggle to find common ground with other opposition groups in parliament. This, many analysts contend, has been one of the major causes of its underperformance in the 2007 legislative elections.

Thirty-three political parties and thirteen independent electoral lists contested the chamber's 325 seats in the 2007 elections. (Thirty seats are reserved for women based on a quota system introduced prior to the previous parliamentary elections, which were held in 2002.) Eighteen parties ran candidates in at least 50 percent of the country's 95 electoral districts. Five parties were represented in almost every district: the two governing parties (the USFP and the Independence Party—al-Istiqlal), the main Islamist opposition party (PJD), the Popular Movement, and the National Rally of Independents.

EXPLAINING THE 2007 AND 2009 ELECTION RESULTS

The results of the 2007 parliamentary elections surprised many observers. The Independence Party finished in first, with 52 seats (16 percent of the popular vote), followed by the PJD with 46 seats (14 percent of the popular vote). The Popular Movement and the National Rally of Independents finished third and fourth, with 41 and 39 seats, respectively. The party that formerly held the most seats, the USFP, was reduced to just 38 seats. The fall of the USFP was widely expected because of a series of internal conflicts and splits within the party as well as the poor record of the governing coalition. However, the strong showing of the Independence Party, the USFP's longtime coalition partner, is puzzling. However, two factors likely played a part in explaining this outcome: (1) the strength of the Independence Party's appeal to traditionally conservative constituencies in Morocco; and (2) the party's strong networks of support in some rural areas.

The PJD's results came as the biggest surprise. Prior to the elections, expectations were high regarding the Islamists' potential gains, especially against the background of Western and domestic polls predicting an unstoppable rise of the PJD. During the final phase of the election campaign, the party leadership expressed high optimism, stating publicly that 70 to 80 seats were within reach and that the party would be the strongest bloc in the parliament. The fact that the PJD added only four additional seats in 2007—going up from 42 in 2002 to 46—stunned the PJD leadership and pundits alike. Initial statements by prominent party figures were characterized by an angry tone and harsh accusations of vote buying by other parties.[17]

Local and international monitoring groups confirmed that the elections were conducted in a fair and transparent manner. Yet there were a number of reports of violations involving vote buying in both urban and rural areas. Remarkably, voter turnout plunged to a historical low of 37 percent, down from 51 percent in the 2002 elections and 58 percent in 1997. Poor participation marred the process despite significant get-out-the-vote efforts by the government as well as by political parties and civil society organizations. Government agencies and various nongovernmental organizations conducted voter education programs, especially in impoverished urban areas, and leading political parties announced and heavily publicized detailed electoral platforms several weeks before the elections. Most platforms tackled the social and economic needs of the population, and, at least in the case of the USFP, the Independence Party, and the PJD, concrete policy measures were included. Despite all these efforts, however, Moroccans' waning level of interest in electoral politics persisted.

The three elections that followed the 2007 parliamentary elections marked the electoral regression of the PJD. In September 2008, the PJD failed to win any of seven contested seats in partial parliamentary elections, which were conducted to replace disqualified MPs.[18] In the municipal elections of June 2009, the PJD ranked sixth, winning 1,509 out of 27,795 seats, equivalent to 5.43 percent.[19] Although the party widened its representation at the municipal level—from a mere 2.1 percent between 2003 and 2009—the net result of its electoral performance deteriorated. While it contested only 17.6 percent of the municipal seats in the 2003 elections, the PJD ran candidates in 39.4 percent of the seats in 2009.[20] Moreover, the PJD's weak presence in rural areas prevented it from winning any seat in the renewal elections for 81 seats of the House of Councilors, held in October 2009.[21]

POSTELECTORAL DILEMMAS

It appears from the outcome of the 2007 election, and the low voter turnout in particular, that the inability of the parliament to play an active role in policy implementation has resulted in a growing disenchantment with parliamentary politics that has dimmed prospects for broader participation in the political process. Wide segments of the population have come to see the parliament as a failed institution that can do little to solve their pressing economic and social problems. It is worth noting that Morocco has sustained one of the highest unemployment rates in North Africa over the past two decades. Continuous efforts to alleviate poverty have had little real effect on the welfare of the country's poor. Major cities such as Casablanca, Rabat, and Marrakesh have become encircled by dilapidated settlements extending into the rural heartland that breed social illnesses such as religious extremism, juvenile criminality, and illegal migration by young people to the developed countries of the West.

Since 1998, many formerly hopeful Moroccan citizens have become increasingly skeptical about the capacity of the various Moroccan political parties to carry out meaningful socioeconomic reforms. In a remarkable turn of events that year that ended decades of political upheaval, the late King Hassan II asked the former opposition parties (the USFP and the Independence Party) to form a coalition government. The two parties, operating in coalition with royalist and regional parties, have constituted the core of every Moroccan government since then. But little progress has come out of this transformation.

The popular hopes of substantive reforms set in motion in 1998 have diminished greatly. The USFP and the Independence Party did well enough in the 2002 elections to cling to leadership of their coalition regime: The USFP won 50 seats in the House of Representatives and the runner-up Independence Party won 46. The two parties' popular appeal was shrinking, however, as demonstrated by the decline in voter turnout (51 percent, down from 58 percent in 1997) and the rise of the Islamist PJD.

Since Muhammad VI ascended to the throne in 1999, the process of political opening has continued. The political sphere has become more diverse, and safeguards for human rights have strengthened remarkably. However, improvements in the political process have stopped short of addressing the two central impediments to democratic transition in Morocco—the concentration of power in royal hands and the absence of credible checks and balances. In addition, as noted earlier, the electoral system, which is based on proportional representation, consistently produces a fragmented parliament whose influence is easily checked by the monarchy. The major outcomes of these structural deficiencies have been diminished parliamentary credibility and weaker political parties.

The deficient performance of political parties, whether governing coalition or opposition, has greatly exacerbated the problem. Over the last ten years, the coalition governments led by the USFP and the Independence Party have failed to develop credible programs to resolve Morocco's severe socioeconomic predicaments. Worse, these governments have been marked by corrupt practices that have jeopardized the historical legacy of the USFP and the Independence Party as opponents of government corruption. The efforts of the parties to reach a balanced distribution of power among the king, the cabinet, and the legislature have yielded no tangible results. The monarchy has systematically balked at introducing constitutional reforms in the areas pertaining to the decision-making powers of the cabinet—specifically those attached to the office of the prime minister—and to the oversight powers of the parliament. The outcome has been a burgeoning mistrust of traditional political forces, which recent efforts by different parties at organizational and programmatic renewal have failed to contain.

Even the fresh and untainted PJD has suffered from this popular discontent. Although the party has managed in recent years to develop stable and increasingly well-organized constituencies in urban centers, especially among the younger segments of the Moroccan population, its popular appeal has remained limited. Instead, the followers of Yassin's al-'Adl have advanced to the forefront of the Islamist spectrum in Morocco, focusing their activism on proselytizing and the provision of social services. With its rejectionist attitude toward the monarchy and its leadership's claim that the whole political system is corrupt and therefore cannot be reformed gradually, al-'Adl's leaders have systematically criticized the PJD for its participation in parliamentary politics and accused the party leadership of being submissive to the monarchy.

The popularity of the fundamentalist opposition rhetoric of al-'Adl among Islamist constituencies has kept the PJD from mobilizing wide segments of the disenfranchised population. As a result, the PJD is increasingly finding itself in a new position in which it has to justify its continued commitment to political participation and to take into account the high cost and low return of this course. Islamist constituencies, it seems, need to be convinced of the validity and indispensability of participation as a strategic choice.

Based on the current discourse observed in the PJD, there appear to be two pro-participation arguments in discussion. The first suggests that participation allows the PJD to use various institutional instruments and methods to protect itself from the ruling establishment's repression. In addition, participation allows the party to maintain its public presence, which, in and of itself, helps it maintain cohesion within its ranks and lively rapport with the constituencies. The second argument suggests that through participation, the PJD can maintain an active public role in the struggle for gradual and meaningful political reform in Morocco. Remarkably, it is evident that the first argument has gained more traction in times of tension with the monarchy, especially after the arrests of al-Badil's leaders, whereas the second has become more relevant in times of relative stability in that relationship. Muhammad Yatim, a prominent leader in both the PJD and al-Tawhid wal-Islah Movement, expressed these ideas when he argued that the advantages of political participation were tremendous and indispensable to any political force striving to achieve positive change in society. He also added that political participation allows political actors to preserve and protect the political gains they have already achieved.[22]

Moreover, the PJD is struggling to redefine a practical and sustainable balance between the pragmatic demands of participation and those dictated by the Islamist frame of reference. Given the restricted political environment in Morocco, the PJD has adopted moderate positions on various societal and political matters. At the same time, it has had to be careful not to alienate wide segments of its constituencies drawn to it because of its religious frame of reference. Doubtless, the task of finding the balance between pragmatism and ideological commitment is becoming progressively more difficult, especially in light of growing popular disenchantment with the political process and the increased significance of strong rejectionist Islamist currents. The PJD has plunged into exhaustive debates about the movement's priorities with the costly consequence of losing its sense of strategic orientation.

Conclusion

Though the Party for Justice and Development failed to meet expectations in the 2007–2009 elections and is now grappling with the many dilemmas of participating in a semiauthoritarian political environment, it has effectively moved from the status of an outsider to that of an insider. The PJD's gains in 2002 were not just a temporary breakthrough, and, in the years since, it has become well entrenched in the Moroccan political process. In the 2007 parliamentary elections, the PJD fielded candidates in 94 of 95 districts, compared with only 56 districts in 2002, and in the 2009 municipal elections, the PJD contested 39.4 percent of the municipal seats, up from 18 percent in 2003. These developments have forced the media and political observers to acknowledge the extent of its political organization and the progressive nature of its agenda. Moreover, the PJD remains in the opposition, which has its advantages, given the considerable popular dissatisfaction with current and former governments. And finally, though the al-'Adl wal-Ihsan (Justice and Charity) movement is popular, it is unlikely to jeopardize the PJD's political clout unless it enters into the political process.

Yet even if the PJD's popularity grows in the coming years, the challenges posed by the concentration of power in royal hands, a semiauthoritarian electoral system and state-sponsored gerrymandering are all likely to persist, limiting the PJD's role in Moroccan politics.

CHAPTER 5

Pushing Toward Party Politics?

Kuwait's Islamic Constitutional Movement

K uwait's Islamic Constitutional Movement, founded in the aftermath of the Gulf War in 1991, is a relatively new political actor in Kuwait. Yet by the standards of Arab Islamist movements, Hadas (the movement's Arabic acronym) is one of the region's most experienced groups in parliamentary and electoral politics. The party can even claim real electoral and programmatic successes, having been integrated as a regular and accepted political force in Kuwait, and operating well within the boundaries of the country's established political process. Hadas has also experimented with a range of political stances, at times entering the government and at others leading vocal opposition. It has emphasized its distinctly Islamic nature but also has chosen to build cross-ideological coalitions for political reform.

But after a series of successes over its first fifteen years, Hadas now finds its political prospects diminished—no matter which course it follows. The party's problems go beyond merely crafting an appropriate strategy, and result from a deeper paralysis in the Kuwaiti political system.

Since its founding, Hadas has dedicated itself to the proposition that it could Islamize Kuwaiti politics and society most effectively by constitutional means. At the time, circumstances for constitutional action were not auspicious, as Kuwait was just emerging from Iraqi occupation. Nor was postwar chaos the only obstacle; the parliament Hadas sought to join had been suspended for five years, long before the Iraqi invasion.

Close to two decades later, there is much to suggest that Hadas's strategy has been vindicated: the restoration of the country's parliament in 1992 allowed the movement to become a major player in the country's political life. The Kuwaiti Islamic movement, of which Hadas is a part, has gained greater influence in society, thriving in spite of the turmoil of regional politics. Hadas has also been part of an on-again, off-again loose parliamentary coalition that has successfully used constitutional prerogatives to pass legislation and question ministers. These parliamentary prerogatives had existed on paper but rarely been used in the past, partly because on two occasions their use had provoked the *amir* to suspend parliament. But for all that it has accomplished, Hadas still has usually found itself standing outside the central structures of political power, pursuing its goals by harassing the government rather than forming it. Moreover, the party has been losing support at the ballot box, in part because of a major electoral reform that Hadas itself helped spearhead in 2006.

Like any political player, Hadas has had to make difficult tactical choices. It rose gradually, and its success owed largely to the party's judiciousness in building alliances and care in picking battles. With the government and the ruling family, Hadas has striven to position itself simultaneously as an opposition movement and as a party accepting gradualism and the limitations of the Kuwaiti political system. With other Islamist forces, Hadas has had to balance between building a broad Islamist coalition and competing (especially with Salafi and conservative tribal political forces) to write an Islamic agenda and win votes. Hadas has had to find a balance with more liberal and secular forces, somewhere between forming broad opposition coalitions and challenging those who have very different visions for Kuwaiti society.

In 2006, Hadas deputies in parliament threw in their lot with a broad opposition coalition, uniting with erstwhile rivals and pursuing a confrontational strategy to pressure the government into enacting electoral reforms. When the government reacted by escalating the confrontation, dissolving parliament, and calling for new elections, Hadas and its partners scored an impressive victory. After the election, Kuwaiti political observers proclaimed that the opposition was now the majority—an untenable situation in any parliamentary democracy, because any opposition movement that won an electoral majority would then form a government. For a brief period, a version of such an outcome seemed possible, allowing Hadas to participate in a coalition that would move

Kuwait toward a regular political party system and perhaps even push the country's political order toward constitutional monarchy (a goal the movement has sometimes articulated). But instead 2006 seems in retrospect to have been the peak of the party's success with the prospects for a broad reform coalition and Hadas's electoral fortunes both in decline.

In this chapter, we will present:

- The evolving environment in which Hadas has operated;
- The evolution of the movement itself;
- Hadas's platform and its attempt simultaneously to advance Islamic causes and more general political reforms;
- The role the movement has played in parliament;
- Hadas's relations with the regime; and
- Its intermittent efforts to build a broad and diverse coalition for political reform.

The Islamic Constitutional Movement in Kuwaiti Politics

The choices and opportunities now facing Hadas can only be understood in the context of Kuwait's unusual hybrid political system. Since winning independence from the United Kingdom in 1961, Kuwait has combined domination by a ruling family (common to all Arabian peninsular states except Yemen) with some of the features of a constitutional monarchy.

THE POLITICAL CONTEXT

Kuwaiti men (and since 2006, women) periodically elect a parliament, a body that has considerable authority over legislation and a limited but real ability to call individual ministers to account. Indeed, parliament may even go so far as to declare itself unable to cooperate with the cabinet, forcing the *amir* to dismiss the cabinet or dissolve parliament and call new elections.

Members of the ruling Al Sabah family traditionally do not compete for parliamentary seats, but they do monopolize top cabinet slots. Until recently, the position of prime minister was always held by the crown prince. On most matters, all ministers (even those not elected) are granted votes in parliament. Many elected deputies win their seats by providing services to constituents or even buying votes. With a population of only 1.1 million, Kuwait's small and restricted franchise, and—until the 2006 electoral reforms—tiny electoral districts have sometimes enabled a candidate to win a seat with fewer than 1,000 votes. For many years, the government managed to manipulate the political system by funneling favors to citizens through allied deputies, thus supplementing its own votes in parliament with a number of "service deputies." Self-styled opposition individuals and movements of various colors—liberal, leftist, or Islamist—have often done well in elections, but political parties have no legal status in Kuwait. Not only are parties disorganized and weak; they also have generally failed to work together even when they have a strong common interest.

The result has been a sometimes feisty parliament that occasionally obstructs government measures but can rarely act positively in pursuit of a well-defined agenda. The legislature can question ministers, air scandals, and appeal to public opinion, but the government has generally been able to cajole the votes or divide the opposition enough to deflect parliamentary pressure. In other words, deputies frequently annoy and embarrass the government, but they can rarely determine the composition of the cabinet or pass legislation over government opposition.

On two occasions when parliament seemed poised to go farther, in 1976 and 1986, the *amir* reacted by dissolving it in a clearly unconstitutional manner, suspending the legislature for five years the first time and for six years the second.

In the period since the Iraqi occupation, however, the opposition has shown greater viability, and the government's ability to divide and conquer has diminished. Opposition MPs have persuaded the prime minister not to select some ministers (including some members of the ruling family) whom they viewed as incompetent or corrupt. Opposition blocs have occasionally also coordinated effectively on particular issues. And the parliament has broken a series of taboos, first bringing down controversial ministers, then forcing cabinet members from the ruling family to resign, and finally, in 2009, formally questioning the prime minister himself. This prospect would have been unthinkable a generation earlier, and the *amir* had sought in recent years to avoid it by calling for early parliamentary elections any time the parliament seemed about to take a bold step. The parliament's greatest success came in 2006, when it pushed through electoral reforms combining Kuwait's 25 districts (each represented by two deputies) into five (each to be represented by ten deputies). Reformers, including Hadas deputies, claimed that this would turn elections from occasions for buying votes from neighbors and campaigning among tribal or family members to a more programmatic and ideological contest. Only after the opposition had won the 2006 elections, which were held under the old system, did the reform pass.

A HISTORIC OPPORTUNITY?

In spite of its scattered democratic and parliamentary features, Kuwait is not a full parliamentary democracy. But Hadas's growing parliamentary power has brought all the tactical dilemmas the movement has faced since its creation into glaring relief.

The government and ruling family have clearly grown resentful of the opposition's strength and made clear that they feel parliament risks overstepping its bounds. But the ruling family itself is increasingly public in its own deep divisions, leaving opportunities perhaps for other political forces to emerge. Grasping such an opportunity—and indeed constructing any possibility for parliament to act positively rather than negatively—has come to rest on the ability of a diverse body to translate partial coincidences of interest into a party-like coalition with a semblance of voting discipline.

Over the past decade, it has thus become clear that further political liberalization in Kuwait depends on forging a successful alliance of forces that have been wary of each other for Hadas's whole life, and maneuvering around a government that continues to be caught flat-footed in response. The potential payoff is enormous: the prospect of moving Kuwait closer toward the constitutional monarchy and party politics that have seemed unreachable ever since the country gained independence.

Forming an Islamic Constitutional Movement in an Unconstitutional Monarchy

The Islamic Constitutional Movement is the political wing of Kuwait's Muslim Brotherhood. Neither Hadas nor the Muslim Brotherhood exists in any legal sense, as the country's legal framework makes no provision for political parties.

The movement's main legally recognized manifestation is the Social Reform Society, a charitable nongovernmental organization that is informally but quite closely linked to the broad Brotherhood movement in Kuwait. Like its sister movements throughout the Arab world, the Kuwaiti Muslim Brotherhood has managed to engage in a range of related but separate activities in the social, charitable, economic, and political realms. Kuwait has experienced periods of political repression, but has escaped the harsh authoritarianism that has characterized many other Arab states. Official repression, when it has come, has not only been gentler but also restricted to the political sphere, allowing the Brotherhood to work fairly freely, with some of its activities legally unrecognized but tolerated and unimpeded.

THE KUWAITI MUSLIM BROTHERHOOD

The Kuwaiti branch of the Brotherhood formed as the "Islamic Guidance Society" in 1952. Following a short period of repression and disarray toward the end of the 1950s, the organization relaunched itself after Kuwait regained independence, and sponsored the creation of the "Social Reform Society," a body that has emerged as one of Kuwait's leading nongovernmental organizations.[1] From its inception up through the 1980s, the Kuwaiti group was often heavily influenced by its Egyptian parent organization. Formal organizational ties existed (until they were broken in 1991), but the model of the Egyptian organization—with its networking activities and organizational efforts—proved far more influential than any formal ties. More important still were personal contacts; Egyptian teachers and other officials came to work in Kuwait as the country's economy developed, and many Egyptian Muslim Brotherhood leaders found the Gulf states far friendlier places to live when the Nasserist regime moved against the organization after 1954. In addition, Kuwaiti students in Egypt were shaped by the example and ideology of the Egyptian movement, particularly during the resurgence of Islamic activism on Egyptian campuses in the 1970s and 1980s. Many of the movement's current leaders emerged from the Islamist student movement of that period. Finally, the Kuwaiti Brotherhood also emulated the Egyptian movement not only in organizing among students, but also in moving into professional associations and seeking to organize groups of followers in fields previously dominated by nationalists and leftists.

The Social Reform Society—the formal organization associated with the Kuwaiti Muslim Brotherhood—focused largely on social, educational, and charitable activities, but the broader movement, though lacking formal status, did enter politics. In parliamentary elections held since independence, the Brotherhood ran candidates for Kuwait's parliament, scoring some modest successes. But for its first three decades, the Islamic movement, like its counterparts in other Arab countries, concentrated mainly on cultural and religious issues. Partly for that reason, the Brotherhood stood strongly against the various leftist and nationalist movements, which seemed far too secular, and sometimes too supportive of governments like Egypt's, which harshly repressed their own Islamic movements. Thus, the Brotherhood hardly seemed like an opposition movement in Kuwait. When the *amir* of Kuwait closed down parliament in 1976, the Brotherhood equivocated; one of the leaders of the Social Reform Society served as a minister after the suspension, and the Brotherhood cooperated with an attempt by the *amir* to amend the constitution as a condition of restoring it. These actions earned the Brotherhood a reputation as a movement too quick to curry favor with the government, creating suspicions that persist among other Kuwaiti political actors to this day.

THE FORMATION OF THE ISLAMIC CONSTITUTIONAL MOVEMENT

Parliamentary life returned to Kuwait in 1981, and the Muslim Brotherhood again won a few seats. These deputies struck a more confrontational pose toward the government than had their predecessors. Indeed, the Kuwaiti parliament as a whole became a more difficult body for the government to manage, resulting in a second suspension of parliament in 1986. This time the Brotherhood took a clearer stand, participating in (though hardly leading) efforts to call for the restoration of parliament. But it was the Iraqi invasion and occupation of Kuwait in 1990 that permanently changed the Brotherhood's political role, resulting in the creation of Hadas.

During the occupation, the Brotherhood helped organize resistance among those who remained in Kuwait. The formation of this resistance led to a shift in the leadership of the movement: younger activists, many of whom remained in Kuwait during the occupation, gained stature at the expense of the older generation and those who had fled. Immediately after the Iraqi withdrawal, younger Brotherhood elements who had led the resistance formed Hadas. At the same time, the Brotherhood broke its international links with the Muslim Brotherhood, which in its eyes had not given sufficient support to the cause of Kuwaiti liberation. The younger generation also attempted to develop political language that had broader appeal. One of the founders of the party explains that when members of the Muslim Brotherhood spoke among themselves, they could argue primarily in religious terms. But when Hadas began attempting to persuade and mobilize voters, it had to find language that demonstrated it could address popular as well as moral concerns.[2]

While other Islamist movements have dithered about forming political parties (and some, like Egypt's Muslim Brotherhood, continue to demur), there appears to have been little controversy over the matter among Kuwaiti Islamists. Criticisms of the move from what might be viewed as the Islamic right—based on rejection of democratic politics or participation in a non-Islamic system—were made gently and then dropped, perhaps partly because Salafi groups (which traditionally avoid regular politics) had themselves followed the Brotherhood into participating in parliamentary elections in the 1980s.

Hadas's status as a party with a distinct organizational identity separate from that of the broader Muslim Brotherhood movement (which has now ceded the political field to it) has allowed it to develop a clear set of electoral strategies. This organizational ability is hampered only slightly by the movement's lack of formal legal status. Even if it is not recognized by law, Hadas has a clear organization and set of governing structures. Its general membership, which is open to those who are recruited and undergo a probationary period, forms a "general assembly," but day-to-day matters are directed by a secretary-general, a secretariat, a technical office—a vaguely named body that activists acknowledge plays a critical role in making decisions—and an eight-member political bureau. The parliamentary bloc's activities are governed by a parliamentary committee, consisting of Hadas parliamentarians and other leaders and experts called upon by the party. In this way, Hadas deputies are kept under the watchful eye of the party leadership. As one former deputy said, "You do not decide to run from the Islamic Constitutional Movement; you are asked to run."[3] Since some leading Hadas members have failed to gain nomination (including past deputies), the statement seems historically accurate.

The result is that, unlike other blocs, Hadas is more than the sum of a few leading personalities. Indeed, the organization shows an ability to gauge the popularity of its various potential candidates and no hesitation in removing leading figures who have not performed well in past votes from its electoral list.

ELECTORAL SUCCESS AND LIMITATIONS

This structure has served Hadas well in elections held since its founding. At a conference of all major Kuwaiti political groups in Jedda, Saudi Arabia, while Kuwait was still under Iraqi occupation, the royal family agreed to restore the parliament, and in the ensuing 1992 elections, Hadas won four of the fifty seats open for contestation.

It may have come as a surprise that a party that had only formed a year earlier was able to mount a successful campaign, but of course, Hadas had decades of Muslim Brotherhood experience to draw on. Hadas leaders themselves had often earned their first electoral credentials at universities, competing with increasing success in student association elections. Muslim Brotherhood leaders who speak on the matter often mention mosques as a primary recruiting ground, but for Hadas, university campuses were, if not a recruiting ground, an important training arena. To this day, Hadas leadership tends to draw on the middle class and professionals—its current secretary-general and his predecessor are both faculty members at Kuwait University—and its student affiliate has a secure grip on Kuwaiti student union elections.

But it should also be noted that as time went on, Hadas supplemented its electoral base by appealing to voters in outlying areas, where tribal identities are stronger—a very different population than older Kuwaiti political forces are accustomed to mobilizing. The ruling family often brought the population in such areas into the political process, in hopes of creating a counterweight to the more central and urbanized areas, where liberals and leftists were strong. The government strategy worked well in the short term—indeed, the government still finds it can co-opt some tribal deputies—but Hadas (and some Salafi groups) found their conservative social agenda was a winning electoral platform.

Islamists were not the only group that made strides in 1992. Overall, opposition groups did extremely well in the elections and made some efforts to coordinate positions so that parliament could play an active role in determining the members of the cabinet as well as government policy and national legislation.

The high hopes for the 1992 parliament were gradually deflated, largely because the government succeeded in playing opposition elements against each other and opposition groups themselves began to focus on some of the issues dividing them.[4] The parliament did manage to press the ruling family to form a broad government (with Hadas itself initially entering the cabinet) and successfully defended some parliamentary prerogatives (such as preventing the government from applying laws issued by decree when parliament was suspended). But in earning membership in the cabinet, an array of formerly opposition forces lost some of their edge, and the ruling family acquired an ability to encourage the various factions to jockey against each other.

Thus, the diverse opposition soon found itself enmeshed in internal squabbles, especially over educational and cultural issues. A leading intellectual, Ahmad al-Rub'i, had been brought into the Cabinet as minister of education in 1992. Al-Rub'i had been a political activist who flirted with revolutionary ideas in his student days; he had entered parliament in 1985 as a member of a leftist bloc. Islamists regarded him with deep suspicion, and when al-Rub'i embarked on a series of educational reforms that aimed to diminish religious influence in the educational system, Islamist deputies attempted to remove him from office. While the move barely failed, the battle between Islamists and other opposition elements soon dominated the parliamentary agenda, resulting in other skirmishes over issues like gender segregation in the universities and amending the constitution to make Islamic *shari'a* the primary source of legislation.

For the next decade, parliament proved itself annoying to the government and ruling family on several occasions, but threatening on none. In 1999, for instance, the *amir* decided to dissolve the parliament after a series of confrontations with the parliament, in which Hadas played a leading role. On this occasion (unlike in 1976 and 1986), he did so constitutionally by calling for immediate elections. In all of the post-invasion elections, Islamist forces did fairly well. Before the formation of Hadas, the Muslim Brotherhood generally held at least one seat, and it enjoyed four in 1985. Hadas itself won between four and six seats in each election (except for 2003, when it won only two), and its close allies often added another seat or two to its parliamentary bloc, leading Hadas to claim four seats in the 2003 elections.

With parliament divided among a range of groups, and a significant number of "service" deputies—those elected on the basis of their ability to obtain government benefits for their constituents, and thus, highly amenable to co-optation—the ruling family deflected the parliament's ambitions to play a more aggressive role in legislation and oversight. The government was aided greatly by a Kuwaiti constitutional oddity referred to earlier: ministers (most of whom do not come from the ranks of elected deputies) may vote in parliament on most issues. In the current cabinet, for instance, ministers give the government seventeen votes from outside parliament's elected membership. With only 50 elected members, the government needs to pick up only a small number of votes to secure a parliamentary majority on many matters. For instance, when parliament voted to extend the vote to women in 2005, the majority of elected deputies actually voted against the move, but they were defeated by a large showing of ministers who supported the change.

Since only elected deputies participate in a vote of confidence, however, parliament can act far more confrontationally in such matters. The prelude to a vote of confidence, an interpellation—the formal questioning of a minister—is a particularly confrontational step, and one previous parliaments had used sparingly. Since the Iraqi occupation, however, deputies have resorted to the device more frequently. Each interpellation becomes a dramatic affair wherein policy debates, allegations of corruption, and mutual recriminations are aired publicly and political rhetoric often escalates. But an interpellation is a negative step against a particular minister's policies or conduct and does not constitute any positive legislative agenda; indeed, it usually leaves hard feelings and deepens divisions. Hadas deputies have often shown enthusiasm for using the tool to push their agenda, moving against ministers it deems hostile to Islamization or overly permissive of practices that offend religious or traditional values.

The combination of the parliament's failure to develop a clear legislative agenda and the periodic, dramatic clashes occasioned by interpellations have inspired the image of an obstructionist parliament. Indeed, parliament has been unable to pursue fundamental constitutional reform designed to make the government more accountable to the society's elected representatives. The *amir* blocked the one positive constitutional step it proposed: a move to amend the constitution to proclaim *shari'a* "the" rather than "a" source of law. Parliament did, however, accomplish a second demand of many deputies—separating the positions of crown prince and prime minister—although mostly as a result of the crown prince's illness and divisions within the ruling family.

THE PARLIAMENT'S BREAKTHROUGH YEAR—AND SUBSEQUENT REGRESSION

In 2006, Hadas helped lead a parliamentary effort that offered the promise of a qualitative shift in Kuwaiti politics. The death of the *amir* led to a confused and unusually public struggle for succession within the ruling family, with parliament unwillingly dragged into the dispute. No sooner had that battle ended than a new crisis erupted over proposals for electoral reform. A coalition of parliamentarians had led the call to reduce the size of Kuwait's electoral districts. Hadas—the best organized political group—embraced the idea enthusiastically, as did other reform-oriented political leaders from liberal and leftist camps. The momentarily unified opposition was supported by a popular movement, led by students organizing both in Kuwait and abroad. The campaign not only stiffened the parliamentarians' backbones; it led to rivals jockeying to claim the mantle of electoral reform.

The coalition of Islamists, other reformers, and students caught the government off guard, causing it (and leaders of the ruling family) to miscalculate badly. The cabinet itself seemed split on the matter and used some clumsy methods (such as attempting to tinker with the reform and referring the matter to the constitutional court), leading the parliamentary reform bloc to mount a full-on confrontation with the government. When some deputies threatened to summon the prime minister for parliamentary questioning on the subject, the *amir* dissolved parliament. Since the pro-reform coalition had mustered a majority in support of its position, he may have felt he had defeated the opposition by forcing an election according to the old rules.

Yet the *amir* had miscalculated: the forces who favored electoral reform won a majority in the new parliament. Hadas, one of the leading members of the reform coalition, performed especially well, with all six of its nominees winning election. The newly seated parliament immediately passed the law creating five electoral districts. Hoping to build on their victory, the various factions in the reform coalition worked as blocs to hammer out a common legislative agenda. Kuwait seemed on the verge of entering an era of party politics, with opposition parties enjoying a parliamentary majority.

And indeed, each of the three blocs in the new parliament attempted to form strong caucuses: one Islamist (uniting Hadas with Salafis and independent Islamists), one liberal (based in the support of some traditional business leaders), and one populist (with support from middle-class Kuwaitis). Much more ambitiously, the three blocs created a "bloc of blocs" that put together a list of legislative priorities that the new parliament would work on. But the new "bloc of blocs" did not survive two achievements: the electoral reform itself and a law on *zakat* (alms) that Hadas managed to place at the top of laws for the short-lived alliance.

In a sense, the "bloc of blocs" threatened the royal family with the prospect of allowing the majority to govern. The *amir* was hardly likely to allow the new majority coalition to form the government, which would have meant surrendering cabinet formation wholly to the elected parliament. But he (and his nephew, the prime minister), did not even seek to favor one bloc over the others, a move that might have fostered the nascent party system while maintaining a strong role for the ruling family. Instead, the ruling family opted to return to an atomizing divide and conquer approach, reaching out to particular deputies, co-opting some members of each group and playing the blocs against one another haphazardly. While Hadas leaders had hoped for a different approach, they allowed their party to get sucked into this strategy. After leading the opposition in 2006, Hadas accepted a cabinet post in 2007. Yet the opposition did not hold a monopoly on disunity. The ruling family's own strategy became increasingly uncoordinated, as prominent members jockeyed with each other in barely concealed maneuvers, often bringing favored parliamentarians into the fray.

Not all the blame for the divided parliament can be placed on the ruling family. The blocs not only fell out with each other, they also began to disintegrate internally. By 2009, matters had progressed to the point that when I asked one Hadas leader to describe his relationship with other Islamists, he despondently replied, "We have a truce." Bemoaning the need to coordinate with other Islamists one by one, he concluded by complaining, "I find liberals easier to deal with than other Islamists."

Parliamentarians squabbled over a whole host of issues and any sense of comity within the body began to break down. In one public forum in 2009, a male parliamentarian prompted a female colleague to walk out when he contemptuously dismissed her remarks as meaningless (*kalam fadi*). At the same time, an exchange between a Shi'i and a Sunni parliamentarian led to the former referring to a previous cabinet (in which several Sunni Islamists had participated) as a "Tora Bora government." A prominent former Hadas MP chided Shi'i parliamentarians for siding with "liberals" against "Muslims," effectively tarring not only his intended targets but implying that those not in the Islamist camp were completely outside the faith.

Yet all this drama amounts to great motion with little movement. The Kuwaiti political system showed itself capable of producing discussion, but not decisions. The real crisis for the country was not the liveliness of the debates but their inconclusiveness. The results might best be termed a system of "divide but not rule," in which parliamentarians are enthusiastic about their prerogatives but cannot use them in pursuit of a coherent agenda. The ruling family can co-opt individual parliamentarians on specific issues, but it cannot lead the body. And confrontations between groups of parliamentarians and individual ministers started to come thick and fast.

In 2008, the *amir* dissolved the parliament after it had served only two years. After only a year, he grew so impatient with the new body that he dissolved it again. And he apparently also seriously considered suspending the body for a third, indefinite period.

ELECTORAL DECLINE FOR HADAS

Unsurprisingly, perhaps, the opposition blocs performed unimpressively in the 2008 parliamentary elections and became almost irrelevant in the 2009 voting. Hadas's hopes for a party system were dashed. Just as worrying, the movement's own electoral performance suffered greatly. In 2008, it lost half its seats, and in 2009, it won only two.

With a law seemingly tailor-made for its purposes and two years of preparation, why did Hadas meet such defeat?

First, Hadas made poor electoral alliances. With each voter allowed to select four candidates, vote-swapping agreements became common, and Hadas found itself more often the target than the beneficiary of such alliances. Some Hadas leaders complained that fellow Islamists—especially in the Salafi camp—deliberately prolonged negotiations over forming alliances and turned at the last minute to another groups to prevent Hadas from finding quick alternatives.

Second, Hadas confused voters with rapid political movements. In 2006, it stood strongly in the opposition. In the 2008 balloting, it posed as a movement above the fray. In 2009, it entered the campaign having brought on the elections by resigning suddenly from the government and launching strong criticisms against those with whom it had just sat.

But one unanticipated feature of the new electoral environment proved especially damaging, and that one was beyond Hadas's control: the rise of sectarian and tribal voting. In both 2008 and 2009, Kuwaiti Shi'a, who are concentrated in a few areas, used the new law as the occasion to consolidate their votes among a few favored candidates, increasing their representation.

And more ominously for Hadas, two of Kuwait's five electoral districts became the exclusive preserve of tribal candidates, selected before the election in illegal but increasingly sophisticated tribal primaries. The work Hadas had done to cultivate this population was rapidly undone as tribes opted for candidates who generally combined intense social conservatism with fierce loyalty to the tribal population—and an insistence on securing government benefits. After the 2008 setback, I heard one Hadas leader privately comment that in selecting candidates for the next elections, "We need more Matran," a reference to the large al-Mutayri tribe. In 2009, one of Hadas's two successes came from a candidate who owed his seat far more to his tribal primary than his Hadas affiliation.

Underlying the rise of sectarian and tribal voting is the reality of a society that has become more difficult to lead. Not only have international contacts and economic prosperity made the society more complex, the previous generation of Kuwaiti leaders deliberately made the political system more inclusive, in hopes of co-opting new voters (which they did for a while).[5] A half-century ago, Kuwaiti politics was the monopoly of the ruling family, leading merchants, and a handful of educated professionals. Even then it could be contentious, and the ruling family reacted in part by folding new groups into the political field to weaken the influence of various opposition groups and critics. Shi'a, Bedouin, and Islamists were often quietly encouraged to organize and become politically active to balance against other groups. The government granted citizenship rights to large numbers of people living on the outskirts of Kuwait City to dilute the influence of those closer to the center. It doled out benefits and access to government services in such areas on a tribal basis in order to encourage the election of service deputies who gave political support to the cabinet in return for constituent benefits.

These various groups now sit together uneasily in a fractious parliament, and they are no longer content to be politically quiescent. Shi'i deputies regularly raise sensitive issues (such as the building of Shi'i mosques). And on the Sunni side, the tamer Islamic Constitutional Movement has been outflanked by a raft of Salafis and independent Islamists.[6] Tribes have transitioned from loyal clients to obstreperous and demanding constituencies and built very effective political machines.

The inclusion of women in the parliament may have complicated matters still further. On the one hand, the election of four female deputies in 2009 brought Kuwait significant positive international attention and thus raised the political costs to the royal family of suspending the body. But on the other hand, the women deputies hardly form a united bloc and their presence has already led to wrangling over issues such as their dress and their committee assignments. (One of the new deputies, Rola Dashti, won a seat on a committee that focuses on negative phenomena in society—a traditional preserve for conservative and Islamist deputies who enjoyed using it to thunder against cultural and social practices they did not like. When Dashti was elected as the committee's *rapporteur,* two Islamist members quit in protest, saying she had no place speaking for a committee whose existence she did not support.)

And greater inclusiveness is a particular problem for a system that is often based on consensus. The system effectively seems to give every small group in Kuwait not merely a voice but also a veto. In a sense, it requires consensus, but it simultaneously makes that consensus difficult to achieve.

Consensus is required both formally (a small number of deputies can launch a grilling and a no-confidence motion) and informally (the cabinet generally reflects a great plurality of political inclinations and constituencies rather than a narrow majority coalition). And the ruling family deals with the citizenry as a collection of individuals, groups, constituencies, and demands, resisting any attempt to deal with parliament as a collection of political blocs. The result is that elections rearrange much but resolve little.

Working to Be Both Islamic and Constitutional

When asked to present their program, Hadas leaders repeatedly refer to their organization's name: they present it as a movement that is both Islamic and constitutional. And indeed, such a description is extremely apt, since much of Hadas's agenda is encompassed by those two features.

HADAS AS AN ISLAMIC MOVEMENT

From its founding, Hadas has focused on two kinds of Islamic causes: implementation of the Islamic *shari'a* and the protection of a fairly conservative vision of Kuwaiti traditions and values.

On the *shari'a,* Hadas has evolved in a practical direction. At the beginning, it focused most of its energies on amending article 2 of the constitution in order to cite the Islamic *shari'a* as *the* rather than *a* source of legislation. The issue was generally popular and the movement garnered support from deputies outside the Islamist bloc to pass the amendment—only to have it vetoed by the *amir.*

While Hadas continues to call for the amendment, it increasingly directs its energies elsewhere. The *amir's* opposition (and perhaps the realization that the amendment may have little practical effect[7]) has led Hadas to insist instead that newly adopted legislation not violate the *shari'a*. More recently, Hadas has shifted its attention from amending article 2 (whose wording vaguely makes the Islamic *shari'a* a principal source of legislation), to article 79 governing the legislative process by asking that a clause be inserted barring any law violating the Islamic *shari'a*. (The article now simply reads: "No law may be promulgated unless it has been passed by the National Assembly and sanctioned by the *amir*.") Hadas also often cites the work of a committee formed by the *amir* to review all Kuwaiti laws and suggest amendments whenever necessary to bring them into compliance with the *shari'a*. While that committee works at a glacial pace, it still earns the praise of Hadas leaders. Finally, the movement has occasionally introduced legislation in parliament to implement various *shari'a* provisions, working, for instance, to advance the law that mandates payment of the *zakat* mentioned earlier.

In this evolutionary development, Hadas has followed a path familiar to several other Islamist electoral movements in the Arab world, from the PJD in Morocco to the Muslim Brotherhood in Egypt and Hamas in Palestine. Namely, while abandoning the Islamic *shari'a* is unthinkable for an Islamist movement, leaders have found that the slogan "implementation of the *shari'a*" often engenders powerful opposition. While Hadas has hardly abandoned its emphasis on the *shari'a*, the path it favors now focuses on gradualism and revision of laws through a democratic legislative process. This both assuages concerns and leads to more practical results.

Beyond its advocacy of the *shari'a*, Hadas also has stressed a second set of issues clustering around a conservative social agenda. Much of that agenda has a strong religious coloration, but it is not always based directly on Islamic law. And on these matters, Hadas has done little to reassure its critics. Indeed, a good portion of the group's electoral support may come from its ability to present itself as the defender of Kuwaiti morals. Whether taking issue with television broadcasts that seem excessively lurid, the availability of books portrayed as insulting to Islam, or mixed-gender classrooms, Hadas has struck strong positions against perceived moral corruption in Kuwaiti society, often using forceful language it eschews on most other occasions.

These cultural issues cause far more public concern than Hadas's relatively gentle calls for implementing *shari'a*, and the controversies over them have led liberal critics to question Hadas's commitment to democratic principles. Hadas shows far more consistency in this regard than its critics charge, supporting liberal political reforms fairly faithfully, but it draws the line when liberalization leads in a cultural direction. Thus, in the 1990s, it supported reforming the press law to diminish licensing requirements, but also insisted that publishing material offensive to religious values be prohibited with criminal penalties, not merely fines. The party argued that justice came before freedom.[8]

Some Islamist movements that aim to build broader coalitions and public support have downplayed cultural issues—most notably, perhaps, Egypt's Muslim Brotherhood in 2005 and Palestine's Hamas in 2006—but Hadas has shown only limited signs of following such a path, as its core constituency would likely regard such a strategy as an abandonment of its basic principles. Occasionally, as will be examined below with regard to women's political rights, debate occurs within the movement over what stance Islamic teachings require, but Hadas more often makes little effort to distinguish between conservative social practices and religious requirements.

Hadas's Islamic identity also influences its stance on a host of other issues. On foreign policy, for instance, it supports Hamas and the Palestinian cause, but unlike most Islamist movements, its position toward the United States is quite mild. Hadas has not criticized the security relationship between Kuwait and the United States. The American failure in Iraq, however, may embolden those who find ties with the United States excessively close. Hadas is generally liberal in its economic outlook, though it also supports a set of financial and commercial enterprises that endeavor to operate along lines consistent with Islamic law.

THE CONSTITUTIONALISM OF HADAS

Hadas's constitutionalism—its interest in operating within the Kuwaiti constitutional order rather than overturning it—has also evolved since the movement's founding. Unlike the movement's evolution on the *shari'a*, the shift in position on constitutional issues has made Hadas more demanding rather than less. While Hadas joined other parties in calling for the restoration of parliament after the Iraqi occupation, throughout most of the 1990s, it was generally more moderate in tone than some of the non-Islamist opposition. But it was protective of parliament's prerogatives under the 1962 constitution—prerogatives that were generally exercised more energetically after the restoration of parliament in 1992 than before.

In recent years, Hadas has also pushed constitutional reform more forcefully in a liberalizing and democratizing direction. As described above, the group aims for narrowly political rather than broadly cultural liberalization, but its convictions are deeply held and doggedly pursued. It joined many fellow Islamic movements by issuing its own detailed reform plan before the 2006 elections. Hadas called in general for more effective popular participation in government, adopting almost stridently democratic rhetoric. Specifically, the group has pressed recently for a political party law and further electoral reforms that have the potential to change Kuwaiti politics fundamentally, leading to more democracy and a pluralistic party system.

Hadas leaders are also no longer afraid to speak of their ambition to create a "constitutional monarchy"—on the British model, rather than that of Middle East monarchies. The more commonly used phrase in Kuwait is "popular government," suggesting a cabinet that reflects the will of the parliamentary majority, rather than the current system, in which key positions are monopolized by the ruling family and parliament targets individual ministers but has little influence over the composition of the government as a whole. While converting the Kuwaiti political system in this way would afford Hadas unparalleled political opportunities, some of its leaders fear that pursuing it too publicly or enthusiastically would be unduly confrontational and could lead to a crisis that endangers the gains it has already made.

There is no escaping the fact that such talk is a direct call for diminishing the ruling family's role in politics. While Hadas has not questioned the idea of a ruling family and generally uses fairly polite rhetoric about it, the group has been increasingly bold in calling for measures that would transfer considerable political authority from the family to institutions accountable to the people and their elected representatives in parliament.

Using and Enhancing Parliamentary Tools

How has Hadas used its parliamentary seats to pursue its broader agenda? On the Islamic front, its parliamentary agenda, like its general approach, has moved from the general to the specific. On the constitutional front, it has sketched out a similarly practical agenda, but has grown more rather than less ambitious.

ISLAM

With regard to Islamic issues, Hadas focused much of its parliamentary effort in the 1990s on provoking public controversies. Some of its initiatives went down to defeat, such as those described above concerning the interpellation of the minister of education or amending the constitution to make Islamic *shari'a* the main source of legislation. Still, they had the general effect of demonstrating the political strength of the Islamic bloc and its talent for outmaneuvering non-Islamist forces in the battle for public opinion. Hadas also racked up a few concrete accomplishments, such as the move toward gender segregation at Kuwait University. But its moral and tangible victories tended to divide the opposition and aggravate fears among Islamists in other political camps.

In recent years, Hadas has shifted its tactics to emphasize areas of common concern with other opposition members. It has joined moves against ministers on the grounds of financial rather than moral corruption, and it has worked on legislation (such as the *zakat* law mandating payment of alms) that enjoys broader support, as opposed to an earlier proposal to found a Kuwaiti equivalent to the Saudi religious police. Nevertheless, the movement has hardly abandoned its interest in advancing a conservative social agenda or defending against perceived attacks on Islam. In so doing, it has struck a strong pose but also positioned itself as more liberal than many independent Islamists and most Salafis.

For instance, Hadas found itself in a battle with liberals on the one hand and Salafis on the other over the nature of Ramadan television programming. Hadas frequently targets the ministries and other government institutions considered liberal bastions, and it charged that state television had aired vacuous entertainment at the expense of religious programming. But when Kuwaiti television broadcast a historical serial on a religious theme, Hadas felt compelled to defend it against Salafi critics. It is precisely this interest in cultural issues that has led Hadas's critics to charge that the movement is easily distracted by superficial controversies over which parliament has little control.

On one intense recent controversy—that of political rights for women —it was the Islamists themselves who were divided. Indeed, the controversy, which played out over several years, was probably the most internally divisive in Hadas's history. Two separate matters were at issue: whether or not women could vote, and whether or not they could run for office. With respect to *shari'a,* many movement leaders felt that there was no real objection to women voting, but some members of Hadas's deeply conservative voter base opposed any change to Kuwait's male-only franchise. Therefore, Hadas expressed its concerns less in terms of Islamic law and more in terms of the barriers to open campaigning in a gender-segregated society. After protracted internal debates, meetings, and conferences, as well as consultation with legal and religious experts, the Hadas leadership ultimately took a more forthcoming position in support of women's suffrage. But more liberal leaders could not coax the movement into going so far as supporting full political rights, under which women could run for office. The matter came before parliament several times and the proposed reforms were consistently defeated, often with Islamist votes. In 2005, however, proponents of women's political rights finally emerged victorious. Because the legislation granted full political rights (not merely the vote) to women, Islamists championed the opposition in parliament.

In the short term, the matter was not only internally divisive but also politically embarrassing. Favoring the vote for women but not full polit-ical rights seemed to many unsympathetic observers like hair-splitting and mindless opposition to change. But in the longer term, the move-ment's defeat may have been a blessing. First, it resolved what had been a divisive debate within Hadas. Second, the addition of women voters may have strengthened Hadas; members recount how one of their lead-ing parliamentarians, Nasser al-Sani', was going down to defeat in the 2006 elections until the women's ballots (cast separately in gender-segregated polling) were counted. Finally, Hadas showed its fealty to the constitutional process: while it lost on the issue in the parliament, it accepted the result. Now, some Hadas leaders talk of eventually fielding female candidates.

CONSTITUTIONALISM

On the constitutional front, Hadas deputies participated with others in defending parliamentary prerogatives. While Hadas had a reputa-tion for being less confrontational than other opposition groups, the ruling family did not always find it much easier to work with Islamist forces than their non-Islamist counterparts. In the 1996 parliament, in which the Islamist bloc held fifteen seats, tensions between parliament and the government grew so strong that the prime minister and crown prince finally asked the *amir* to dissolve parliament—the first time Ku-wait had moved to early elections.

More specifically, Hadas staked out strong positions in the 1990s on financial corruption in public bodies, with one of its leading parliamentarians—Nasser al-Sani', now the party's secretary-general—developing specific expertise in issues of accountability in public funds. Hadas deputies attempted not only to investigate officials but also to provide a firm legal basis for public integrity by urging passage of financial disclosure laws. To prove the sincerity of their dedication to the issue, Hadas deputies have disclosed their own financial holdings. Hadas leaders have also claimed to be willing to hold members of the Islamist movement to the same standards of financial probity that they expect of others.

Over the past few years, Hadas has moved beyond general support for parliamentary prerogatives and opposition to corruption to supporting efforts at more comprehensive political reform. Not only was Hadas an integral part of the coalition that brought about the 2006 electoral reform, it supports a series of other political reforms to make the Kuwaiti political system both more democratic and more partisan. While Hadas enthusiastically supported the move from 25 districts to five, it has also signaled support for making Kuwait a single electoral district. This would necessitate a system of proportional representation with a party list, and perhaps force the issue of a political party law (which the movement supports) onto the country's political agenda.

Hadas has also more gingerly explored the issue of the current electoral boundaries; each of the current five districts was formed merely by combining five of the older districts, without addressing the serious imbalances created by those older boundaries. The current electoral districts are uneven in size, with outlying areas—and their more tribal and socially conservative populations—underrepresented. Redrawing boundaries would almost certainly strengthen Hadas, but it would also be extremely divisive, since it would undercut the older, longer settled areas, which are populated in part by Kuwait's most powerful families, many of whom look at the outlying districts as coarse and less than truly Kuwaiti.

Outside of electoral reform, Hadas pursues a variety of other liberalizing political reforms, with the caveat, noted above, that its support for liberalization rarely leaves the political for the social or cultural realm. Hadas generally embraces causes associated with political rights. It is particularly attentive to the problems of Kuwait's *bidun* population (bidun literally means "without" and refers in Kuwait to those who reside in the country without citizenship), although critics do not see

Hadas's stance as altruistic, since many *bidun* are members of the same tribes whose votes Hadas covets. Hadas does not have a monopoly on political reform issues, but it does participate with other movements in developing other proposals, such as those to enlarge parliament (because a greater number of deputies might allow the body to widen its legislative and oversight activities to new fields) or change parliament's bylaws (to allow more work to be done in committees to address the concern that it has been more a debating society than a working body).

With an ambitious agenda and only a handful of deputies, Hadas's achievements will necessarily rely heavily on its relations with the government and other political groups in Kuwait. What partnerships and rivalries has Hadas built and how do these affect Hadas's past record and likely future course?

Coping With a Wary but Tolerant Government

The history of Hadas's relationship—and that of the broader Kuwaiti Muslim Brotherhood movement—with Kuwait's rulers displays several features familiar to other Arab states. As happened in Jordan, Syria, and Egypt, for instance, the Muslim Brotherhood was born in a far more tolerant political environment than is the norm in much of the region today. The movement used this more permissive atmosphere to concentrate initially on a broad range of activities: missionary, educational, and charitable work. The Brotherhood only dabbled in politics by running candidates on a limited scale in parliamentary elections. As Arab politics grew increasingly ideological in the 1950s and 1960s, the Brotherhood became an adversary of various leftist and nationalist movements. In Jordan in those decades, or in Egypt in the 1970s, the government often regarded the Brotherhood as a potential counterbalance to radical movements on the opposite side of the political spectrum. Perhaps most like the Jordanian Brotherhood, the Kuwaiti movement was deemed by outsiders as willing and able to reach political accommodation with the government. Kuwait was thus spared the harsh confrontations that occurred between the Islamist movement and the regime in Egypt, Algeria, and Syria.

The period since the Iraqi occupation has seen Kuwait's Brotherhood strike out in a different direction. At first, it did so by establishing a party-like organization distinct from the movement as a whole—a step also taken by the Brotherhood in a few other, but hardly all, Arab states. In Kuwait, though the party organization lacks legal recognition, it has nonetheless been able to avoid becoming subordinate to the broader Islamist movement, unlike some countries, in which the party is legal but weaker vis-à-vis the movement, such as Jordan. What marks Kuwait as truly different, however, is the extent to which the political party has been incorporated as a normal political group.

To be sure, there are tensions between the Kuwaiti Muslim Brotherhood and the government. Since the mid-1980s, and especially since the formation of Hadas, the movement has increasingly positioned itself as part of the political opposition, prompting the government to respond with the divide-and-conquer tactics described above. The possibility that the parliament will overcome such tactics and actually move to restrict the role of the ruling family has sometimes made for a stormier relationship than existed in the past. Nor are the tensions between the government and the movement restricted to the political realm, as the Muslim Brotherhood is very active in the charitable arena domestically and internationally. In the 1990s, the Egyptian government held Kuwaiti Islamist charities responsible for funding the radical Islamist opposition, and since 2001, Kuwait's other allies (most notably the United States) have pressured the government to monitor and restrict the role of Kuwaiti Islamic charities.

To date, neither the more confrontational domestic conditions nor the escalating international pressures have led the Kuwaiti government to engage in the tools of harassment used in Jordan or the harsh (if calibrated) repression employed in Egypt. Yet ironically, the Kuwaiti movement has never been legally recognized, unlike its fellow travelers in less permissive countries. Hadas itself has had to develop a clear leadership structure, fund and manage campaigns, and create platforms and party publications without any legal status. The Kuwaiti government's foot-dragging on electoral reform and reluctance to legalize political parties is explained largely by its fears that such steps would only strengthen Hadas and perhaps lead other opposition groups to develop similar organizational skills.

Hadas therefore risks entering a period of greater tension in its relationship with the government. Remarkably, the possibility of an "unconstitutional dissolution" of parliament—dissolving the body, suspending the clauses of the constitution that allow for parliamentary elections, and allowing the *amir* and an unaccountable cabinet to rule by decree—is being seriously discussed in Kuwait for the first time since the restoration of parliament in 1992. There are far less extreme options available to the government, such as mollifying the reformers or seeking to divide them, and a full confrontation between the Islamic movement and the government seems unlikely. Kuwait's relatively permissive political atmosphere will probably survive, but the current tension is forcing all political actors to develop new strategies.

Yet if the current period carries a significant threat of confrontation, it also offers Hadas some opportunities to participate in government. Hadas leaders have entered the cabinet on several occasions. Twice, they did so without obtaining the movement's support, leading Hadas to disown them. But on two other occasions, a Hadas leader accepted a cabinet portfolio with the movement's blessings. These have not always been happy experiences, as the movement has obtained a say in policy—and, according to some critics, a host of government jobs for some of its followers—but as only one voice in a very cacophonous body, which is ultimately required to support a set of policies it has only limited ability to influence.

Coordinating With Rivals

Perhaps because it gyrates between opposition and support for the government, Hadas provokes suspicion among its rivals. Other political actors charge the movement with being both too reluctant to confront the government and too close to radical Islamists. Both sets of doubts originate not only in recent events but also in political rivalries that date back to the 1960s, making them not easy to dispel.

SUSPICIONS OF THE ISLAMIC CONSTITUTIONAL MOVEMENT

As far as Hadas's reputation for being insufficiently dedicated to political opposition, such suspicions are based in part on the Islamist movement's priorities in Kuwait. Like its counterparts in other Arab countries, Kuwait's Islamist movement is not solely a political party following an electoral logic, but a wide-ranging effort to enhance the Islamic nature of society in the social, economic, and cultural realms. The diverse activities associated in which the movement participates lead it to value protected social spaces, and an overly confrontational or politicized attitude might endanger aspects of the movement that benefit from official acquiescence. Hadas's formation did change the Islamic movement's behavior to some extent, since it resulted in a wing of the movement that specialized exclusively in electoral and political work. Hadas had a particular interest in pressing for greater political liberalization—from which it would likely benefit—and indeed currently presents itself explicitly as an opposition political group.

But even in the 1990s, when Hadas emerged as an opposition party, its potential partners continued to see it as too quick to cut separate deals with the government to protect the status of the Islamist movement more generally, especially in the educational and charitable arenas. While there the diverse opposition groups share a rough consensus on the requirements of political reform—an enhanced role for parliament, greater fiscal transparency, genuine political accountability, electoral reform, and diminished dominance of the ruling family over the government—Hadas's potential partners often charge the movement with insufficient enthusiasm for the cause. In the 1990s there may have been some truth to this claim, as Hadas was quite willing to concentrate on elements of its agenda that set it against other opposition elements (especially in the cultural realm), but in the last few years, its dedication to political reform has run quite deep.

Yet while some critics charge that Hadas is only lukewarm in its opposition to the government, others suspect that it actually conceals radical sentiments. Part of this fear comes from recent events in the region; while Hadas and the Kuwaiti Muslim Brotherhood more generally have completely eschewed violence, it is not uncommon for critics to charge in private that Hadas differs from more radical groups only in its ability to put forward a gentler image. As long as political violence is common in the region, Hadas can probably do little to dispel such doubts, which are based on nothing Hadas has said or done but instead on the enthusiasm with which some radical Islamist groups elsewhere have embraced violent means.

But while fears of violent inclinations on the part of Hadas may be groundless, non-Islamist actors sometimes advance a more subtle critique of the movement based on its program. While Hadas claims to (and indeed always does) act through constitutional and legal mechanisms, its vision of Kuwaiti society is explicitly based on the need to cultivate Islamic values. For non-Islamists, this is easily and perhaps naturally portrayed as an attempt by Hadas to impose a specific—and highly conservative—interpretation of proper Islamic practice on the society as a whole. Such a critique of Hadas's platform is essentially secularist in nature, and for that reason is not always voiced in public debates; the argument that religion and morality are strictly personal concerns finds little resonance in most of Kuwaiti society. But in liberal and some elite circles, Hadas is viewed as authoritarian not by its political practices—which are difficult to criticize—but by the content of its program. The milder Hadas approach on the Islamic *shari'a* has not yet reassured such critics, and each move by Hadas deputies to raise a cultural issue only deepens their fears. For this reason, Hadas will likely always have difficulty moving beyond tactical cooperation among opposition forces toward a joint strategic program.

Even within Islamist ranks, Hadas finds rivals as much as partners. Among Kuwait's Sunni population, Hadas is in the unusual position of coexisting with Salafi parties. (In many Arab countries, Salafi movements eschew electoral politics altogether.) The willingness of Kuwait's Salafis to run for parliament has diminished the ideological gap between the Muslim Brotherhood and Salafis that existed in an earlier period (who were suspicious that the Muslim Brotherhood was too willing to compromise on religious matters). In recent years, Hadas has worked with representatives of Kuwait's various Salafi strains to form an Islamic bloc in the parliament.

Hadas's relationship with Kuwait's Shi'i Islamists is more complicated. Some of Hadas's attempts to adopt elements of *shari'a* rest on Sunni rather than Shi'i legal interpretations. Thus, Hadas was forced to make concessions to Shi'i deputies when pursuing legislation to mandate payment of the *zakat*. Hadas deputies argued that Shi'a, like non-Muslims, were free under the proposed law to do the same as non-Muslims and consider the fairly small mandatory *zakat* payment a tax while privately pursuing their own charitable activities—a view that offended the Shi'a, who objected to being lumped together with non-Muslims. Despite such awkward situations, Hadas often attempts to reach an accommodation with Shi'i Islamist deputies, but it is hampered by its parliamentary partnership with Salafis, most of whom take a far less tolerant attitude toward Shi'i Islam. As a result, Shi'i Islamist deputies vote with the populist bloc rather than the Islamist one.

Perhaps the most critical factor in the course of Kuwaiti politics is the ability of the very disparate groups constituting the opposition to work together toward a common reform agenda. The rewards of successful coordination would be substantial indeed for all groups, but the suspicions among the movements run very deep. In particular, as is the case in other Arab countries, many non-Islamists with a history of political opposition have come to regard the Islamist movement as a greater adversary than the government. The possibilities for forging a common reform front are real; indeed, they are being actively explored. But they are playing out against a backdrop of rivalry and distrust.

Conclusion: Can an Opposition Coalition Reform Kuwaiti Politics?

Hadas has found its fate tied up in a long-standing division within Kuwaiti politics about the nature of the constitutional order.[9] The ruling family has regarded the constitution and parliament as its gifts to the Kuwaiti people. In their view, the rulers have agreed to consult with the population on major matters but retain ultimate authority. On two occasions, they have taken back their gift for several years. For much of the Kuwaiti opposition, the constitution is seen instead as a contract between the ruling family and the population, whereby the population agrees to allow the family a leading role so long as it operates within the bounds of the constitutional order. In their view, such a contract cannot be unilaterally abrogated by either side.

Thus, when the *amir* opened the regular session of Kuwaiti parliament in October 2006, speaking of respect for "separation of powers," he meant something quite different than what many parliamentarians believe the phrase means. To the *amir,* in insisting that it play an extensive role in government, parliament risks overstepping its bounds. For opposition parliamentarians, the ruling family is refusing to allow constitutional institutions to operate with full authority. Ominously, the increasing tensions have occasioned a flood of rumors that the *amir* is considering an "unconstitutional dissolution" for a third time. In response to steady questioning, the *amir* once stated that the idea of such a step had not crossed his mind, which hardly seemed a categorical denial. In 2009, he was widely reported to have agreed in a family gathering to dissolve the parliament, only to change is mind hours later. He has spoken openly of forming an upper house of parliament—most likely an appointed body on the Bahraini model, which would circumscribe the actions of the existing elected body. Such a step would require a constitutional amendment and thus the assent of the parliament, unless the *amir* imposed the new body by fiat.

Like many Islamist movements, the Kuwaiti Muslim Brotherhood has an agenda that reaches far beyond political reform. It is working for the long-term Islamization of Kuwaiti society. Thus the movement hesitates before throwing in with a confrontational political opposition for fear that it will endanger its current position and subordinate its long-term agenda to short-term political maneuvering. But in Kuwait, the formation of Hadas has pulled the Muslim Brotherhood fully into the political process and tied its fate to the cause of political reform perhaps more than anywhere else in the region. In a few areas, such as the interest in developing a legally recognized political party, Hadas is even willing to go further than other elements of the opposition coalition—despite the traditional distrust of partisanship by Islamist movements. If the political opposition succeeds in its program of investigating corruption, strengthening the legislative and investigative abilities of parliament, and moving toward ideological and programmatic politics, the rewards for Hadas could be rich. This has drawn Hadas into an attempt to form an alliance with a group of liberal and populist politicians whose political values and orientations have historically made them very wary of Islamists.

In this context, Hadas faces some very hard choices. It stands on the brink of achieving a greater level of political influence than almost any of its sister movements enjoy, but that may require it to become more comfortable with its role in the opposition and on its cooperation with forces it has traditionally regarded as unsympathetic to the Islamist movement's religious, cultural, and moral values.

Yet in less than two decades, Hadas has managed to emerge as the Arab Islamist party most thoroughly integrated as a normal political actor. Its leaders are frustrated because they feel that in a sense they have become more democratic than the political system in which they operate—and perhaps more than Kuwaiti society is ready for. Kuwaiti democracy may be faltering—not because the Islamists are challenging it, but because they have not yet found a formula for deepening it.

CHAPTER 6

Between Government and Opposition

The Case of the Yemeni Congregation for Reform

Within the spectrum of Islamist parties and movements that participate in legal politics in the Arab world, the Yemeni Congregation for Reform (Islah) represents a unique case. Unlike most such movements, when Islah first entered Yemen's political scene in 1990, it was an ally of the ruling General People's Congress (GPC), but it turned against the GPC and became the leading opposition party by the end of the decade. Islah also lacks an ideologically motivated membership and a clear ideological or political narrative. The group is primarily composed of traditionalist and tribal groups that share only a loose commitment to Islamizing the Yemeni state and society.

This chapter examines Islah's role in Yemeni politics and the characteristics of its parliamentary participation. It seeks to address four questions:

1) Under what conditions did Islah decide to participate in Yemeni politics, and has its participation changed the nature of the country's political game?

2) Why did Islah abandon the ruling coalition to join the opposition?

3) What are Islah's parliamentary priorities and has its legislative platform changed since the 1990s?

4) Have Islah's internal structures, decision-making processes, and rhetoric on key policy issues changed over time as a result of its participation in Yemeni politics?

Islah's Entry Into Yemeni Politics: Post-Unification Developments

An analysis of the Yemeni Congregation for Reform requires an understanding of the tribal character of Yemeni society and the tension this creates within the party between its rather weak ideological orientation and its engagement in tribal politics.

Tribalism has deep historical roots in Yemen, and continues to permeate the political, social, and economic life of the country today. Contrary to the institutions of the modern state, which are organized around the two principles of universal citizenship and equality of all under the law, tribalism sustains different rules for state and society. In Yemen today, the tribe is the main point of reference for its members and the collective guarantor of their interests. The state and its resources are often used to achieve the tribes' parochial goals. By the same token, political actors—primarily the ruling establishment and opposition parties—lobby tribes for loyalty and support. The pervasive tribalism means that political life revolves to a significant extent around tribal personalities, rather than ideologies and political programs. Patronage is thus an influential political tool.

The strength of tribalism, the weakness of modern state institutions, and the lack of common identity among Yemen's citizens have affected Islah and its place in the country's politics. These forces influence the party's internal dynamics and its external political behavior, making them more opaque and harder to define. Moreover, Islah has not had the long experience with semi-pluralist politics that has shaped Islamist parties and movements elsewhere in the Arab world. Islah developed its political culture as an ally of the ruling GPC. As a result, Yemeni Islamists understand politics in terms of loyalty, patronage, and connections. This has further diminished Islah's ability to engage in internal debates leading to a cohesive ideological narrative about the Yemeni state and society, to a clear programmatic concept of what positions can be justified in Islamic terms, or to a common stance on key policy issues. Indeed, a striking feature of Islah is that leading party members have repeatedly made contradictory statements on issues. These include Islah's relations with the ruling GPC, the party's commitment to the opposition role Islah has been fulfilling since it joined the Joint Meeting Parties (JMP), and the party's position with regard to the ongoing tensions in the North and South of Yemen.

Islah is one of many political parties that formed shortly after the unification of North and South Yemen in 1990. No fewer than 50 parties contested the newly unified country's first parliamentary elections in April 1993, including Islah. The late Shaykh 'Abdullah al-Ahmar, the former head of the Hashid Tribal Confederation, who enjoyed good relations with the GPC (the party that had ruled North Yemen before unification), and President 'Ali 'Abdullah Saleh (leader of North Yemen from 1978 to 1990 and of Unified Yemen since 1990), played a key role in establishing Islah in 1990. Al-Ahmar remained the president of Islah's Supreme Board—the party's powerful executive body—from 1990 until his death in 2007.

In forming Islah, al-Ahmar and his compatriots brought together members of the GPC and members of the Yemeni Muslim Brotherhood. Al-Ahmar convinced the Yemeni Muslim Brotherhood, other Islamist elements, and a number of influential tribal personalities to join together and establish Islah. Thus, the party emerged as an alliance of three distinct groups: the tribal forces headed by al-Ahmar; the Yemeni Muslim Brotherhood, which has provided the party's organizational and political backbone; and a number of conservative businessmen, represented initially by Muhammad 'Abd al-Wahab Jabari, who became a member of Islah's Supreme Board.[1] After its formation, Islah initially remained an ally of the GPC, cooperating with its effort to marginalize the Yemeni Socialist Party (YSP), the former ruling party of South Yemen.

The Muslim Brotherhood comes from the Sunni community, which represents slightly more than 60 percent of the Yemeni population (the next largest is the Zaydi Shi'i community, which is estimated to represent 30 to 35 percent of the population) and it emerged in North Yemen in the early 1960s. Like other Islamist parties and movements in the Arab world, it drew inspiration from the Egyptian Muslim Brotherhood, and the founders of the Yemeni branch, such as the prominent Shaykh 'Abd al-Majid al-Zindani, were students at Egyptian universities in the early 1960s. The Muslim Brotherhood component of Islah—influential primarily in urban centers such as Sanaa, Taiz, and Ibb—helped shape the party's ideology and political platform. The first article of Islah's basic law defines it as a "popular political organization that seeks reform of all aspects of life on the basis of Islamic principles and teachings." Shaykh al-Zindani became the president of Islah's Central Shura Council—the party's national legislative body—in 1995 and stayed in office until 2007.

Given Islah's origins as an alliance of a motley array of groups, it is not surprising that the party's ideology has remained vague and its platform ambiguous. Throughout the 1990s, Islah could be best described as a conservative party that promoted tribal and religious values. It believed in *shari'a* as the sole source of legislation and the foundation of a comprehensive vision to reform Yemeni state and society. Over time, especially after Islah moved away from its alliance with the GPC, the party has opened up to democratic ideas. Today, Islah accepts democracy as compatible with the Islamic concept of *shura* (consultation) and rejects all forms of dictatorship. It also recognizes the right of secular parties and movements, such as the YSP, to participate in Yemeni political life. Islah bases its own participation on respect for the constitution and the pluralist rules of the political game it enshrines.[2]

While Islah's ideology and platform have been weak from the outset, over time its tribal character has grown more influential. The post-unification era in Yemen marked the emergence of tribes as powerful stakeholders in political life, especially in parliamentary and local council elections. Yemen's tribalism had been reinforced during the civil war in the North between 1962 and 1967, when some tribes fought with the republican forces, which were backed by the Nasser regime in Egypt, while others defended the traditionalist Imamate rule. Ultimately, however, the tribes were all motivated by the desire to acquire weapons and financial assets. Guns and money reaffirmed the role of tribes and tribal leaders as protectors of their members, and tribes became more effective in providing security and social services in their territories, which increased their leverage in negotiations with the state.

As a result, the state's legitimacy diminished in tribal areas. Governments in North Yemen recognized the *de facto* influence of the tribes and were forced to delegate the task of maintaining order to tribes that took their side. The Hashid Confederation, long headed by Islah founder Shaykh al-Ahmar and considered one of the most influential groups in North Yemen, has maintained its strength since unification. And inevitably, the Hashid Confederation's role has strengthened the tribal faction over other elements in Islah.

Islah's tribal constituencies are concentrated in rural areas, above all in the northern Hashid territory in the governorates of Sanaa and Amran. The growing role of tribal leaders in Islah has added to the ambiguities and confusions inside the party. Tribal leaders are known to shift their loyalties and stances across the political spectrum to secure tribal interests. Moreover, some leaders of the same tribe or clan are found in the GPC, while others belong to Islah, a conscious effort to adapt to changing political circumstances and lessen the impact of either of the two parties on the tribes. The divided loyalty and shifting positions of tribal leaders have helped undermine Islah's ability to develop a clear ideological and programmatic vision.

Islah's Islamists, popular in urban centers, have never acquired the muscle of the tribal constituencies, but have always played a major role within the party. This is particularly true of the Muslim Brotherhood component of Islah, which is the largest in terms of members and, above all, the most efficient politically and organizationally. Like other Islamist groups in the Arab world, the Yemeni Muslim Brotherhood is a predominantly urban movement, with strongholds in universities and professional associations. Within Islah, the Muslim Brotherhood has developed a clear and elaborate approach to political participation on the basis of its endorsement of democratic procedures, which it claims do not contradict Islamic values and teachings.

For the movement, political participation complements religious and social activism, since Islam presents a holistic approach to various aspects of life, including politics. Thus, political activism is understood and framed as part of da'wa, the preaching of Islam. In the 1990s, the movement came to accept pluralism, acknowledging the right of other parties to propagate nonreligious ideologies and platforms.[3] The Yemeni Muslim Brotherhood has evolved from a religious movement to a political party under the banner of Islah. It rejects the idea of establishing an Islamic state, considering the concept of a theocratic state problematic. It separates religion from the state, but combines religion and politics in its activism.[4]

There are other Islamist elements within Islah in addition to the Muslim Brotherhood. Some party figures are close to Salafi groups. Salafism, which was introduced to Yemen in the last three decades and influenced by Saudi Wahhabism, has a different concept of politics than the Muslim Brotherhood. Salafis are skeptical of political participation and denounce democratic procedures as non-Islamic. Yet parliamentary and local elections in Yemen have demonstrated that some Salafis and their followers still vote for Islah candidates as the best available option.

Since its inception, Islah has undergone several changes, yet it is still far from being a unified party with a clear ideology and program. This lack of unity has weakened the party's role and activism in Yemeni politics. Between 1990 and 1997, Islah was an ally of the ruling GPC and participated in the coalition government from 1994 to 1997. However, in 1997

Islah switched sides and joined the Yemeni Socialist Party and other parties in opposing the GPC. Islah leaders justified this step on the grounds of the GPC's and President Saleh's unwillingness to introduce significant democratic reforms. Since 1997, Islah has gradually become the leading opposition party in Yemen, especially since joining the JMP.

However, Islah's new political role as an opposition party has remained contested internally. While alive, Shaykh al-Ahmar never withdrew his support for President Saleh. Salafi leaders in Islah have been particularly critical of the alliance with secular parties, mainly the socialists and the Nasserites in the JMP. Some of them have also denounced Islah's move to the opposition as violating Islamic prescriptions about the relationship between the ruled and their rulers, which, they maintain, necessitate obedience to the ruler.[5]

Islah's break with the GPC led to an opening of the party toward the South. In the parliamentary elections of 1993, Islah had won all its 62 parliamentary seats in North Yemen.[6] In the elections of 1997, it won some seats in the South. Although the party has remained predominantly a northern party, Islah's opening toward the South and its later alliance with the Yemeni Socialist Party has led to a second set of significant changes in the party, mainly related to the reduction of the influence previously enjoyed by tribal leaders. A clear indicator is the changing composition of Islah's parliamentary bloc since 1993. Whereas 60 of Islah's 62 MPs elected in 1993 had tribal affiliations, their number decreased in the parliament of 1997 to 24 out of 53 MPs and later to 11 out of 45 in the parliament of 2003. Clearly, tribal dominance within Islah has decreased since its break with the GPC. This has lessened the party's dependence on tribal leaders and created a more receptive internal environment for the party's activism. Tribal leaders, as noted, are highly volatile politically, tending to put the personal and business interests of their tribal constituencies over political stances and policy platforms.

Another aspect of change in Islah is that it has created charitable, religious, and educational institutions to enlarge its power base through the delivery of social services, following a pattern common among Islamist parties and movements in the Arab world. For example, the Islah Social Welfare Society (ISWS) engages in health awareness campaigns, religious education, illiteracy eradication, and relief donations, mostly directed to the urban poor, during the holy month of Ramadan. ISWS coordinates its activities with the Muslim Brotherhood and explicitly displays its adherence to the movement's ideology. Businessmen and tribal leaders affiliated with Islah also provide charity and welfare services in their areas. Religious leaders within Islah concentrate on mosque preaching, Islamic schooling, and university education to maintain their constituencies. A pivotal role in this regard has been played by Shaykh al-Zindani, who founded a well-known religious university—al-Iman University—and inspired the creation of the so-called Virtue Councils in early 2009, whose mandate is to safeguard religious morality in Yemeni society.

Switching Sides—Islah's Participation in Yemeni Politics

Most Islamist parties and movements that participate in party politics in the Arab world do so from the opposition benches. In a few cases, as is the case with the Islamic Constitutional Movement in Kuwait and the Algerian Society for Peace, Islamists have joined coalition governments either for short periods of time (Kuwait) or as junior parties with limited access to real power (Algeria). The Yemeni Congregation for Reform represents a different experience altogether. Islah switched sides, moving from an ally of the ruling GPC to an opposition party. However, this move has been far from complete because of Islah's unwillingness to break with the GPC at all levels and because influential leaders within Islah have remained critical of its alliance with the opposition. The result is a party that regularly goes back and forth between the government and the opposition on key political issues and whose policy platform lacks clarity and vision.

At the beginning, the Islamist platform of Islah did not push it away from the alliance with the ruling GPC. Throughout most of the 1990s, Islah remained a close ally of President Saleh, motivated by several factors. First, many of those who joined Islah originally belonged to the GPC or were supporters of the northern regime it represented. Second, leading members of the two parties belonged to the same well-established tribal, business, and personal networks that form the Yemeni elite. Third, both the GPC and Islah shared a history of rivalry with the Yemeni Socialist Party and the secular ideology it propagated.

In 1990, after the unification of North and South Yemen, Islah entered the political fray in Yemen to support the leadership of the former northern regime against the southern Yemeni Socialist Party (YSP). The GPC-Islah alliance developed into an electoral and parliamentary coalition in 1993. Ranking second in the 1993 parliamentary elections after the leading GPC, Islah joined the coalition government of the GPC and YSP, which, however, lasted for only one year due to ongoing tensions between the northern and southern leadership. In 1994, Islah joined the GPC's war against the Yemeni Socialist Party, which ended with the latter defeated and its leaders exiled.[7] In the aftermath of the civil war, the GPC and Islah formed a coalition government (1994–1997), in which Islah was originally given the position of deputy prime minister and five portfolios: justice, electricity, local administration, health, and fisheries. Later, in 1995, Islah secured an additional ministerial portfolio.[8]

However, the defeat of the YSP in the civil war created a new dynamic in Yemeni politics, because the strengthened GPC could dispense with its alliance with Islah. In the lead-up to the 1997 parliamentary elections, there were incipient signs of disagreements between the GPC and Islah on their electoral platform as well as on candidates. Although opposition parties started pointing to those disagreements, the GPC and Islah continued to assert their strategic alliance. Disputes between the two parties revolved around several key issues.

There were differences as to the mechanism through which power would be divided in the South, where the YSP's defeat had left a power vacuum. The GPC was also worried about the possibility that Islah would seek to expand its influence beyond the political space the regime was willing to grant it as a junior partner in the ruling coalition and pose a challenge to it. Like the experience with Islamists of other ruling parties in the Arab world, the GPC was fearful of the well organized and popular Muslim Brotherhood component inside Islah, anticipating it would reach out to constituencies in the South and organize them. Finally, the GPC was consumed with its effort to strengthen its own power base and control over Yemeni state and society. For example, the GPC had adopted a policy of modernizing the educational system to contain the influence of the Muslim Brothers and other Islamist elements affiliated with Islah in schools and universities. In the second half of the 1990s, this policy led to the closing of some religious educational institutions controlled by Islah, deepening its disagreements with the GPC.[9]

In light of these measures, Islah's leadership chose to exert pressure on its ally by initiating a campaign questioning the integrity of the parliamentary elections of 1997; it called the voter registries flawed and alleged the GPC had misused state resources in the lead-up to the elections.

However, it remained unclear whether the intention of Islah's leaders was to pressure the GPC to broker a new electoral deal with it or to break away from the alliance.

The final move toward the break between the GPC and Islah was largely the result of the GPC's conviction that it could end the alliance with Islah without great electoral losses. In the lead-up to the parliamentary elections in 1997, the GPC secretary general announced that his party wanted to achieve a "comfortable majority." Convinced that the GPC was intent on securing this comfortable majority without its allies, Islah protested this policy, warning of a GPC conspiracy against democracy in Yemen and positioning itself close to opposition parties, such as the Yemeni Socialist Party and the Nasserites. The socialists and Nasserites were determined to boycott the elections, viewing them as having the sole objective of granting President Saleh and the GPC false democratic legitimacy. Islah, however, was unwilling to go this far and in the end, severed its cooperation with the opposition and took part in the elections.

Islah secretary-general at the time, Muhammad 'Abdullah al-Yadumi, claims that the GPC had threatened to declare a state of emergency and abort the democratic process if Islah boycotted the 1997 parliamentary elections. Al-Yadumi says that Islah had considered joining the boycott of several opposition parties, but the threat of a government declaration of a state of emergency led it to conclude that participation in the elections was in the interest of the Yemeni people and democracy. In al-Yadumi's words, "Participation in the elections was going to protect what there is of the democratic margin for participation, so we participated."[10]

In the 1997 election campaign, Islah coordinated with the opposition on some issues, such as petitioning for electoral safeguards and for a transparent update of the voter registries. However, having decided to participate in the elections, it turned against cooperation and dropped its demands for safeguards. Islah ended up participating as the GPC's chief competitor and won 53 of the 301 parliamentary seats, second to the GPC's 187. After the elections, Islah joined neither the GPC in a coalition government nor the opposition camp. It preferred to play the game of accommodating the regime rather than completely severing ties. Islah's leaders, especially Shaykh al-Ahmar, still viewed the GPC and President Saleh as strategic allies.

The 1997 parliamentary elections thus unleashed a period of great ambiguity in the relations between Islah and both the ruling GPC and the opposition parties. In the presidential elections of 1999, Islah named President Saleh as its candidate. Before the 2003 parliamentary elections, however, Islah joined the Opposition Supreme Coordination Council— which originally included the YSP and four smaller parties—to form a new opposition coalition, the Joint Meeting Parties. JMP developed a collective electoral platform, making the GPC their common enemy and demanding the introduction of democratic safeguards and significant political reforms. They also coordinated on candidates. The results of the 2003 elections meant the return to parliament of the YSP, which won seven seats, and the Nasserites, which won three. Islah saw its pool of seats decline from 53 to 45.

Yet even joining the JMP did not stop Islah's leaders, especially Shaykh al-Ahmar, from supporting President Saleh and making several political deals with him and the GPC. In the 2006 presidential elections, al-Ahmar endorsed Saleh for the presidency against the JMP's candidate, Faysal bin Shamlan, who was supported by Islah as a party. Al-Ahmar's support for the president and the continued coordination between the two men explain why the GPC parliamentary bloc elected al-Ahmar speaker of parliament repeatedly from 1993 till his death in 2007.

Since 2003, Islah's practice of switching sides between the GPC and the opposition has continued. In 2005, al-Ahmar called Saleh incapable of reforming the government and declared that it had become impossible to reach electoral or political agreements with the GPC. In the lead-up to the 2006 local elections, which were held on the same day as the presidential elections (September 20, 2006), Islah's leadership announced its full support of the JMP. However, the GPC and Islah negotiated a political agreement on how to reform the government through introducing democratic and decentralization measures, and al-Ahmar supported Saleh in the presidential elections.

Recently, Islah has displayed the same ambivalence over the question of postponing the parliamentary elections scheduled for April 27, 2009, for two years. When the GPC declared that the security threats facing Yemen in the North and South made it necessary to delay the election and requested parliament to do so, Islah's parliamentary bloc protested vehemently. Its MPs accused the GPC of conspiring against democracy and free and regular elections, called on President Saleh to block any postponement, and threatened to boycott the political process. Yet a few days before the election date of April 27, 2009, Islah joined the GPC and other parties represented in parliament in voting for postponement, but demanded immediate reform of the electoral system.[11]

Several factors explain why Islah has never opted to break completely with the GPC.[12] First, Islah does not see itself as an alternative to the GPC. Its Islamist platform and its move toward the opposition in the last years have not led the party to reconsider the objective of reforming state and society in Yemen through consultation and coordination with the ruling GPC. Second, channels of communication between the two parties have always remained open, even in the periods of heated electoral competition at the national and local levels. Third, key figures in Islah's leadership, such as Shaykh al-Ahmar and Shaykh al-Zindani, have maintained enduring relationships with President Saleh and periodically assured him that Islah neither aims at replacing the GPC nor at challenging the power of the president.[13] Indeed, the death of Shaykh al-Ahmar in 2007 has had a negative impact on relations between the two parties and is a key reason for Islah's growing opposition to the government.[14]

On the other hand, the very nature of the GPC and Islah as umbrella organizations for tribal, conservative, and religiously inspired groups has meant that they have been competing for the same constituencies, producing ongoing tensions between them. More votes for the GPC mean fewer for Islah in many cases, and vice versa. The GPC has viewed the growing electoral success of Islah in the South as a direct challenge. In the 1997 parliamentary elections, for example, the GPC sought to defeat Islah candidates in the governorates of Ibb and Ta'iz, because Islah had scored significant electoral victories there in 1993.[15]

Attempts at regulating competition failed repeatedly. Both sides were unwilling to compromise. In the 1997 elections, the GPC and Islah agreed that the GPC would run uncontested in 100 out of the 301 electoral districts and Islah in 50, while they would compete in the remaining 151 districts. In practice, however, both the GPC and Islah ran candidates as independents in the districts where they were not supposed to participate.[16]

The GPC has systematically resorted to additional means to defeat Islah at the polls. Since 1997, GPC candidates have capitalized on their party's access to the state's financial resources and media outlets to influence elections. The GPC has also used the armed and security forces to instigate clashes with opposition supporters. In the 2006 local elections, the GPC notched up its competition with Islah by trying grassroots politics and providing social services in urban and rural areas for the first time. GPC candidates attempted to attract voters through field visits and the provision of services. Tribal leaders were specifically targeted to convince them to limit their contacts with Islah or to run for office with the backing of the GPC.[17] GPC maneuvering and patronage resulted in significant losses for Islah and the JMP. Islah's share in the local councils dropped from 23 percent of the seats after the 2001 elections to less than 10 percent. The YSP's share decreased from 4 to 3 percent.[18]

On another level, the GPC's leadership, specifically President Saleh, has played in recent years on the contradictions within Islah between those groups in favor of the party's alliance with the JMP and those which are skeptical of it. Most recently, Shaykh al-Zindani, who has frequently criticized Islah's alliance with the YSP, was rewarded by the president. Saleh endorsed al-Zindani's efforts to form Virtue Councils.

The GPC has also used the differences between the Muslim Brotherhood and the Salafi components of Islah to create a state of instability inside the party. Salafis have been encouraged to move out of Islah and form new political parties. Salafi shaykhs and conservative preachers have been promoted by the government to replace preachers affiliated with the Muslim Brotherhood in various mosques. The government's aim has been twofold: one, to limit Islah's control over mosques, which has helped the party in constituency building and electoral mobilization; and two, to deepen the rift within Islah between the Muslim Brothers and the Salafis. However, as noted the actual participation of Salafis as a group in Yemeni politics has remained minimal due to their scattered location and traditional teachings that forbid participation in politics.

Although far from being complete and unquestioned among its rank and file, Islah's gradual shift toward the opposition has helped the party to mature as a political force. Islah has abandoned the more simplistic slogans and arguments of the 1990–1997 period, such as "Islam is the solution" and the denunciation of secularism. It has become more pragmatic and accommodating in its attitude toward nonreligious opposition parties, mainly the YSP. The security challenges facing the Yemeni state in the North (the Houthi rebellion in Saada) and in the South (the separatist movement and al-Qaeda) have made Islah see its role in the tribal areas of the North and its alliance with the southern-based YSP as essential pillars in keeping Yemen together and preventing the collapse of the state. Islah's policy platform has also come to focus increasingly on pushing for political and socioeconomic reforms, fair representation of

Yemeni parties in state institutions, and active participation of the opposition in decision making and in fighting corruption.

In addition, Islah's ideology and vision have evolved while participating as an opposition party. It has presented itself, like other Islamist parties and movements in the Arab world, as a party pressing for political change from within an authoritarian political system, using peaceful methods. Islah has underscored its commitment to democratic mechanisms by regular participation in national and local elections and acceptance of their results, despite regime manipulation. Like other Arab Islamists, this participatory vision has been religiously legitimated by equating democracy with the Islamic concept of *shura*.

Islah's positive evolution in the opposition, however, does not mean that the party's ambiguities or its constant switching between the government and the opposition sides will cease any time soon. Islah's accommodating attitude toward nonreligious parties and its acceptance of pluralism have not led the party to abandon the view of *shari'a* as the sole basis for organizing state and society in Yemen. The dissatisfaction of several strong leaders in Islah with its current course and the ongoing communication between them and the GPC have prevented the party from adopting a clear opposition platform. The JMP, for their part, have never stopped questioning Islah's commitment to the alliance. Divisions between the Muslim Brothers and the Salafis within Islah have prevented the party from taking concrete stances on issues pertaining to the role of religion in politics, especially since *shari'a* provisions were enshrined in the constitution early in the 1990s. From the time al-Zindani began pressing for the formation of the Virtue Councils in July 2008 until their formation in early 2009, Islah leaders remained divided between support and skepticism, and the party could not reach a unified position.

Islah's ambiguities and internal divisions have harmed the party electorally and politically on various occasions. Most significantly, they have impeded the party's legislative role and its performance in successive Yemeni parliaments. In contrast to other Islamist parties and movements, such as the Moroccan Party for Justice and Development and the Egyptian Muslim Brotherhood, which over time have developed well-organized parliamentary blocs with clear legislative priorities and active parliamentary participation, Islah has never reached a level close to that.

Islah in Parliament—Legislative Priorities and Performance

Islah's role in parliament has to be evaluated against the background of two realities of Yemeni political life since unification in 1990. First, since it started to contest parliamentary elections in 1993, Islah has been losing seats while the GPC has been increasing its representation. Second, in the last two decades Islah has changed its position in Yemeni politics from a partner in the ruling coalition with the GPC (until 1997) to alliance with opposition parties grouped in the JMP.

Since entering Yemeni politics, Islah's representation in parliament has fallen gradually from 62 seats out of 301 in 1993 to 53 in 1997, and then to its current tally of 45 after the 2003 elections. The other major opposition party in Yemen, the YSP, which boycotted the 1997 parliamentary elections and participated only in the elections of 1993 and 2003, has fallen precipitously from 56 seats in 1993 to 7 in the current parliament. Meanwhile, the GPC increased the number of seats it won from 123 in 1993 to 187 in 1997 to 229 in 2003. This partly reflects the growing institutional and political dominance of the GPC, which emerged at the end of the 1990s as the country's uncontested ruling party. Islah has become the major opposition party facing the GPC. However, its ability to compete with the GPC has been diminishing, and it leads an opposition that has suffered substantial parliamentary and political losses between 1993 and 2003.

In the parliamentary elections of 1993, Islah ran based on an electoral platform that spelled out the party's coalition with the GPC, its commitment to religion (Islam is the solution) and exposed its uncertainty with regard to democratic mechanisms. It finished second after the GPC, besting the YSP.

The 1997 elections reflected the outcome and effects of the 1994 civil war between the North and the South. The war ended with the defeat of the South and enactment of a new electoral law in 1996 (law 27/1996) that banned former southern leaders from participation in political life, dealing a blow to the YSP, which boycotted the elections. The GPC won a clear parliamentary majority of 62.1 percent—187 seats, compared to 40.5 percent in 1993. Islah's approximate share of the popular vote fell to 17.6 percent from 20.9 percent in 1993, resulting in 53 seats. In 1997, Islah's candidates ran on a quasi-opposition platform, criticizing the GPC's dominance over Yemeni politics and the lack of democratic safeguards in the electoral process.

In the 2003 elections, Islah's losses continued. Only 45 of its parliamentary candidates were elected and the party's share of the vote fell to 14.9 percent. Despite the parliamentary representation of the YSP and other opposition parties, the GPC's dominance reached unprecedented heights. President Saleh's party secured 76 percent of the parliamentary seats, 229.

Islah more skillfully presented its opposition platform in the lead-up to the 2003 elections. In line with other opposition Islamist parties and movements in the Arab world, Islah's platform called for gradual, peaceful democratic reforms and for a fair distribution of political power between the GPC and other parties. The fact that *shari'a* provisions had been enshrined in the constitution in 1994 prevented Islah, unlike other opposition Islamists, from putting forward the application of *shari'a* as the keystone of its opposition platform. *Shari'a* was replaced by calls for democratic reform, political change, better governance, and measures against corruption.

The growing dominance of the GPC over Yemeni politics and the shrinking role of Islah have been also demonstrated at the local level. After the local elections in 2001, the GPC's representation in local councils was 61 percent against Islah's 23 percent. The YSP controlled 4 percent of the seats in local councils—mainly in the southern governorates—and independents 12 percent. Like the parliamentary elections in 2003, the local elections in 2006 enhanced the majority status of the GPC. The ruling party ended up securing over 80 percent of the seats on local councils. Islah's share of the popular vote declined to less than 10 percent, the YSP's to 3 percent, and that of independents to approximately 5 percent.

As a party with a declining presence in a parliament dominated by the president's party, Islah, especially after its move toward the opposition since 1997, has behaved like a small party trying to have some impact on key legislation and policy issues. Unlike other opposition Islamists in the Arab world, Islah's positions and activities in parliament have not reflected a comprehensive platform. They have been characterized by ambiguity and switching sides between the GPC and opposition parties, the two characteristics that shape Islah's overall role in Yemeni political life.

From 1993 to 1997, Islah's parliamentary bloc assisted the GPC bloc. Until 1994, the parliamentary agenda was influenced by the post-unification struggles over the distribution of power between North and South Yemen. This resulted in a bitter conflict between the North-based

GPC and Islah, on the one hand, and the South-based YSP on the other. The Islamist platform of Islah was used effectively to discredit the socialist agenda of the YSP. Indeed, the ideological controversies between the YSP socialists and Islah's religious leaders, such as Shaykh al-Zindani, who systematically described the YSP as an atheist organization, added to the tensions between North and South.

After the YSP's defeat in the civil war in 1994, the GPC and Islah formed a government with Islah as the junior partner in the ruling coalition. Its parliamentary bloc focused in the post–civil war phase on ensuring the conformity of Yemeni legislation with *shari'a* provisions. President Saleh had rewarded Islah for its support during the civil war by accepting its demand to enshrine *shari'a* in the constitution. In December 1994, the GPC and Islah parliamentary blocs amended article 3 of the constitution to make *shari'a* the source of all legislation. The amendment was the clearest sign of Islah's adherence to an Islamist platform between 1993 and 1997. However, the party failed to capitalize on it to introduce further legislative changes. Several religious leaders in Islah disapproved of the education law, which was passed by the GPC and the YSP before 1994, and obliged the government to close down some of the educational institutes that taught *shari'a* and *fiqh* (Islamic jurisprudence). Islah's parliamentary bloc failed to change the education law.

After the elections of 1997, Islah's legislative priorities and performance have been shaped by its changed position in Yemeni politics as a result of joining the opposition. Islah has used its participation in parliament to underscore its commitment to democratic mechanisms and its recognition of the legitimacy of the existing state's legal framework, but also has called for the introduction of political and economic reforms. Contrary to its legislative initiatives before 1997, Islah's parliamentary bloc has devoted less attention to legislation related to religious and moral issues. Islah has acted only when the GPC has proposed laws that contradict some *shari'a* provisions, trying to block them.

Since the parliament of 1997–2003, Islah's legislative priorities have changed and it has come to seek the following: constitutional amendments aimed at a fairer distribution of power between the government and the opposition, reforms in electoral laws and laws pertaining to political rights, improving parliament's oversight of the government's socioeconomic policies, and a reduction in corruption. To a lesser extent, it has also sought religious legislation. These priorities became clearer after Islah and the JMP agreed in January 2003 to a joint electoral platform for the 2003 elections and a joint parliamentary platform.

Concerning constitutional amendments, Islah's bloc voted in 2000 for two government-sponsored amendments that extended parliament's term from four to six years and the president's term from five to seven years. In endorsing the two amendments, Islah assumed that lengthening parliament's term would provide more stability in the legislative process and partially free the parties from the influence of powerful electoral constituencies, such as tribes. Islah expected the longer parliamentary term to make it easier to introduce political and economic reforms.

Rhetorically, Islah defended the amendment to the president's term as a way to make the country more stable. In fact, its defense reflected the support of key Islah leaders, including al-Ahmar and al-Zindani, for President Saleh. However, in 2007, when Saleh proposed through the GPC additional constitutional amendments to shift Yemen from a presidential to a parliamentary system and to reduce the presidential term to five years and set an upper limit of two consecutive terms, Islah's bloc refused to fall in line. Islah parliamentarians criticized the president's initiative as undemocratic and designed to sustain his and the GPC's dominance of Yemeni politics. Throughout 2008 and most of 2009, the two parties along with smaller parties have been discussing these proposals.[19]

As for electoral laws and laws pertaining to political rights, Islah MPs have systematically attempted to block the initiatives of their GPC colleagues they find undemocratic in spirit. However, the GPC has been able to ignore Islah's opposition in most cases because of its comfortable parliamentary majority.

Several examples follow. In 2000, Islah MPs opposed the bills on local councils, which entailed the appointment of governors by the Ministry of Interior. Islah demanded that governors should be directly elected like members of the local councils. The GPC majority passed the law.[20] The parliament again took up the law of local councils in 2008. The GPC bloc suggested an amendment providing for the election of governors by the members of local councils instead of the appointment of governors by the president. Islah MPs opposed this seemingly democratic amendment, because it clearly favored the GPC, which has controlled more than 80 percent of the local council seats since the 2006 local elections. They renewed their demand for direct election of governors, but in vain. Parliament passed the GPC amendment.[21]

In 2006, the GPC and the JMP parties, including Islah, signed an "Agreement of Principles" aimed at organizing the presidential and local council elections of September 2006. The agreement, which was preceded by parliamentary passage of a new law for elections and referenda (law 26/2006), changed the composition of the Supreme Commission for Elections and Referendum (SCER). It added two JMP members, making four in all, as compared to five members who were appointed by the GPC. The agreement also stipulated that the subelectoral committees, which were responsible for the validation of voter lists and the supervision of the election process, would be composed of 54 percent GPC-appointed members and 46 percent JMP-appointed members. The agreement also emphasized the neutrality of the military and security services, public money, and public media during the elections.[22]

After initial euphoric statements, Islah MPs became disenchanted with the inner workings of the committee in the early days of validating the voter lists. Islah claimed that the SCER failed to carry out its mission. It accused the GPC members in the commission of obstructing the validation process, expelling election observers from civil society organizations, and using the security services to intimidate JMP commission members.[23] The presidential elections ended with an overwhelming victory for the GPC candidate, President Saleh, over the JMP candidate, Faysal bin Shamlan. Saleh won 77.2 percent of the vote. The local elections also were a sweeping victory for the GPC.

In 2008, Islah MPs proposed a new law to ensure the judiciary's independence and reinforce the separation of executive and judicial authority. Islah's bill aimed at changing the practice of the appointment of judges by the Minister of Justice, which gives the executive considerable influence over the judiciary. The bill would have created a general assembly, composed of senior judges, to nominate judges eligible for high judicial offices. The assembly's nominations would have needed the approval of the parliament and the president.[24] Islah's legislation was referred to a parliamentary committee for study, and no decision had been reached as of October 2009.[25]

In 2008, the Islah bloc also proposed a law to grant and protect free access to information. It was endorsed by other opposition MPs and widely supported by civil society organizations and various professional associations. Even so, the GPC majority brought down Islah's legislation. Later last year, the cabinet adopted a different bill prepared by the

National Information Center, a government agency, and moved it to the parliament for deliberations. The government's proposal would impose severe restrictions on access to information, including harsh penalties for journalists—up to six months in prison—for publishing any information deemed by the authorities to be politically sensitive or a threat to Yemen's national security or its foreign relations. As of October 2009, the parliament had yet to pass the government's bill.[26]

Islah MPs have devoted significant attention to social and economic issues. In its electoral platforms of 1997 and 2003 as well as in several declarations of programs, Islah has repeatedly criticized the government's failure to improve the living conditions of Yemenis by introducing just and effective social and economic policies. Like their Islamist colleagues elsewhere in the Arab world, Islah MPs have gradually mastered the technique of supporting their criticism of the government's failure with numbers demonstrating social and economic hardship—for example, more than 45 percent of the Yemeni population live on $2 a day, 18 percent live on $1 a day, and the unemployment rate runs as high as 35 percent. However, Islah has confined its parliamentary activism on social and economic policies to criticism of the government and largely failed to increase effective parliamentary oversight powers or develop alternative policies.[27] Failure to develop alternative, concrete policy measures in the socioeconomic realm brings Islah closer to the majority of Islamist parties and movements that participate in Arab politics. The Moroccan Party for Justice and Development, the Egyptian and Jordanian Muslim Brotherhoods, and Algerian Islamists have been all heavily criticized for their inability to develop concrete policy platforms that address issues such as poverty, unemployment, and social services.

Since 1997, the Islah bloc has been disapproving of the government's annual budget and abstaining from voting on fiscal issues. Islah's opposition to GPC-backed bills on social and economic issues has remained largely ineffective because of the GPC's parliamentary dominance. For example, the Islah bloc opposed the new income tax law in 2005, the law of wages and salaries in 2007, and various privatization measures that allowed foreign investors to own real estate in Yemen in 2009. In all three cases, the GPC majority passed the legislation. Islah MPs have succeeded in introducing amendments to only to a few GPC bills. Most recently, in 2009, the Islah bloc amended the micro credit law meaningfully. The bill circulated by the government gave the central bank the right to confiscate the borrowers' property in case of failure to pay back government loans. Islah viewed this as contradicting *shari'a* provisions and demanded its removal. Before passage, the legislation was amended to grant the central bank only the right to refer borrowers in default to the judicial authorities.[28]

Out of 119 parliamentary questions that Islah MPs addressed to the government between 2003 and 2009, 41 raised issues pertaining to Islamic teachings and morality. These issues varied from selling alcoholic beverages in some provinces and showing "indecent movies" in hotels to the closing of religious schools. However, with regard to religious legislation, Islah MPs have succeeded in recent years in amending only two bills based on their Islamist platform. In 2005, the Islah bloc cooperated with the GPC majority to make *shari'a* part of the curriculum of the state police academy, an amendment to law 10/2001.[29] In 2009, most Islah MPs were among the parliamentary majority that rejected government-proposed amendments of civic status laws (law 14/2002 and law 20/1992) to raise the eligible age of marriage for women from fifteen to eighteen years. In the end, after taking into consideration the opinion of the parliamentary Islamic Codification Committee, a parliamentary majority approved raising the age of marriageable women to seventeen years.[30]

The parliamentary debate on raising the age of marriage for women has revealed how differently various Islah MPs interpret their party's Islamist platform and relate it to religious legislation. Some Islah MPs voted for the government's proposal, while others, especially Islah representatives in the Codification Committee, denounced it as contradicting *shari'a* and threatening the moral integrity of women.[31]

An earlier incident revealing the internal divisions among Islah MPs in interpreting the Islamist platform occurred in May 2008, when President Saleh called on religious scholars to form "Virtue Councils" to further moral practices and ensure compliance with Islamic teachings in society. Shaykh al-Zindani and Shaykh Hammud al-Zarihi, both prominent figures in Islah, were among 25 scholars who established these councils. The Virtue Councils held several meetings, in which the scholars called for a ban on alcohol consumption, a prohibition on women working for private companies, supervision of beaches and public places, and other measures intended to enforce virtues and fight vice. Several Islah members, mainly clerics and preachers, later joined the Virtue Councils.

As a result, Islah was heavily criticized by its partners in the JMP and various civil society organizations, which feared that the formation of Virtue Councils would further diminish individual freedoms in the name of religion. Islah was forced to state publicly that as a political party it would not interfere in issues of morality and so does not approve or disapprove of the Virtue Councils. The statement also described the decision of Islah members to join the councils as personal and not reflecting a party line.

Although the official stance of Islah toward the Virtue Councils has demonstrated a measure of practical separation between its political activity and its religious elements (the Muslim Brotherhood and the Salafis) influential inside it, it has also brought to the surface the internal divisions within Islah in interpreting its Islamist platform. Islah could not disown the formation of the councils or denounce an initiator, al-Zindani, a prominent party figure. It needed to accommodate him and his influential followers, lest it lose their backing. But the party also had to respect its members who distanced themselves from al-Zindani's initiative, seeing it as an apolitical enterprise with which the party should not be associated.[32]

Overall, Islah's impact on the legislative process has been rather limited since the party moved to the opposition side in 1997. Between 1994 and 1997, when it participated with the GPC in a coalition government, Islah scored its clearest legislative victory: the 1994 amendment to article 3 of the constitution that made *shari'a* provisions the source of all legislation. Islah's efforts since 1997 to push for democratically inspired constitutional and legal amendments and to strengthen parliamentary oversight of the government's policies have largely failed because of the uncontested dominance of the GPC in parliament. Islah MPs are outnumbered both in plenary discussions and in the standing committees, which review legislative proposals and presidential decrees after their first discussion in parliament.[33]

Although Islah's long-standing ambivalence toward President Saleh and the GPC and its internal divisions have hindered the party's parliamentary activism, more than anything it has been the concentration of power in the hands of the president and the ruling party that has greatly curbed Islah's legislative success. At this level, the experience of Yemeni Islamists corresponds to the wider regional pattern of Islamist parties and movements, which have proven ineffective opposition groups in parliaments controlled by authoritarian regimes.

Trajectories of Evolution—
Impacts of Political Participation on Islah

In spite of its limited impact in parliament, Islah has continued to contest elections at the national and local level and to play politics by the rules. Apart from the 1994 civil war, in which the party joined hands with the GPC to defeat the YSP, Islah has upheld its commitment to peaceful participation in political life since its formation in 1990. Islah's emerging acceptance of democratic procedures and pluralism during the 1990s has evolved, so that today it is an uncontested pillar of the party's ideology and role. Indeed, its experience in the JMP has demonstrated Islah's willingness to cooperate with ideologically and programmatically different parties and to develop a joint electoral and parliamentary platform to push for reforms in Yemen.

Yet Islah has had to overcome various obstacles to participate in politics. Operating in an authoritarian regime, in which the president and his party dominate political life and strip checks and balances among government branches of their meaning, has forced Islah, since its move toward the opposition in 1997, to sustain its ties with the regime to have some influence over key political choices. Islah also had to overcome its own mixed constituency and its internal divisions to take part in politics. The tribal, Muslim Brotherhood, and Salafi elements of Islah have prevented the party from developing a clear ideology and platform. As the analysis of the party's legislative priorities and performance has shown, the Islah parliamentary bloc has been forced to strike a balance between tribal and political interests, between different interpretations of the party's Islamist platform among influential leaders, and between those who see Islah as part of the opposition JMP and those who denounce cooperation with the JMP and still view the GPC as an ally. The result has been continued ambiguities in Islah regarding its ideology and platform and a wide skepticism on the outside as to where the party really stands.

These characteristics have made the experience of Islah different from that of other Islamist parties and movements in the Arab world, though not completely. Of course, most Arab Islamists who also participate in politics from the ranks of the opposition have managed to sort out much of their initial ideological ambiguities and to articulate clear parliamentary platforms. Islah has not so far. Still, Islah, like other Islamists, has had to account to its constituents for achieving only limited reforms and justify its continued commitment to reform. Like Islamists elsewhere, Islah has justified itself through a mixed narrative: first, economic and political reforms are framed as long-term and gradual processes of change, requiring patience on part of their advocates. Second, peaceful participation is presented as the best available option to challenge the authoritarian regime while assuring peace within Yemeni society. This last argument resonates well in a country like Yemen, which went through long periods of instability in the past and seems to be entering a new one now. In fact, the growing security and instability threats in the North and South of Yemen have been used effectively by Islah to justify its participation in legal politics and its ongoing contacts with the regime as essential in preserving Yemen from state failure or disintegration.

Islamist parties and movements have become institutionally more complex and amenable to internal democratic procedures while participating in party politics. For example, the Moroccan Party for Justice and Development has kept a functional separation between the religious movement and the party, while the Egyptian Muslim Brotherhood has maintained such a functional separation between the movement and the parliamentary bloc. Islah's internal evolution too has been toward growing institutional complexity.

The organizational and decision-making structure that Islah has developed contains six legislative and executive levels: the General Congress, the Central Shura Council, the Supreme Board, the General Secretariat, the Judiciary Board, and local congresses and councils in each of the 20 governorates of Yemen. According to its bylaws, at all these levels, Islah bases decision making and leadership formation on the concept of shura, which compels party members to deliberate and put into practice a participatory approach.[34]

The General Congress of Islah, the party's main executive body, amended in a meeting in March 2009 different articles of Islah's bylaws to allow for greater internal democracy, decentralization, and participation. A significant example is the amendment of article 12 of the bylaws. Before the amendment, article 12 gave the General Congress the right to elect from its own members the delegates of the local congresses of Islah. The amended article 12 stipulates that members of the local councils will elect the delegates of local congresses directly. Also, in the same meeting, the General Congress amended article 14 to transfer the responsibility for electing the members of the Central Shura Council, the party's internal parliament, from the General Congress itself to local congresses.

These two recent amendments demonstrate Islah's willingness to improve the inner workings of its executive and legislative bodies by introducing a high degree of both internal democracy and of decentralization of decision-making powers from the national to the local levels. They shed another positive light on Islah's strategic commitment to democratic procedures. It is worth noting that the amendments to article 12 and 14 were pushed not only by the local councils of Islah, which benefit from them, but also by several key figures in the leadership following extensive debates within the party.[35]

Unlike the democratizing drive of Islah manifested in the interplay between the party's national and local levels, two key features of internal democracy in political parties—mobility and change in leadership—have been largely missing. Shaykh al-Ahmar remained president of Islah's powerful Supreme Board from the party's formation until his death in 2007. In fact, the fourth and last confirmation by the General Congress of al-Ahmar in his position, which took place shortly before his death, violated Islah's bylaws stipulating that the term of the Supreme Board president can only be renewed three consecutive times. Shaykh al-Zindani remained president of Islah's Central Shura Council for three consecutive terms from 1995 till 2007. In 2007, al-Zindani was replaced as council head by Muhammad Ibn Ajlan, who had been vice president between 1995 and 2007. Al-Zindani was then elected to a seat on the party's Supreme Board.[36]

The lack of mobility and change in the top leadership positions, which does not make Islah any different from other parties in Yemen, has also shaped the wider composition of the Central Shura Council. Since Islah's formation, influential tribal and religious members have systematically controlled more than a two-thirds majority in the council (100 out of 130 seats).[37] Only in leadership positions at the local level, which are determined through internal elections for candidates to run for leadership in local congresses and councils, has Islah shown itself able to display a high degree of mobility and change. The last round of elections for the local congresses and councils, held in January 2007, confirmed this trend.[38]

Another trajectory of evolution among most Islamist parties and movements in the Arab world is their gradual opening toward women. Here too, Islah's experience has resembled the wider Islamist spectrum.

Islah's discourse on women has changed over time, from an initial skepticism of female political activism to an acceptance of it driven by political and pragmatic considerations. In 1998, women were elected for the first time to Islah's Central Shura Council; they won seven seats. Currently, seventeen women hold seats in the council. In the March 2009 meeting of Islah's General Congress, the party's bylaws (article 36) were amended to allow for greater female representation, and a section for women was added to the General Secretariat.

Islah's gradual opening toward women has been propelled mainly by its electoral competition with the GPC. Like Arab Islamists elsewhere, Islah has always had significant female constituencies—currently, they are 18 percent of party membership. However, women were largely ill-represented within Islah and kept out of leadership positions and election candidacy in the 1990s. In recent years, especially after Islah's poor showings in the presidential and local elections in 2006—Islah did not nominate a single female candidate for the 7,000 contested seats in the local councils—party leaders have come to realize the importance of mobilization among women and therefore the need to better represent them in the party's legislative and executive bodies.

Still, as with various policy and political issues, internal division has plagued Islah's opening toward women. Some tribal and religious leaders have opposed it, based on a conservative interpretation of *shari'a* provisions, while others have recently pressed for the introduction of female quotas at all levels of the party.[39] Owing to the party's internal division, Islah's parliamentary bloc has consistently declined in the last three years to subscribe to various GPC proposals aimed at introducing a 10–15 percent female quota in the parliament, 20–25 percent in the local councils, and 10 percent in the State Consultative Council.

Conclusion

The Yemeni Congregation for Reform shares many characteristics with other Islamist parties and movements in the Arab world, but it also has a number of key differences. Like other Islamist movements, Islah has a faith-based ideology and platform, albeit loose, and it participates in party politics with the aim of achieving constitutional and socioeconomic reforms. It has also gradually become committed to following democratic procedures both internally and in Yemeni national politics.

However, Islah differs from most other Arab Islamists in that it combines tribal influences with those of the Yemeni Muslim Brotherhood and Salafi groups. Compared to Islamists elsewhere, Islah shows a higher degree of internal division on key issues, such as its relationship with the ruling establishment, women's participation in politics, the interpretation of its Islamist platform, and how that translates into political action. Moreover, unlike other Islamists, Islah began participating in politics as a junior partner in a ruling coalition and did not join the opposition until several years after its establishment. The practice of switching sides between the government and the opposition has been a hallmark of Islah and continues to make it an exception among its Islamist counterparts.

CHAPTER 7

Hamas

Battling to Blend Religion, Politics, Resistance, and Governance

The Palestinian Islamic Resistance Movement—known by its Arabic acronym, Hamas—traces its origin to two sister movements, the Egyptian Muslim Brotherhood and the Jordanian Muslim Brotherhood, and its ties with both organizations remain deep. But it has operated in a very different political environment—and a radically changing one as well, in which Hamas has had to shift from a movement that is largely underground to one that governs. Its response to that environment—as well as its efforts to change it in the most radical ways—makes its experience extremely unusual and interesting to students of Islamist movements, not because it is typical but because of the ways it tests the limits of participation. In this chapter, we will:

- Show how the political context has shaped Hamas as a movement (one that shares some organizational features and goals with its sister Brotherhood organizations, but also one that confronts very different problems)
- Explore the evolution of Hamas's ideology and platforms, especially as the movement has stepped up its level of political involvement
- Examine the effect of governing on Hamas
- Explore the future prospects of the movement and of Palestinian politics in light of Hamas's rise.

Political Context

Hamas presents itself, especially forcefully in recent years, as a movement closely following the example of the "mother movement," Egypt's Muslim Brotherhood. Indeed, Hamas emerged very much from elements of the Palestinian Muslim Brotherhood and draws the sympathy of Brotherhood chapters throughout the world.

But the Palestinian Brotherhood emerged in a very different context from that of its fellow movements, and that context is critical to understanding its evolution. To make things more complicated, Hamas emerged in the 1980s not just out of the Brotherhood but very much in reaction against the patterns that organization had established. Like the Palestinian Muslim Brotherhood—which it eventually both replaced and subsumed—Hamas has built itself in reaction to the political context in which it operates. But the pre-Hamas Brotherhood and Hamas have reacted to that context in sharply different ways, demonstrating that context shapes much but it does not determine the Islamist response.

The interest of the Egyptian Muslim Brotherhood in Palestine's cause dates back to the 1930s, and the feelings were slowly reciprocated. Palestinian supporters of the Brotherhood slowly coalesced; they were just forming their independent branch as the British Mandate for Palestine drew to an end.[1] As volunteers from other Muslim Brotherhood movements joined in the fighting in 1947 and 1948, the connection between the Brotherhood and the Palestinian cause was firmly fixed. But for the following four decades that connection led to few political results.

In the wake of the 1948 war, the Palestinian Brotherhood, like the Palestinian population generally, was divided among four locations. First were those who lived within the borders of the new state of Israel; they came first under martial law and then under fairly restrictive political conditions. Eventually, in the 1980s and 1990s, an Israeli Islamic movement arose that built on both the memory and the model of the Muslim Brotherhood; it eventually split over the issue of participation in elections. The Islamic movement in Israel has a branch that allies itself with other Israeli political parties at the national level and works to represent the country's Palestinian citizens. But another branch rejects participation at the national level (participating only in local government) and vociferously criticizes the Israeli polity in Islamic terms. Close ideological (and sometimes personal) ties developed between the more radical branch of the Israeli Islamic movement and Hamas, but organizational separation was imposed both by the different contexts in which they operated and the sharp security ramifications that would have followed from a more formal set of ties.

The second location where the Palestinian Muslim Brotherhood operated was in the West Bank and Jordan. With Jordan's annexation of the West Bank, the West Bank Palestinian Muslim Brotherhood was thoroughly integrated into the Jordanian Brotherhood organization— an institutional linkage that (as the study of the Islamic Action Front in this volume explores in more detail) has begun to pose problems for the organization, political stance, and identity of the Jordanian movement in the past few years.

Third, the Muslim Brotherhood operated in Gaza, administered by Egypt until 1967. The movement there came under some of the same restrictive conditions suffered by the Egyptian movement, though it retained its separate identity and soldiered on despite the repression of the Nasserist period.

Finally, some Palestinian Muslim Brotherhood elements found their way to other countries, especially in the Arabian Peninsula. Along with Egyptian exiles, Palestinian Brotherhood members played a role in establishing the Muslim Brotherhood in countries such as Kuwait, but as those chapters gradually struck local roots, a separation developed between the local organization and those whose political horizons lay back in their homelands.

This geographical dispersion and the unpromising political environment induced the remnants of the Brotherhood still active to turn their attention away from the political sphere, but its leaders worked to make a virtue out of this necessity. Deciding that their immediate task was to make the society more Islamic, they worked in religious, educational, and other fields.

The 1967 war brought critical changes for the various arms of the Palestinian Islamist movement, the ultimate effect of which was to produce the conditions that allowed for the emergence of Hamas and the re-entry of the Brotherhood into politics and resistance. But the short-term effect was very much in the other direction. The aftermath of the 1967 war brought the West Bank and Gaza back into direct contact; it also placed both locations under Israeli control. But rather than lead the Brotherhood into resuming an interest in politics, the immediate effect was to lead the Brotherhood to continue focusing on other realms, leaving "resistance" to a host of other Palestinian groups. While the Brotherhood's political positions, when enunciated, were hardly friendly to Israel's policy (or even its existence), the organization's continued insistence that Palestine had to become more Islamic before it was liberated seemed a welcome gift to Israeli security officials who allowed the Islamists some freedom to pursue their social and religious activities.

Criticized by other Palestinian movements for abandoning politics, the Muslim Brotherhood retorted that the circumstances were not appropriate and that their efforts would be more effective if devoted to improving Palestinian society and piety. The collection of leftist and nationalist ideologies prevailing in Palestinian resistance circles at the time repelled many Islamists. When Islamists became active, it was just as much to contest the local influence of non-Islamist groups as it was to resist Israel. Thus, from an Israeli perspective, Islamists were a welcome counterweight to various other Palestinian groups interested in organizing the population for political ends and resistance to occupation. The occupiers therefore gave Muslim Brotherhood members some freedom to organize as long as they maintained their distance from the national struggle.

And for a while they did. In the 1970s and 1980s, Islamist and non-Islamist Palestinian organizations saw themselves as bitter rivals, sometimes battling for control of Palestinian organizations as well as Palestinian loyalties. To the Islamists, the nationalist and leftist forces seemed to have abandoned religion; to the nationalists and leftist forces, the Islamists were leading Palestinians to a dangerous political quiescence. But the Brotherhood itself was beginning to move in a different direction. In the West Bank and especially in Gaza, a new generation of activists wished to drag the organization in a more active direction and use its growing sphere of social activities as the base for a more political orientation. In Kuwait, Jordan, and Egypt, a new generation of leaders also arose, seeking to build an Islamic resistance movement.

By the late 1980s, those efforts coalesced in the launching of a new movement that came to call itself the Islamic Resistance Movement, or Hamas. Hamas was formed by Brotherhood activists in order to ensure that there was an Islamist participant in the national struggle. Hamas was most visible in Gaza, but there was clear diaspora activity behind its launch as well, and West Bank Islamists joined in early on as well. When the first Palestinian uprising erupted against the Israeli occupation, Hamas played a prominent role in attacking Israeli targets. The underground resistance organization thus quickly became far more active and dominant than the Brotherhood that had spawned it. The rivalry with other Palestinian movements actually increased during this period, as each set out to assert leadership over the growing wave of Palestinian resistance activities. The decision to enter politics came at a time when other Islamist groups in the Arab world were also stepping up their political involvement. Hamas's founders were probably vaguely influenced by this trend. But they may also have been inspired by the Iranian revolution (while Iran was hardly a model, the idea of an Islamic-colored revolutionary movement was appealing), and perhaps it was competition from a splinter Islamist group (Islamic Jihad) that helped prompt the switch to resistance. The decision, however, was not a sudden one: while the early history of Hamas is still shrouded in secrecy, it is clear that there was much planning and debate in Islamist circles throughout the 1980s (not only in Gaza but also among supporters in the Arab world) about whether, how, and when to take up arms.

Within a short period, Hamas had subsumed much of the Brotherhood in the West Bank, Gaza, and Palestinian diaspora. It retained some features of its origins as a clandestine resistance organization, notably a partially underground character. Unlike other Brotherhood movements that strive to operate through legal channels where possible, Hamas accorded the Israeli occupation no legitimacy and showed no qualms about illegal and violent activities. An early set of arrests of its leaders led the movement to establish a military wing that operated clandestinely and kept some distance from those parts of Hamas that operated more openly. The construction of a distinct military wing began as a security measure, but it cemented the inclination of the movement to develop different branches with different spheres of activity and emphases. Part social movement, part military organization, part political party, and based simultaneously in the West Bank, Gaza, and the diaspora, the various wings of Hamas coordinated remarkably well, given their geographical separation and varying sets of activities.

In the late 1980s, Hamas began to portray itself as an Islamic alternative to the various nationalist and leftist groups that had dominated the Palestinian political scene for a generation. The Islamist group did not reject cooperation with the other movements but its terms for entering the Palestine Liberation Organization (PLO)—the umbrella organization then gaining acceptance as the "sole legitimate representative of the Palestinian people"—which included a large bloc of representatives in all PLO bodies proved too high a price for the PLO leadership.

Beginning in 1993, the signing of the Oslo Accords by PLO leader Yasser Arafat fundamentally changed the political environment for Hamas. The agreement between the PLO and Israel created a new entity, referred to by Palestinians as the "Palestinian National Authority" (PNA), which governed civil affairs for Palestinians in the West Bank and Gaza as well as security affairs in most Palestinian cities in those areas. The PNA worked to establish itself as the basis of a Palestinian state, creating ministries, writing laws, and drafting a constitutional framework, and, in 1996, holding presidential and parliamentary elections.[2]

Hamas joined with some small Palestinian factions in rejecting the Oslo Accords and declared that the Israeli occupation had not ended; neither would its resistance to that occupation cease. Indeed, in the early Oslo period, Hamas stepped up its use of violence by increased targeting of Israeli civilians (especially after the massacre of Palestinian worshippers by an Israeli settler in Hebron in 1994).

But if Hamas claimed that the Israeli occupation had not ended, it still could not ignore the difficulties caused by the creation of the PNA; the new environment offered some severe challenges to Hamas. There were now Palestinian security forces to contend with, and Hamas followers clashed with those forces from the beginning. The PNA came under heavy pressure from Israel and the United States to move against Palestinians who continued violent resistance, and Hamas found itself coming under severe repression, especially after its bombing campaign of 1994. In addition, the PNA quickly established patterns of patronage that largely obscured the distinctions between Arafat's personal political machine, the Fatah party, and the institutions of the proto-state—leaving Hamas and its followers (somewhat willingly, perhaps) partially out in the cold. And the prospect of statehood also allowed the PNA some measure of popular support as it built its structures and even (at least early on in the Oslo process) when it moved against Hamas.

Oslo and the PNA also offered some opportunities for Hamas. Day-to-day oversight of civil affairs in the West Bank and Gaza passed from Israeli to Palestinian hands, giving Hamas a bit more freedom to maneuver, especially in nonpolitical affairs. Hamas's standing in Palestinian society sometimes placed limits on what PNA security officials felt comfortable in doing. Indeed, local branches of Fatah and Hamas sometimes joined with smaller factions in a series of ad hoc consultative bodies known as the "National and Islamic Forces" (when the second intifada broke out in 2000, this structure provided an institutional basis for some limited cooperation).

Palestinian elections posed a particularly vexing issue for Hamas: the movement was anxious both to prove its popular standing but also to withhold its blessing from any part of the Oslo process.

In the second half of the 1990s, Hamas's approach to the new environment was worked out in practice. First, its leaders proclaimed that while they would defend themselves if forced, they wanted no part of violence among Palestinians and would therefore react with restraint to PNA forces. They largely held true to this stance, even when their leaders and followers were arrested and tortured. Second, after some hesitation and considerable internal debate, the movement decided not to enter the 1996 elections. A splinter group did run candidates, scoring very modest successes. Hamas had still flirted with the idea of participation and followed this with suggestions that it would actually compete in municipal elections (a stand that made Fatah repeatedly postpone them). Third, the movement generally scaled back its "resistance," anxious not to provoke PNA repression or popular ire for provoking harsh Israeli countermeasures. Finally, Islamists in general turned their emphasis from the political sphere—where the cards were temporarily stacked against them—to social, educational, and charitable work.

The eruption of the second intifada in 2000 constituted a turning point every bit as portentous for Hamas as the Oslo Accords. Suddenly "resistance" was the common denominator for all Palestinian groups, and Hamas quickly took a leadership role. As Hamas's activism and political relevance rose rapidly, Israel moved sharply against it, successfully assassinating a series of Hamas leaders. But here Hamas's work in building itself as an organization that could operate independently of the skills or charisma of particular individuals paid off handsomely—the devastation in the movement's senior ranks (and in some local cadres) seemed to leave no permanent scar on the movement's capabilities.

When the second intifada began to subside, Hamas had emerged with its political credentials in Palestinian society enhanced; the organization was far healthier than any of its rivals; and it had avoided any taint of association with a PNA that was seen by many Palestinians as not merely irrelevant and impotent but venal as well.

This is one of the central paradoxes of Hamas and its performance: even though it is dedicated to radically changing existing political realities, the movement is perhaps at its most impressive in the way it adapts itself and profits from those same realities.

The Political Platform of Hamas

Hamas had the luxury of developing its political positions in the late 1980s at a time when it was completely devoid of any political responsibilities. The new movement could strike the strongest rhetorical positions, outbid Fatah (then attempting simultaneously to rush out in front to lead the intifada, and enter into indirect negotiations with Israel), and take an uncompromising position on armed resistance. Has the political integration of Hamas led it to modify these positions? Perhaps, but so far only in an ambiguous manner that leaves plenty of escape routes back to its original positions.

The movement's founding ideological document—the 1988 Hamas Charter—is a rambling document, infused with religious references, unstinting dedication to the liberation of Palestine as an Islamic cause, invocations to resistance, and uncompromising positions on national issues. It includes fleeting and conspiratorial references to entities as tenuously connected to the Israeli–Palestinian conflict as the Rotary Club; the document also goes beyond merely framing the conflict as one between religious communities to shrill references to the "Protocols of the Elders of Zion" and Jewish Nazis and "merchants of war."[3] It is this last set of features in particular that is likely responsible for the evident embarrassment on the part of many Hamas leaders regarding the Charter; indeed, the document is almost never quoted by those in a movement not known for bashfulness or reticence in any other respect.

But if blatant bigotry and strange conspiracy theories have declined as themes, what of the movement's insistence on the religious nature of the conflict, its emphasis on resistance, and its uncompromising position on a solution? Between the publication of the Charter in 1988 and the 2005 decision to enter parliamentary elections, there were definite signs of evolution in all three areas, though general and reversible.

Hamas continued without interruption to define itself as a religious movement, identify Palestine as an Islamic cause, and use religious symbolism and rhetoric. Yet many Palestinian observers noted the movement edging away from these themes and began describing Hamas during this period as a nationalist movement in religious garb. That description almost certainly goes too far, but close observers of the movement noted that leaders and statements began tilting far more heavily toward casting the conflict with Israel in political rather than religious terms.[4]

If Hamas—as the Movement of Islamic Resistance—could not disavow Islam, neither could it abandon its commitment to resistance. But its emphasis certainly did shift. In part this was due to the new realities imposed by the Oslo Accords and the creation of the PNA, a Palestinian entity but one involved in coordinating security measures with Israel. Hamas declared that the Oslo Accords were illegitimate and that resistance was still justified, called for an end to Palestinian security cooperation with Israel, and carried out some of its most intensive campaigns of violence early in the Oslo process. But a combination of factors—the pressure of public opinion, the desire to avoid confrontation with the PNA, and the opportunities to build other aspects of the organization in the space provided by Palestinian autonomy—led to a gradual shift in the movement's short-term priorities. The movement continued sporadic action throughout the 1990s and leapt to action as soon as the second intifada broke out. But having found an ability to calibrate the level of its violent activities according to its calculation of the international and domestic environment, Hamas proved willing to consider temporary cessations of resistance. Israel refused to negotiate directly any cease-fire with the movement (gravitating between grudging cooperation and active sabotage of third-party efforts), but the PNA was willing to plead with Hamas to cease operations. As part of intra-Palestinian understandings, Hamas was willing to hold its fire unilaterally. Beginning in 2002, Hamas cooperated with a series of such efforts. Indeed, after that year, Hamas would generally hold Israel responsible for any eruption of violence. The clear implication (however much Hamas would have insisted otherwise) was that resistance is to be used for the present only in response to immediate provocation rather than as a tool for ending the occupation.

Finally, what of Hamas's uncompromising position that an Islamic state should be constructed in all of Palestine? The stance has never been repudiated, but Hamas has also advanced a suggestion at various times that it could accept an extended truce with Israel. The precise terms and length of that cease-fire have varied; at its most generous, Hamas leaders have suggested that the truce could extend for a generation.

All three of these trends—the vague and incomplete but still discernible downgrading of religion, resistance, and rejection of a negotiated settlement—were accentuated by Hamas's entry into the political process. That entry came with the movement's 2005 decision to enter parliamentary elections. The move to run candidates was a very difficult step for Hamas. Indeed, elections had been a periodic topic of intense internal debate since the Arab–Israeli negotiations begun in the early 1990s prompted various proposals to elect an interim body to administer Palestinian affairs. When the elections finally were held, in 1996, Hamas declined to participate, but the decision was more tactical than strategic. As talk of a second set of elections increased in Palestinian and international circles as a device for renewing the PNA's institutions, Hamas activists realized that the question might confront them again. Intensive discussions over what they termed the "politicization" of the movement took place among Hamas cadres and what such a step would mean for a movement that retained an armed wing and still dedicated itself to resistance. Neighboring Islamist movements were consulted for advice (and generally suggested that Hamas enter the elections if it wished but avoid winning them). In the end, Hamas proclaimed that it could pursue politics without abandoning resistance and negotiated an agreement with other PLO factions that facilitated its participation in the 2006 elections.

In assembling an electoral platform for the 2006 elections, Hamas drew on its vague ideological evolution. It drew on general Islamic symbols but downplayed almost all specific elements of its religious agenda, forswearing any attempt to Islamicize the legal or educational system. On resistance, the movement coupled its entrance in the campaign with an extended cease-fire. Hamas leaders began to stress (in a marked change in tone from its earlier days) that resistance could take many forms and that armed action was a means and not an end. Regarding Israel, Hamas's new skill at evasion led it to announce that it would enter into negotiations only on practical matters of daily life—and that its entrance into the PNA and the Parliament would require no more, since international relations were the domain of the PLO and its leader, not the PNA, which oversaw internal matters only. The completely moribund state of the Israeli–Palestinian peace process made it possible for Hamas to change the subject away from issues of war and peace to those of competence and corruption.

It was Hamas's ability to put forward a comprehensive reform platform that led to its victory. Here, the movement very consciously emulated the strategy of its sister movements elsewhere in the Arab world by greatly elevating the issue of political reform. Even more than elsewhere, this proved to be a winning formula—more so than Hamas bargained for, as Fatah's venality, disarray, and string of policy failures led to its humiliation at the polls.

Hamas's unexpected electoral success placed it in a position where it was forced beyond merely rhetorical navigation of its contrasting commitments. It tried to sketch out a consensus program. When the figure it designated to serve as prime minister, Isma'il Haniyya, presented his cabinet to the parliament in March 2006, many Palestinians observed that the tone and the content of the speech could have been written by a Fatah leader. How did moving from opposition to government affect the movement?

Hamas and the Regime—and As the Regime

For all the uniqueness of its situation prior to 2006, Hamas's relationships with official actors often differed from those of its fellow Islamist movements in the Arab world only by degree. Hamas was treated as a pariah internationally, especially among Western governments (regional regimes were often more ambivalent and some—such as the Syrian, Iranian, and Qatari—actually supported the movement).[5]

Domestically, the regime—actually both the PNA and Israel—saw the movement as a threat and was capable of using harsh tools against it. (Hamas was unusual for a Muslim Brotherhood movement primarily in its willingness to embrace violence—but it did so by insisting that it would only act against Israeli targets. While it actually did employ violence against Palestinian rivals, it was far more restrained and sometimes quite embarrassed and defensive in justifying the use of violence domestically.) The PNA itself vacillated among efforts to suppress, ignore, and co-opt Hamas, always mindful of the movement's strong standing in Palestinian society.

Thus Hamas's 2006 electoral victory brought a fundamental change: no longer could Hamas be treated as an opposition movement. It had the power to enter government. No party—international, regional, or domestic (and certainly not Hamas itself)—was certain how to react.

From March 2006 until June 2007, Hamas led the Palestinian cabinet, and for the latter part of that period with some participation from other factions in a broad national unity government. But throughout, Hamas' ability to govern was frustrated: it was unable to use its parliamentary majority due to a combination of Fatah obstructionism and Israeli arrests (a large number of its deputies and some of its ministers were arrested after the capture of Israeli soldier Gilad Shalit). The government was in a permanent state of fiscal crisis, denied most of its tax revenues (which under the Oslo arrangements were collected by Israel). International assistance plummeted; European donors were willing to pay only some salaries and then only so long as they went directly to civil servants, bypassing the Ministry of Finance. The president, who headed the rival Fatah movement, constantly threatened to upend the constitutional order in order to oust Hamas; Fatah activists organized strikes against the Hamas-dominated cabinet; and foreign governments (including the United States, Egypt, and Jordan) seemed interested in training and arming potential rivals.

The movement tried to be far more faithful to constitutional procedures and legal mechanisms than Fatah had ever been. But Hamas proved unable to follow this formula for long. International boycott, fiscal strangulation, intermittent violence with Fatah, and crippling strikes by public employees all made governing difficult. For the most part, Hamas appeared to hold its fire against Israeli targets, but it hardly did so in a way that inspired confidence or credibility in Israel (especially after the capture of Gilad Shalit). More seriously, Hamas hesitated in moving against (or even verbally distancing itself from) other Palestinian groups that did launch attacks.

Faced with crisis on every front, the movement's first impulse was to work again toward a national unity government, but that proved difficult indeed. A short-lived truce with Fatah in early 2007 made possible the creation of a national unity government, but that agreement began to fray quickly, especially on the streets of Gaza. In addition, because the arrangement was based on "respecting" international resolutions and PLO agreements, some within Hamas worried that the movement was getting sucked into a diplomatic process it deeply opposed. In an unusual step, a senior movement leader (Mahmud al-Zahhar) publicly criticized the program of the national unity government on the floor of the Parliament on precisely these grounds before bowing to party discipline and voting to grant it confidence.

The temporary success of unity efforts was undermined by a variety of international and domestic parties (the Quartet of parties mediating the

Israeli–Palestinian conflict, which largely refused to deal with the new government; elements of Fatah that continued to use violence against Hamas; and elements within Hamas itself who worried that the movement was getting trapped). In June 2007, as fighting between Hamas and Fatah in Gaza escalated, and some movement leaders concluded that there was a concerted effort to oust them from all positions of political power, Hamas seized power in Gaza (and was ousted in the West Bank).

Hamas now had complete control of the government, but only within Gaza. Moreover, its control did not extend to the borders, which were closed and monitored by Gaza's Egyptian and Israeli neighbors. Limited as it was, however, control of Gaza led to a deep transformation of the nature of Hamas as a movement. The signs were often missed by observers, who looked past organizational issues to search only for signs of ideological transformation and indication of acceptance of a two-state solution. On that diplomatic front there were only tantalizing and still extremely ambiguous hints of shifts. Hamas leaders would speak of a long-term armistice, but on terms that were diplomatically unpromising. They accepted a state on the 1967 lines, but made clear that they did not see that as a resolution of the conflict with Israel. There were plenty of hints of a shift but never one that cut a rhetorical route of retreat.

It was on the organizational level that Hamas changed far more clearly—its leaders took a series of steps that it had always claimed to seek to avoid, unmistakably building a governing apparatus in Gaza that elided the distinction between party and government. In an unambiguous fashion, Hamas came to take on some of the features that characterized Fatah in the 1990s; in this regard, Hamas's leaders began to resemble the people the movement's founders warned them against.

As made clear above, Hamas never rejected political participation in principle, but it entered the political field carefully and after a prolonged series of internal deliberations. When it won the parliamentary elections in January 2006, it took several steps to show it would not repeat Fatah's imperiousness and clumsiness: it publicly eschewed many of the perquisites of political authority and leaned toward technocratic expertise rather than political credentials in assigning some key cabinet positions.

But from the beginning there were signs of strain. While Hamas claimed that it could pursue "resistance" and politics simultaneously, increasingly its interest in governing led it to favor a temporary modus vivendi with Israel. In addition, the fidelity of Hamas to constitutional procedure began to decay as the constitutional order it defended seemed to offer only worthless paper guarantees that its electoral victory would lead to a measure of authority

The movement also claimed that it would avoid the mistake made by Fatah in melding itself to the PNA. In Hamas's eyes, Fatah had not only been deeply corrupted as a movement; it had also corrupted the Palestinian Authority (PA) itself (turning the proto-state into an instrument of party patronage and even brutal domination). And Fatah paid an even higher price in the process: it lost the ability to survive as a coherent movement outside of the power it exercised through the PA. Thus, when Israel turned against the PA in 2001 and 2002, Fatah found itself so wedded to the ministries, administrative bodies, and security services it had created that the movement began to disintegrate into ill-coordinated branches. In the intifada, Fatah found itself torn between "resistance" and governing, unable to accomplish either goal effectively. Hamas, by contrast, insisted that it would require high PA officials to resign their positions within the movement. That pledge was initially honored.

After June 2007, Hamas abandoned many of its pledges to maintain fidelity to resistance and legality. In a series of steps, Hamas thoroughly insinuated itself into all aspects of social, political, and economic life in Gaza and continued to seek a modus vivendi, however temporary and tension-filled, with Israel.

First, it abandoned most pretenses of living within the PNA's constitutional framework. It appointed ministers who executed their duties without having the legally required approval of the Legislative Council. When the speaker of the parliament was released by Israel in the West Bank ('Aziz al-Dwayk, elected on the Hamas ticket), Hamas was just as resistant as Fatah to having him resume his post (since it might have meant reviving a parliament in which Fatah had a working majority as long as most Hamas deputies were held by Israel).

Hamas also took sharp retaliatory actions against Fatah, closing the rival movement's offices, arresting its supporters, and even preventing most Fatah delegates from Gaza from leaving to attend the 2009 party congress in Bethlehem. It sought to bring nongovernmental organizations (NGOs) under its sway (for instance, flooding them with new pro-Hamas members in a bid to take over formerly nonpartisan bodies), tried to stack student council elections, and barred hostile newspapers.

Hamas turned the countermeasures taken by the West Bank government into ways to solidify the movement's control over the Gaza PA.

When most civil servants in Gaza still on the payroll of the Ramallah-based Ministry of Finance struck, Hamas filled the gap by hiring its own officials. When judges decided largely to continue following the Ramallah-based Supreme Judicial Council, Hamas created its own ad hoc judicial framework and hired its own judges. And when teachers struck, at the direction of their Ramallah-based union, Hamas dismissed most of them and hired its own. (When the union called off the strike after the Israeli military campaign in Gaza last winter, only some teachers were allowed to return.)

Hamas abandoned some of the pretense of building a security apparatus separate from the movement. The original seizure of power in Gaza in 2007 was more the work of the movement's militia than of the official security forces, belying Hamas's claim that this was a war between the legitimate PNA and Fatah. Hamas continued to use its armed wing to handle internal dissent, including a violent suppression of Salafi jihadists in the summer of 2009.

In all these respects, Hamas's actions had a familiar ring to them—they resembled those taken by Fatah when it originally built the PA in the 1990s. The resemblance even extended to the economic realm. In the 1990s, the economic arrangements of the Oslo Accords led to a system of PA monopolies and border crossings that were dominated by a group of top officials. The Oslo provisions regarding moving goods in and out of Palestinian areas were a dead letter for Gaza, but the tight restrictions imposed on the tiny strip by Israel and Egypt have led to an oddly similar political result as the Oslo arrangements: what went in and out (in terms of commodities and even currency notes) was monitored, licensed, controlled, and taxed by Hamas and the Gaza PNA. Officials used this system carefully to tax and regulate, constructing a fiscally sound administration in the midst of terrible economic devastation and international boycott.

The eerie resemblance between Hamas after 2007 and Fatah after 1994 began to extend to rhetoric. After the violent showdown with a Salafi jihadist group in Rafah, Hamas officials began to sound remarkably like Fatah officials after their violent clash with Hamas supporters in Gaza fifteen years earlier. In both instances, there was talk of the need to accept the legitimate security forces and the rule of law, a sharp denunciation of opponents for using weapons for purposes other than national goals, an attempt to blame the dissidents for initiating the violence, and dark, sometimes wildly implausible allegations that external hands were somehow involved in sparking the violence.

By tightening its grip on the reins of governmental control, eliding the distinction between public authority and private organization, developing an economic system effectively sustaining the party-state, and allowing a military wing to rise in influence, Hamas seemed to be following Fatah's pattern of the 1990s.

Hamas—a movement that prides itself as being the "un-Fatah" in almost every respect—would have bitterly rejected the argument that by its actions it was reincarnating its rival. In fact, there were several critical differences between the two movements. First, while Hamas managed the political economy of the Gaza Strip to solidify its hold on power, its members were implicated in only a fraction of the graft and venality that characterized Fatah during the Oslo years. Second, Hamas as a movement retained far more coherence than Fatah. Neither movement was free of divisions and rivalries, but Hamas was more able to make decisions and far more able to have internal dissidents accept their losses. Hamas has shown some ability to operate in accordance with its internally established procedures, even as it remains under siege and partly underground—in 2008, for instance, the movement was able to carry out internal elections of the kind that Fatah steadily postponed until it was jolted by its 2006 repudiation.

Hamas further differed from Fatah in the continued viability of its external leadership. While those Fatah leaders who chose to remain outside of Palestine were pushed to the edge of the movement, Hamas's political bureau, headquartered in Damascus, continued to play a leading role in diplomacy and decision making.

Finally, Hamas failed to imitate Fatah in its acceptance of a negotiated peace with Israel. But here the picture was complicated. The effectiveness of Hamas's entrenchment in Gaza certainly did obscure the long-term goals of the movement for the liberation of Palestine. As much as movement leaders insisted that Hamas's horizons were hardly limited to Gaza, they were unable to articulate any strategy in public for moving beyond their tiny party-state. In addition, they clearly pursued a cease-fire with Israel, even going beyond Fatah in willingness to impose it on other groups.

Hamas and the Palestinian Political Outlook

When viewed over the past two decades, Hamas's self-confidence is easy to understand—the movement has progressed enormously. What began as a small network of groups attempting to push Palestinian Islamists in the direction of active and violent resistance to Israel now is a deeply rooted movement that occupies the attention of the world's top decision makers. Hamas's leaders have been masters of improvisation in the past to great success, and they seem confident that there is no reason to be more purposive now.

But having achieved such success, the movement's leaders now find themselves confronted with some difficult choices about their priorities and even Hamas's identity. Hamas's leaders have promised their followers that they can resist Israel, govern, and reform Palestinian society on Islamic lines. But those goals increasingly pull the movement in very different directions. Since its startling triumph in Palestine's January 2006 elections and especially since its seizure of power in Gaza in June 2007, Hamas is showing signs of strain over which path to emphasize.

One path emphasizes the group's Islamist agenda. The Muslim Brotherhood, since its founding in Egypt 80 years ago, has always emphasized reforming the individual and the society along Islamic lines. For many years, Palestinian members of the Muslim Brotherhood emphasized personal and social reform at the expense of politics and the national struggle: Palestine could be liberated, they held, only after it had become more thoroughly Islamic. Hamas was founded by Brotherhood activists frustrated with such passivity and tired of taunting by more secular Palestinian nationalists that they were contributing nothing to the liberation struggle. The founders of Hamas insisted that there was no need to postpone resistance and that they could take direct action against the Israeli occupation while pursuing Islamicization of Palestinian society.

Yet since it won the 2006 parliamentary elections, Hamas has given mixed signals about its religious agenda. Religious issues were deliberately played down in the electoral campaign, and the group did not use its parliamentary majority to rush through any religiously inspired education. It kept the existing school curriculum, moving only to modestly expand the classroom time devoted to religious instruction. But since its seizure of power in Gaza in June 2007, some movement activists have shown impatience: they seek to use Hamas's dominant political position to bring Palestine's legal framework and public life into line with Islamic values and teachings.

A second path for Hamas emphasizes resistance—literally, the movement's middle name. Hamas was born in an effort to participate in what Palestinians term their "revolution." While a latecomer to armed action, the Oslo process left Hamas as the most prominent movement dedicated to continued resistance. During the second intifada, when some other movements (including parts of Fatah) returned to violent activity, Hamas still posed as the vanguard of Palestinian resistance to Israel.

Yet as with its Islamist agenda, Hamas's pursuit of resistance has been eclipsed since it began entrenching itself in government. From March 2006, when it formed the PNA cabinet, until June 2007, when the PNA split in two, Hamas came under enormous international pressure to renounce violence. It responded with a half-measure: while it completely rejected the international calls in theory, in practice it held its own violent activities to a minimum. Since June 2007, this pattern has actually become more pronounced. Hamas has generally sought a cease-fire with Israel, while disavowing any intention of reaching a permanent settlement or disarming. It has, of course, fired rockets from Gaza—but with the declared aim of securing a cease-fire on more favorable terms. Moreover, when an indirectly negotiated cease-fire has prevailed, Hamas has not only largely observed it but also enforced it on other factions.

Hamas's third path is that of governing. For a normal political party, this would be the most preferred course of action: to run in elections, seek and win a majority, and then implement its preferred policies. But Hamas has not seen itself as simply a political party. Indeed, it dithered for over a decade before finally deciding to enter the parliamentary elections of 2006; after it won an overwhelming parliamentary majority, Hamas still sought to avoid governing alone, preferring a coalition. Even when they took office, Hamas ministers still prided themselves on disavowing the perquisites of official position (ostentatiously taking public transportation to work on occasion, for instance).

This reluctance to enjoy power was not merely expressed on a symbolic level. Hamas leaders present their movement as the un-Fatah in every respect. While Fatah melded itself to the PNA Authority after it was formed in 1994, Hamas made clear it would follow a different path. Fatah had become addicted to political power, mired in corruption, and unable to sustain itself with any coherence and purpose when the Palestinian Authority came under Israeli assault. Fatah leaders showed a proclivity for writing the law as they wished and then violating it when it did not suit their needs. Hamas leaders in 2006 promised to follow a different path: they would reluctantly govern, but they would insist upon a distinction between party and government. The Basic Law—the Palestinian Authority constitution—would be scrupulously observed. Some senior ministers even went so far as to disavow statements by Hamas leaders outside the government, claiming that only the cabinet could speak for the Palestinian Authority.

But Hamas took a very different direction after seizing power in Gaza in June 2007. Suddenly the movement appeared far less reluctant to wield political power. It fought, both effectively and ruthlessly to retain it, at least in the Gaza Strip. No longer the un-Fatah, Hamas has harassed political opponents, sought to bring civil society under its sway, bent (and even broken) the law when it suited its purposes, and forgotten the distinction between movement and government.

Hamas has tried to date to follow all three paths at the same time: it has promised Islam, resistance, and good government. But what to do when these pull in different directions—as they increasingly do? How can it pursue resistance against Israel without endangering its ability to govern Gaza? Can it stress greater religious observance without making its rule a bit more onerous and exposing itself to international criticism and even embarrassment?

The movement's ideology as well as its structure would seem to suggest that governance is a means and not an end; the ends are Islamicization and liberation through resistance. But increasingly Hamas is behaving in precisely the opposite manner. Since its decision to enter the parliamentary election, Hamas has chosen the path of governing whenever there was a fork in the road. It has, for instance, downplayed Islamic law, held its fire against Israel, suppressed jihadist groups, and dug itself deeply into governing positions in Gaza.

For the self-styled "Islamic Resistance Movement" to place governing above Islam and resistance may seem to be a surprising choice—and indeed, it is, for many Hamas followers and observers. The movement's leaders seem to wish to show that they can rule Gaza efficiently and pursue international diplomacy, even if it means postponing other parts of the group's mission.

For the short-term future, all indications are that the emphasis on governing will continue. But the constituencies for religion and resistance remain strong. Hamas leaders have shown an impressive ability to work out differences in the past and there is no reason to believe that dissidence about short-term goals will lead to schism. But whether the newfound interest in governing will transform and even tame the movement has yet to be decided.

CHAPTER 8

Conclusion

Arab parliaments are a frustrating arena for political activity, and Islamist movements are now discovering precisely why. They must decide whether the fruits of parliamentary participation outweigh the frustrations. The movements examined in this book are poised to continue their parliamentary activities, but they are doing so with more realistic expectations of the limitations in this strategy.

Islamist movement leaders and their extensive grassroots bases have been disappointed in the return on their investment in political participation. While they have many successes to claim, their involvement has failed in three regards:

- They had hoped to break through barriers of restricted political pluralism and effect true reform, redistributing power between ruling elites and opposition movements.

- They sought constitutional and legislative amendments that would increase legislative institutions' power relative to that of the executive, and they wanted to institute effective systems of checks and balances.

- Some wanted to overcome a history of conflict with intellectual elites and form flexible alliances with secular opposition movements; others could not escape an absolutist ideological approach to politics.

Islamists also wanted to expand the scope of religion in the public sphere and foster an organic link between the Islamization of society and political participation. But their actions led political elites to sever their connections with Islamic proselytizing and charity activities, which form the backbone of the Islamists' social role and are the mainstay of their popular and electoral bases. The increased focus on political participation simultaneously led to attacks from less politically oriented Islamist forces, which accused the politically active groups of pragmatism, implying they had strayed from the true faith and Islamic law.

Challenges of Islamist Participation

The Islamists' less impressive showing—recent electoral losses in some countries and steadily deteriorating prospects in others—has sparked discussions about future strategies within some Islamist movements. The groups face three major challenges.

1. *The first major challenge:* Coming up with new arguments that can convince their popular bases that, despite poor payback in the short run, they must persist in participatory politics.

An analysis of recent interviews with and statements by prominent Islamist figures reveals two basic categories of justificatory argument. The first stresses the value of the mechanisms of political participation, especially in activities related to parliament and legislation, by focusing on how such action allows movements to counter the maneuvers of ruling elites and their security agencies. It also makes clear that participating in parliaments allows for regular public broadcast of Islamist demands, which helps preserve movement cohesion and sustain popular support. Participation has shortfalls, but it is highly effective in offering Islamists a wider audience for their ideals and providing legitimate ways to oppose elites' efforts to constrain Islamist participation.

The other set of arguments focuses on what we might describe as maximalist motives inspired by Islamists' desire to prove themselves to be responsible politicians, committed to participatory politics under all circumstances (including successive setbacks) and dedicated to advocating peaceful change and incremental reform. A parliamentary strategy effectively refutes criticisms and suspicions of Islamist motives and goals harbored by ruling elites and secular opposition movements.

We further note that the more precarious the situation of an Islamist movement, the more it tends toward the minimalist position. This is increasingly the case with the Egyptian Muslim Brotherhood when tensions between it and the government intensify. By contrast, the more relaxed the relationship between an Islamist movement and the government, the more it tends toward the maximalist position, as with the Constitutional Movement in Kuwait.

2. ***The second major challenge:*** Finding a sustainable and practical balance between the requirements of political participation and the demands of ideological commitment. The realities of restricted pluralism and the ruling elites' domination of the political system strategically and tactically compel Islamists to adopt compromising positions on major social issues (although the nature of these necessary compromises varies considerably). These same realities also compel them to develop pragmatic understandings with ruling elites and/or secular opposition movements to increase the paybacks from political participation. However, Islamists are torn between this need and their ideological convictions; they have a reasonable fear of sacrificing the distinctiveness of their political rhetoric and programs and alienating broad, influential segments of their supporters.

Striking a balance between pragmatism and ideological commitment grows increasingly difficult, if not impossible, when political participation produces unsatisfactory results. We have seen two reactions in play. One is to retract earlier compromise positions and revert to ideological stances. For example, the draft platform of Egypt's Muslim Brotherhood called for the creation of a religious body with legislative oversight functions and opposed, on the basis of Islamic jurisprudence, the candidacy of a Copt or a woman as head of state. The other course, followed by the Justice and Development Party (PJD) in Morocco, is to engage in a long debate on the essential political component of Islamist movements, the relative weight of political pragmatism with respect to ideology, and the priorities of political participation. The strategic ambivalence of such an extensive debate could prove costly to the movement (but would be fascinating for the scholar and observer).

3. ***The third major challenge:*** Rethinking the substance of the relationship between Islamist movements' proselytizing and political components, then devising the best possible structures for organizing those components institutionally. The opening of opportunities for political participation during the past few decades has

led some Islamist movements to introduce a functional separation between proselytizing and politics. They do so by creating political parties, fronts, and associations that are institutionally autonomous, then allowing those new entities to attach increasing importance to political participation as a means for promoting change and reform. On the other hand, it is unclear whether combining proselytizing and politics is a disadvantage under conditions of closed or limited opportunities for political participation and sustained political repression.

Growing in Crisis

Islamist leaders boast about their patience and long-range vision; they insist that they are not overly seduced by short-term opportunities or discouraged by momentary setbacks. But in the first decade of the twenty-first century, many of them seized the moment and focused their energies on parliamentary elections. In Egypt the Muslim Brotherhood launched its most intensive election campaign in the 2005 parliamentary elections. In Morocco the PJD sensed that it might be able to form the cabinet. In Jordan the Islamic Action Front (IAF) dropped its electoral boycott and returned to parliament. In Palestine Hamas entered its first parliamentary elections and won them. In Kuwait Hadas joined a cross-ideological coalition to force electoral reform. And in Yemen, al-Islah switched from junior partner of the governing party to the leader of the opposition.

With the exception of Hamas, none of these movements sought a parliamentary majority; even Hamas showed signs of having given little thought to the possibility of victory. The movements sought to run, but either deliberately sought to avoid governing or anticipated at best participating in a coalition. The modesty of these goals was based not on any modesty of the Islamist vision but on a sound reading of two aspects of the prevailing political environment in most Arab countries. First, although Arab parliaments are generally democratic and powerful on paper, in practice they are limited in both respects. Most are dominated by a governing party or a fragmented group of parties and independents, many of them deeply co-opted. Their paper powers over legislation and government oversight rarely are exercised effectively. Second, existing regimes generally see Islamist movements as the most effective and threatening opposition. Arab regimes are sometimes willing to outmaneuver Islamist adversaries rather than fully suppress them, but those same regimes are quite capable of showing a far less subtle and even brutal side if Islamists make too much of the resultant openings. Most movements had only a short-term reach; winning a parliamentary majority and using it to govern were beyond them. Once again, Hamas was the exception that proved the rule. Most other movements were far more limited in their goals.

But even more modest goals were not often met. The electoral opportunities delivered far less than the movement's leaders—and their most enthusiastic followers—hoped. The Egyptian Brotherhood formed the most powerful, cohesive, and disciplined opposition in the country's parliamentary history but had few legislative achievements. The Moroccan PJD was kept out of the cabinet. The Jordanian IAF saw its representation diminish and the unity of its ranks severely threatened. Hamas was unable to use its parliamentary majority to do more than run the Palestinian Authority cabinet for a year. Kuwait's Hadas faced electoral embarrassment. Yemen's al-Islah discovered that opposition in an authoritarian system offers even scantier authority than supporting the government.

Is participation in an Arab parliament meaningless? How do the movements themselves evaluate their experience? Why did they enter the parliamentary fray in the first place? Islamist leaders are fairly consistent across countries in explaining their motivations for running in parliamentary elections. First, campaigns allow them an opportunity to reach broader audiences with their message of religion and reform. When they win seats, that campaign soap box is converted into a protected institutional base for issuing proclamations, statements, and proposals that can reach broader domestic (and even international) audiences. Parliamentary seats mean greater media access, greater freedom of travel, official status (and thus a cover for contact with foreign diplomats), and the ability to introduce draft laws and question ministers.

Second, participation in parliamentary elections allows Islamist leaders to present their movements as having broad constituencies and many supporters. Vocal opponents of existing regimes can produce powerful critiques of rulers' policies and practices, but few other than Islamists can show that their critique has any persuasive power outside of seminars and salons. Parliamentary elections generally reward those who are well-organized and disciplined; this has made them favorable turf for Islamist mobilization.

Third, Islamist leaders often speak of participation in elections as more a duty than an opportunity. In their eyes, existing rulers are often unable or unwilling to pursue the public interest, so societies turn to the Islamist alternative expecting virtuous leaders to guide them to better solutions. In their own view, Islamists are pulled into parliamentary politics by their own people, not propelled by their own ambitions. Abandoning the political field would encourage a surrender to despair.

Fourth, parliamentary politics offers the opportunity to develop a new set of skills. Over the past half century (and sometimes longer), Islamist movements have learned to organize their members, educate sympathizers, serve youths, support the poor, provide access to medical care, and support Islamic international causes. Parliamentary politics, however, is a distinct field. Elections require cultivation of expertise in canvassing, electoral advertising and sloganeering, and mobilization. Participation in parliament requires those skilled in research, drafting, and investigation. Both elections and parliamentary activity lead Islamist movements to cultivate the abilities to work with potential allies, forge coalitions, and develop political programs. Islamist movements that move more heavily into parliamentary elections and legislative activity enrich and broaden their experience and develop new avenues for pursuing their religious and reform agenda.

Islamists are acutely conscious of the need to improve their performance in Arab parliaments and realize that progress toward democratic reform will continue to be meager. Morocco's PJD saw its popularity dwindle in the 2007 elections—even though it gained four additional parliamentary seats, bringing its bloc up to 46 out of 324 seats. The party found itself eliminated again in the Independence Party's ruling government coalition, but it is now actively campaigning to extend its base of support to new sectors of society. In particular, it is targeting the urban middle class and the rural poor, both of which had been outside its reach and were more attracted to left-wing parties (particularly the Socialist Federation, a partner in the ruling coalition). Toward this end, the PJD is pursuing three strategies. Its platform gives greater priority to economic and social policies over religious and identity concerns; its parliamentary bloc is pushing more intensively for comprehensive constitutional reform aimed at gradually reducing the powers of the monarchical executive and promoting a more effective balance of power; and its outreach includes confidence-building with the left through partial alliances and/or power-sharing at the municipal level in some areas.

The Kuwaiti Islamic Constitutional Movement and the Yemeni Islah are similarly devoting greater attention to matters of constitutional reform. The Egyptian Muslim Brotherhood is working to reach an understanding with the ruling elite over the conditions for Islamist participation in politics. In Egypt, such an understanding could ease tensions between the government and the Brotherhood.

If this is what Islamist movements seek to do—communicate to new audiences, show the movement's strength, answer its people's needs, and develop new skills—then how much have the efforts of the past decade or two accomplished? The first goal—communicating to new audiences—unquestionably has been met. Islamist movements now find themselves more able to (and more skilled at) reaching beyond their own followers to broader publics, skeptical liberals, and even foreign diplomats and researchers. They have attracted more attention and found ways to address each of these groups.

The second goal—illustrating strength—also has been achieved, but sometimes at considerable cost. Islamist groups have communicated very effectively that they have followings; if anything, they now have a more imposing image than they might deserve. Although they speak for a significant part of the society, none can claim a majority. Yet the feeling that they would win any free election remains widespread. They sometimes pay a high price for this reputation. Existing regimes can come to see Islamist movements as a threat when they focus on elections and parliamentary activity. In Egypt, the 2005 election was followed by a wave of repression; the PJD remains an outcast with regard to government formation in Morocco; the Jordanian regime increasingly sees the IAF as a security threat; and some Islamist leaders say privately that Hamas has paid a very high price indeed for winning the 2006 parliamentary elections.

Islamist leaders have the least to show for their efforts in meeting the third goal, serving constituents. The movements have entered politics, developed platforms and drafted laws, questioned ministers, and aired scandals—and had little concrete to show for all these efforts. Sometimes the foot soldiers of the movements have found themselves harassed, arrested, or detained. On most occasions, Islamist parliamentarians find themselves outvoted.

Finally, in the area of developing new skills and improving their performance, Islamist movements have been remarkably successful, but the fruits of that success are rarely tasted. Islamist campaigners are often the most professional; Islamist parliamentarians often the most serious and dedicated; and Islamist political strategists often the most able to sketch out steps that go beyond the next twenty-four hours. But the inability to deploy most of these political skills in the service of other movement objectives might be the Achilles' heel of the parliamentary effort.

In sum, Islamist movements in Arab parliaments have shown themselves to be able and articulate, but they have not effectively reassured regimes nor produced concrete achievements. Given this uneven record, we are forced to speculate that the coming years likely will see a limited de-emphasis of parliamentary strategies. The movements studied here are too involved in politics, too proud of their achievements, and too invested in what they have built to beat a wholesale retreat from politics. We expect Islamists to compete in subsequent parliamentary elections. But we also expect that they will place fewer of their hopes (and, in some countries, perhaps fewer of their energies) in a parliamentary strategy, instead contenting themselves for the foreseeable future to reap the limited gains that parliamentary activity offers without viewing it as the sole or even primary strategy for realizing their vision of Islamic reform.

Notes

CHAPTER 1

1. One important exception was Richard P. Mitchell, *The Society of Muslim Brothers* (London: Oxford University Press, 1969).

2. One of the best examples of this approach—partly because it combined a broad ideological approach with a more empirical political analysis—was John Esposito and John Voll, *Islam and Democracy* (London: Oxford University Press, 1996).

3. The leading examples of this newer work are Carrie Rosefsky Wickham, *Mobilizing Islam: Religion, Activism and Political Change in Egypt* (New York: Columbia University Press, 2002); Quintan Wiktorowicz, *The Management of Islamic Activism: Salafis, The Muslim Brotherhood, and State Power in Jordan* (Albany: State University of New York, 2001); and Janine A. Clark, *Islam, Charity, and Activism: Middle-Class Networks and Social Welfare in Egypt* (Baltimore, Md.: Johns Hopkins University Press, 2003).

4. See Judy Barsalou, "Islamists at the Ballot Box: Findings from Egypt, Jordan, Kuwait, and Turkey," United States Institute of Peace Special Report no. 144, July 2005. See also Jillian Schwedler, *Faith in Moderation* (Cambridge: Cambridge University Press, 2006).

CHAPTER 2

1. We have taken part in these debates. See Nathan J. Brown, Amr Hamzawy, and Marina Ottaway, "Islamist Movements and the Democratic Process in the Arab World: Exploring Gray Zones," Carnegie Endowment for International Peace, Carnegie Paper no. 67, March 2006, http://www.carnegieendowment.org/files/cp_67_grayzones_final.pdf; Amr Hamzawy, Marina Ottaway, and Nathan J. Brown, "What Islamists Need to Be Clear About: The Case of the Egyptian Muslim Brotherhood," Carnegie Endowment for International Peace, Policy Outlook, February 2007, http://www.carnegieendowment.org/files/ottaway_brown_hamzawy_islamists_final.pdf.

2. Amr Hamzawy and Nathan J. Brown, "Can Egypt's Troubled Elections Produce a More Democratic Future," Carnegie Endowment for International Peace, Policy Outlook, December 2005, http://www.carnegieendowment.org/files/PO24.brown.hamzawy.FINAL1.pdf.

3. One of us (Nathan J. Brown) has explored the relationship between elections and semiauthoritarianism in "Dictatorship and Democracy through the Prism of Arab Elections," in Nathan J. Brown, ed., *The Dynamics of Democratization: Dictatorship, Development, and Diffusion,* forthcoming.

4. In Egypt, the most notable movements sprang from the thought of Sayyid Qutb, a Brotherhood leader who viewed existing political and social systems as non-Islamic. The current leaders of the Brotherhood repudiate the most extreme elements of Qutb's ideology but they have not disowned Qutb himself, provoking suspicions among some movement critics.

5. There is a growing body of work on the reemergence of the Brotherhood. Among the leading writings in English are Carrie Wickham, *Mobilizing Islam: Religion, Activism, and Political Change in Egypt* (New York: Columbia University Press, 2002), and Mona El-Ghobashy, "The Metamorphosis of the Egyptian Muslim Brothers," *International Journal of Middle East Studies,* vol. 37, issue 3, 2005, p. 391.

6. For a complete record of seats contested and won by the Muslim Brotherhood in the People's Assembly elections since 1976, see Appendix A.

7. We draw here on our earlier discussion of the draft platform in "The Draft Platform of the Egyptian Muslim Brotherhood: Foray into Political Integration or Retreat into Old Positions," Carnegie Endowment for International Peace, Carnegie Paper no. 89, January 2008, http://www.carnegieendowment.org/files/cp89_muslim_brothers_final.pdf.

8. "Intikhabat (2005) al-ikhwan yaktasihun wa-l-watani mahzur jamahiriyan" [The 2005 Elections: The Brotherhood Sweeps and the National Democratic Party Fails Popularly], Nuwwab Ikhwan, January 20, 2007, http://www.nowabikhwan.com/Index.aspx?ctrl=press&ID=15d18904-d747-4f05-9eb1-6b3471a5100c.

9. Noha Antar, "The Muslim Brotherhood's Success in the Legislative Elections in Egypt 2005," report produced by EuroMeSCo, paper no. 51, October 2006, p. 14; and "al-barnamaj al-intikhabi li-l-ikhwan al-muslimin 2005" [The 2005 Electoral Program for the Muslim Brotherhood], Ikhwan Online, http://www.ikhwanonline.com/Article.asp?ArtID=15548&SecID=0.

10. "Al-ikhwan al-muslimun al-misriyyun yudashinun sahifatahum al-jadida bi-hujum dar 'ala hizb al-tajammu' al-yasari wa yatahimun al-wafd bi-annahu mikhlib qat al-hukuma" [The Egyptian Muslim Brotherhood Inaugurate Their New Newspaper With Malicious Attacks on the Leftist Tajammu' Party and Accuse the Wafd of Being "in the Clutches of the Government"], *Al-Sharq al-Awsat,* January 3, 2003, http://www.aawsat.com/details.asp?section=4&article=144808&issueno=8802.

11. "Egypt's Muslim Brothers: Confrontation or Integration?" International Crisis Group, Middle East/North Africa Report no. 76, June 18, 2008, pp. 12–13.

12. "Reforming Egypt: In Search of a Strategy," International Crisis Group, Middle East/North Africa Report no. 46, October 4, 2005, pp. 19–20.

13. 'Isam al-'Iryan, "Towards the Renaissance," *Al-Ahram Weekly,* no. 771, December 1–7, 2005, http://weekly.ahram.org.eg/2005/771/op71.htm.

14. Ahmad al-Khatib, "Al-ikhwan yas'un li-l-tahaluf ma'a al-mu'arada fi muwajahat al-hazr al-dusturi" [The Brotherhood Seeks to Ally With the Opposition in Challenging the Constitutional Prohibition], *al-Masry al-Youm,* April 1, 2007, http://www.almasry-alyoum.com/article2.aspx?ArticleID=53198.

15. Hisham Salam, "Opposition Alliances and Democratization in Egypt," United States Institute of Peace, 2008, http://www.usip.org/print/resources/opposition-alliances-and-democratization-egypt.

16. For a general overview of the parliamentary priorities and activities of the Muslim Brotherhood for the People's Assembly of 2000–2005, see "hisad al-dawra al-rabi'a li-nuwwab al-ikhwan" [The Harvest of the Fourth Session for the Brotherhood's Deputies], Ikhwan Online, http://www.ikhwanonline.com/article.asp?artid=7777&secid=251; 'Abd al-Mu'iz Muhammad, "Al-dawra al-rabi'a li-l-barlaman al-misri . . . nazra taqwimiyya" [The Fourth Session of the Egyptian Parliament . . . an Assessment], Ikhwan Online, http://www.ikhwanonline.com/article.asp?artid=7528&secid=251; 'Abd al-Mu'iz Muhammad, "Nuwwab al-ikhwan yaqimun al-dawra al-khamisa li-l-barlaman al-misri" [The Brotherhood's Deputies Begin the Fifth Session of the Egyptian Parliament], Ikhwan Online, http://www.ikhwanonline.com/article.asp?artid=12983&secid=251; and for the 2005–2010 People's Assembly, see "Kutlat al-ikhwan . . . arba' sanawat min al-'ata'" [The Brotherhood's Parliamentary Bloc . . . Four Years of Performance], Nuwwab Ikhwan, August 29, 2009, http://www.nowabikhwan.com/index.aspx?ctrl=press&id=4e661d31-5fad-422e-b98e-38abee7168e4; Muhammad Husayn, "Kutlat al-ikhwan . . . hisad mashraf wa zakhm raqabi" [The Brotherhood's Parliamentary Bloc . . . Impressive Harvest and Intensive Oversight], Nuwwab Ikhwan, June 27, 2007, http://www.nowabikhwan.com/index.aspx?ctrl=press&id=d19436fa-2bf1-47d3-9cf3-c3b9a0cfba07.

17. Only once (in the 1990 elections) did the movement decide to join with most opposition movements to boycott the People's Assembly elections totally; this came in response to severe government restrictions.

18. "Hisad al-dawra al-rabi'a li-nuwwab al-ikhwan" [The Harvest of the Fourth Session for the Brotherhood's Deputies].

19. "Kutlat al-ikhwan . . . arba' sanawat min al-'ata'" [The Brotherhood's Parliamentary Bloc . . . Four Years of Performance], Nuwwab Ikhwan, August 29, 2009, http://www.nowabikhwan.com/index.aspx?ctrl=press&id=4e661d31-5fad-422e-b98e-38abee7168e4.

20. For example, the 2004 Initiative for Reform expressed a need for "Canceling ill-reputed laws, especially the Emergency Law, Political Parties Law, Public Prosecutor's Law of Practicing Political Rights, Press Law, Syndicates Law and others." For general background on initiative see Gamal Essam El-Din, "Brotherhood Steps Into the Fray," *Al-Ahram Weekly,* no. 681, March 11–17, 2004, http://

weekly.ahram.org.eg/2004/681/eg3.htm; and Dr. Sayed Mahmoud al-Qumni, "The Muslim Brotherhood's Initiative as a Reform Program: A Critical Review," paper presented at the Brookings Institution Conference on Islamic Reform, Washington, D.C., October 5–6, 2004.

21. "Reforming Egypt: In Search of a Strategy," International Crisis Group, Middle East/North Africa Report No. 46, October 4, 2005, p. 19.

22. 'Abd al-Mu'iz Muhammad, "Madha qadama al-ikhwan fi-l-barlaman?!" [What Did the Muslim Brothers Present in the Parliament?!], Ikhwan Online, September 18, 2005, http://www.ikhwanonline.com/Article.asp?ArtID=14480&SecID=529.

23. There are 12,000 judges in Egypt for more than 35,000 polling stations; see Gamal Essam El-Din, "Debate Heats Up Over Article 76," Al-Ahram Weekly, no. 740, April 28–May 4, 2005, http://weekly.ahram.org.eg/2005/740/eg7.htm. The Brotherhood Bloc stressed that the overseeing committee should be headed by the president of the Supreme Constitutional Court and should include four judges of the Court of Cassation. Its supervisory role should include the correction of voters' lists, and extend to all stages of the elections. See Muhammad, "Madha qadama al-ikhwan fi-l-barlaman?!" [What Did the Muslim Brothers Present in the Parliament?!].

24. 'Abd al-Mu'iz Muhammad, "Al-ikhwan wa-l-dawra al-thaniyya . . . ma'rakat al-ta'dilat al-dusturiyya" [The Brothers and the Second Session: Battle of the Constitutional Amendments], Ikhwan Online, July 7, 2009, http://www.ikhwanonline.com/Article.asp?ArtID=51222&SecID=251.

25. "Huquqiyyun yarsadun tajawuzat wa intihakat bi-marakiz al-iqtira'" [Jurists Watch Out for Excesses and Violations at Polling Stations], al-Arabiya, March 26, 2007, http://www.alarabiya.net/articles/2007/03/26/32904.html.

26. For our analysis of the constitutional amendments, see Nathan J. Brown, Michele Dunne, and Amr Hamzawy, "Egypt's Controversial Constitutional Amendments," Carnegie Endowment for International Peace, Web Commentary, March 2007, http://www.carnegieendowment.org/files/egypt_constitution_webcommentary01.pdf.

27. Adil Sabri, "Nusus ta'dilat dustur misr wa atharaha al-mutawaqa'a" [The Texts of Constitutional Amendments in Egypt and Their Expected Impacts], Islam Online, December 2006, http://www.islamonline.net/servlet/Satellite?c=ArticleA_C&cid=1168265499761&pagename=Zone-Arabic-News%2FNWALayout.

28. Khalid Abu Bakr, "Abu al-futuh: al-ikhwan akbar mutadarrir min ta'dil al-dustur" [Abu al-Futuh: The Muslim Brothers Are Harmed Most by the Amendment of the Constitution], Ikhwan Online, December 26, 2006, http://www.islamonline.net/servlet/Satellite?c=ArticleA_C&cid=1168265498797&pagename= Zone-Arabic-News%2FNWALayout.

29. Bakr, "Abu al-futuh: al-ikhwan akbar mutadarrir min ta'dil al-dustur" [Abu al-Futuh: The Muslim Brothers Are Harmed Most by the Amendment of the Constitution].

30. 'Abd al-Satar Ibrahim and 'Abduh Zayna, "Misr: a'la lajna barlamaniyya tuwafiq 'ala muqtarahat mubarak bi-ta'dil al-dustur wa siyaghat al-mawwad al-jadida" [Egypt: The Highest Parliamentary Committee Agrees With Mubarak's Suggestions of Constitutional Amendments and the Drafting of New Articles], Al-Sharq

al-Awsat, January 9, 2007, http://www.aawsat.com/details.asp?section=4&article=400769&issueno=10269.

31. "Bayan hawla madd al-'amal bi-qanun al-tawari' 3 sanawat ukhra" [Statement on Extending the Emergency Law for Another 3 Years], Ikhwan Online, April 1, 2003, http://www.ikhwanonline.com/Article.asp?ArtID=247&SecID=0.

32. Ahmad Salih and Hani Adil, "Al-tafasil al-kamila li-jalasat al-barlaman bi-madd al-'amal bi-qanun al-tawari'" [Complete Details for the Parliamentary Session on Extending the Emergency Law], Ikhwan Online, May 26, 2008, http://www.ikhwanonline.com/Article.asp?ArtID=37555&SecID=0.

33. Muhammad Husayn, "hasan yastajawib al-dakhiliyya wa yatahimha bi-qatl al-misriyin 'amdan" [Hasan Questions the Interior Ministry and Accuses It of Deliberately Killing Egyptians], Nuwwab Ikhwan, November 14, 2008, http://www.nowabikhwan.com/index.aspx?ctrl=press&ID=5df3ffe2-9f73-447a-bedf-04b6484e37a0.

34. Muhammad, "Madha qadama al-ikhwan fi-l-barlaman?!" [What Did the Muslim Brothers Present in the Parliament?!].

35. "Qanun ikhwani li-ilgha' habs al-sahafiyin wa-l-atiba' al-misriyyin" [A Brotherhood Law to Cancel the Detention of Egyptian Journalists and Doctors], Ikhwan Online, http://www.ikhwanonline.com/Article.asp?ArtID=4993&SecID=250.

36. Amira Howeidy, "The Battle Is Not Over," *Al-Ahram Weekly,* no. 801, June 29–July 5 2006, http://weekly.ahram.org.eg/2006/801/fr2.htm.

37. 'Abd al-Mu'iz Muhammad, "Al-barlaman al-misri yuqirr qanun al-sulta al-qada'iyya wasat rafd al-ikhwan wa-l-mu'arada" [The Egyptian Parliament Approves the Law of Judicial Authority Amidst the Rejection of the Muslim Brotherhood and the Opposition], Ikhwan Online, June 27, 2006, http://www.ikhwanonline.com/Article.asp?ArtID=21502&SecID=0; "Subhi yuqadim mashru'an jadidan li-qanun al-sulta al-qada'iyya" [Subhi Presents a New Draft for the Law of Judicial Authority], Nuwwab Ikhwan, July 8 2007, http://www.nowabikhwan.com/index.aspx?ctrl=press&ID=5713b819-11f0-4901-b1f7-fb4d68c297da.

38. 'Abd al-Mu'iz Muhammad, "Awwal qanun mushtarak bayn al-ikhwan wa-l-jabha al-wataniyya 'an tanzim al-ahzab al-siyasiyya" [The First Joint Law Between the Muslim Brotherhood and the National Front on Organizing Political Parties], Ikhwan Online, June 13, 2006, http://www.ikhwanonline.com/Article.asp?ArtID=21151&SecID=250.

39. "Muwafaqa 'ala mashru' qanun ikhwani li-ilgha' al-habs al-ihtiyati" [Agreement on a Proposed Brotherhood Law to Abolish Preventive Detention], Nuwwab Ikhwan, April 29, 2007, http://www.nowabikhwan.com/index.aspx?ctrl=press&ID=06a183a7-a5ab-4ec7-a67c-0a5c22a77ec9.

40. "Mashru' qanun li-munahida al-ta'dhib bi-misr" [Anti-Torture Draft Law in Egypt], Ikhwan Online, January 4, 2004, http://www.ikhwanonline.com/Article.asp?ArtID=3948&SecID=0.

41. 'Abdullah Shehata, "Bayumi yu'add mashru' qanun yasmah bi-huriyat insha'at al-jam'iyyat al-ahliyya" [Bayumi Prepares a Draft Law Granting the Freedom to Establish Civil Associations], Nuwwab Ikhwan, December 24, 2009,

http://www.nowabikhwan.com/index.aspx?ctrl=press&ID=87539445-0784-4eb6-b3e6-42c7cd37d446.

42. Ahmad Salih, "100 na'ib yarfadun qanun man' al-tazahur fi duwar al-'abada" [100 Deputies Oppose a Law Prohibiting Demonstrations in Houses of Worship], Ikhwan Online, April 2, 2008, http://www.ikhwanonline.com/Article. asp?ArtID=36060&SecID=250; Ahmad al-Bahiri, "Jadal azhari hawl mashru' qanun «man'a al-muzahirat fi-l-masajid» . . . wa-'ulama' ya'tabirun munaqishat barlamaniyan khatwa li-«kabt al-huriyat»" [Debate in al-Azhar Around the Draft Law Prohibiting Demonstrations in Mosques . . . Religious Scholars Consider Parliamentary Discussion a Step Towards Crushing Freedoms], al-Masri al-Yawm, December 12, 2007, http://www.almasry-alyoum.com/article2.aspx?ArticleID=860 70&IssueID=886; Ahmad Ramadan, "Qanun man'a al-tazahur fi dur al-'abada . . . mu'amara jadida 'ala misr" [Law Prohibiting Demonstrations in Houses of Worship . . . a New Conspiracy Against Egypt] Ikhwan Online, December 25, 2007, http://www.ikhwanonline.com/Article.asp?ArtID=33080&SecID=250.

43. 'Abdullah Shehata, "Radi yaqtarih mashru'a qanun yulaghi hazr al-nashr" [Radi Suggests a Law to Abolish Censorship, Nowab Ikhwan, February 27, 2009, http://www.nowabikhwan.com/index.aspx?ctrl=press&ID=6cccdcc3-3870-4cae-b59f-fd2b68fb22fb.

44. Article 169 of the Egyptian Constitution.

45. For crime, see al-Zuhra al-'Amir, "Jara'im 2009 . . . misr bi-l-lawn al-ahmar" [Crime in 2009 . . . Egypt Embarrassed], Ikhwan Online, January 1, 2010, http://www.ikhwanonline.com/Article.asp?ArtID=58573&SecID=271.; for sexual harassment, see Ahmad Salih, "Muhakimat barlamaniyya jadida li-fashl al-nizam" [New Parliamentary Hearings on the Failing of the Regime], Ikhwan Online, March 10, 2009, http://ikhwanonline.com/Article.asp?ArtID=46289&SecID=250.; for illegal migration, see "Al-hijra ghayr al-shar'iyya . . . al-hulm wa-l-alm" [Illegal Migration . . . the Dream and the Pain], Ikhwan Online, http://www.ikhwanonline.com/Article.asp?ArtID=11769&SecID=271.

46. Social expenditure reached 42 percent of the annual budget of 2004/2005, raising the wages of workers in the health and education sectors.

47. 'Abd al-Mu'iz Muhammad, "Al-fasad wa-l-rashwah mas'ulan 'an al-inhiyar al-iqtisadi" [Corruption and Bribes are Responsible for the Economic Collapse], Ikhwan Online, October 8, 2005, http://www.ikhwanonline.com/Article. asp?ArtID=14889&SecID=0.

48. Internal debt reached 330 billion EGP and external debt reached 28.7 EGP. See 'Abd al-Mu'iz Muhammad, "Hasad al-dawra al-rabi'a li-nuwab al-ikhwan (3)" [Harvest of the Fourth Round for the Muslim Brotherhood's MPs (3)], Ikhwan Online, July 21, 2004, http://www.ikhwanonline.com/Article.asp?ArtID=7776&SecID=251.

49. "Barlaman misr yunaqish istijwaban li-l-ikhwan 'an al-din al-'am" [The Egyptian Parliament Discusses an Inquiry from the Brotherhood on Public Debt], Ikhwan Online, January 18, 2004, http://www.ikhwanonline.com/Article. asp?ArtID=4178&SecID=0.

50. Between 2000 and 2004, the Egyptian government ran an average annual deficit of 2.65 percent. See "Statistical Abstract of the ESCWA Region for 2005," United Nations Economic and Social Commission for Western Asia, http://css.escwa.org.lb/Abstract/chap09/index.asp.

51. In November 2003, the CAO became subject to the supervision of the President of the Republic, a development which MP Hamdi Hasan criticized.

52. Forty-nine thousand of these cases were concentrated in the oil sector, Ministry of Culture, municipalities, and the Housing sector. "Al-hukuma al-misriyya tasbah fi bahr min al-fasad" [The Egyptian Government Swims in a Sea of Corruption], Ikhwan Online, November 16, 2003, http://www.ikhwanonline.com/Article.asp?ArtID=3443&SecID=0; "nuwwab al-ikhwan yutalibun bi-fath malaff al-fasad min jadid" [The Brotherhood's Deputies Demand Re-opening the Issue of Corruption], Ikhwan Online, December 25, 2004, http://www.ikhwanonline.com/Article.asp?ArtID=9951&SecID=0.

53. The 100 billion Egyptian pounds was the cumulative sum of assets lost in financial corruption cases and illegal money making (drug trafficking, money laundering, bribes, and so on). Several MPs criticized, based on the CAO report, the government for the unnecessary spending of 521 million EGP to buy cars for ministers and finance their travels with research committees. They claimed that the amount spent could have raised the salaries of state employees by more than 20 percent; "Al-hukuma al-misriyya tasbah fi bahr min al-fasad" [The Egyptian Government Swims in a Sea of Corruption], Ikhwan Online, November 16, 2003, http://www.ikhwanonline.com/Article.asp?ArtID=3443&SecID=0; Salih Shalabi, "nuwwab al-ikhwan yaftahun malaff fasad al-hukuma al-misriyya" [Brotherhood Deputies Open the Issue of the Egyptian Government's Corruption], Ikhwan Online, http://www.ikhwanonline.com/Article.asp?ArtID=19025&SecID=271.

54. "'Al-sayid hazin': bidun islah siyasi yatadahur ay iqtisad" [al-Sayid Hazin: Without Political Reform Any Economy Declines], Ikhwan Online, http://ikhwanonline.com/Article.asp?ArtID=4989&SecID=250.

55. "Mustafa 'iwad allah: siyasat al-khaskhasa 'afqadat misr sharikatha wa sharadat 'amalha" [Mustafa 'Iwad Allah: The Policy of Privatization Drove Away Egypt's Companies and Workers], Ikhwan Online, February 17, 2004, http://www.ikhwanonline.com/Article.asp?ArtID=4828&SecID=0 ; "Hasanayn al-shura: 100 miliyar jinih taklifa al-fasad sanawiyan bi-misr" [Hasanayn al-Shura: 100 Million Pounds Lost to Corruption Every Year in Egypt], Ikhwan Online, February 24, 2004, http://www.ikhwanOnline.com/Article.asp?ArtID=4979&SecID=0.

56. Ahmad Sabi', "'Al-adli: nuhadhir al-hukuma min istinzaf al-ihtiyati al-naqdi" [al-Adli: We Warn the Government Against Exhausting the Monetary Reserves], Ikhwan Online, http://www.ikhwanonline.com/Article.asp?ArtID=5216&SecID=250.

57. Ahmad Sabia', "Misr: nuwab al-ikhwan yas'alun ayn qanun man' al-ihtikar?!" [Egypt: The Brotherhood's Deputies Ask Where Is the Law Prohibiting Monopolies?!], Ikhwan Online, http://www.ikhwanonline.com/Article.asp?ArtID=5445&SecID=250.

58. Al-Sayid Zayid, "Duktur al-ghazali: li-l-ikhwan ru'ya iqtisadiyya lakin al-mushkila fi-l-tatbiq" [Dr. al-Ghazali: The Brotherhood has an Economic Vision but the Problem is the Implementation], Islamyoon, August 14, 2008, http://islamyoon. islamonline.net/servlet/Satellite?c=ArticleA_C&cid=1218614721545&pagename= Islamyoun/IYALayout.

59. "Nass radd al-kutla 'ala al-muwazana" [The Text of the Bloc's Reply to the Budget], Nuwwab Ikhwan, June 11, 2008, http://www.nowabikhwan.com/Index. aspx?ctrl=press&ID=2eb8f08f-0635-4ee4-97f6-304e2a2a2c75.

60. Hani Adil, "Isqat 11 istijwaban bi-l-tasfiq li-l-hukuma" [11 Parliamentary Questionings Dropped to Government Applause], Ikhwan Online, March 22, 2009, http:// www.ikhwanonline.com/Article.asp?ArtID=46762&SecID=250.

61. "Al-husayni yuqadim mashru' qanun li-tashdid 'uqubat al-ihtikar" [Al-Husayni Proposes Draft Law to Strengthen the Punishment of Monopolies], Nuwwab Ikhwan, January 13, 2008, http://www.nowabikhwan.com/index. aspx?ctrl=press&ID=220cf723-b3a3-4c14-93f6-1d6b48796b2f.

62. "Mujaz li-ada al-kutla khilal al-dawr al-barlamani 2009" [A Summary of the Bloc's Performance in the 2009 Parliamentary Session], The Muslim Brotherhood, 2009, (unpublished).

63. Sahib al-Sharif, "Istijwab li-radi yatahim al-hukuma bi-ihdar amwal al-manh" [Radi's Parliamentary Questioning Accuses the Government of Wasting Grant Money], Nuwwab Ikhwan, December 24, 2008, http://www.nowabikhwan.com/ index.aspx?ctrl=press&ID=64e11870-e2f3-4162-a8be-c076e3898a44.

64. Muhammad Jamal 'Arifa, "Wasat al-intiqadat: intikhab malakat jamal misr" [The Center of Criticism: Choosing "Miss Egypt"], al-Arabiya, April 24, 2004, http://www.alarabiya.net/articles/2004/04/24/2721.html.

65. 'Abd al-Mu'iz Muhammad, "Azmat al-mudhi'at al-muhajabat bi-misr bi-marahiliha al-niha'iyya" [The Crisis of Veiled Television Presenters in Egypt in its Final Stages], Ikhwan Online, January 25, 2005, http://www.ikhwanonline.com/Article. asp?ArtID=10372&SecID=391.

66. In fact, the Muslim Brothers focused mostly on this issue in the 1979 assembly, when Brotherhood deputies proposed a series of laws to bring Egypt's legislative framework into line with its interpretations of Islamic law..

67. "Majlis al-sh'ab yuwafiq 'ala madd fatrat 'umada al-azhar ila thalath sanawat" [The Egyptian Parliament Agrees to Extend the Terms of al-Azhar's Leaders to Three Years], Nuwwab Ikhwan, December 19, 2006, http://www.nowabikhwan. com/index.aspx?ctrl=press&ID=30b63109-bc1f-4cd5-8631-be8afb8df649.

68. 'Abd al-Mu'iz Muhammad, "Mashru`at qawanin qadamaha al-ikhwan ahrajat al-hukuma" [Draft Laws Presented by the Brotherhood Embarrass the Government], http://www.ikhwanonline.com/Article.asp?ArtID=14597&SecID=251.

69. "Iqtirah bi-l-barlaman al-misri bi-intikhab shaykh al-azhar" [Proposal in the Egyptian Parliament to Elect the Shaykh of al-Azhar], Ikhwan Online, http:// www.ikhwanonline.com/Article.asp?ArtID=4876&SecID=251.

70. Ahmad Yusuf, "Istijwab li-biha' yatahim al-hukuma bi-tafkik jami'at al-azhar" [Biha's Parliamentary Questioning Accuses the Government of Dismantling

al-Azhar University], Nuwwab Ikhwan, http://www.nowabikhwan.com/index.
aspx?ctrl=press&ID=89b6241b-e518-4a43-aae7-d720572d9025.

71. Radi claimed that the intelligence apparatus is interfering in the appointment of
Mosque preachers as well as the preparation of Friday speeches. See Khalifa
al-Dasuqi, "Radi yu'add mashru' qanun yamnah al-'ulama' hasana" [Radi Prepares
Draft Law Granting Religious Scholars Immunity], Nuwwab Ikhwan, October 25,
2007, http://www.nowabikhwan.com/Index.aspx?ctrl=press&ID=eda54edc-0627-
452c-9bb0-91f2856e2f0b.

72. Muhammad Husayn, "Radi yastajawib zaqzuq li-tafwidihi al-amn fi-idarat
al-masajid" [Radi Inquires of Zaqzuq on his Entrusting State Security with the
Administration of Mosques], Nuwwab Ikhwan, http://www.nowabikhwan.com/
index.aspx?ctrl=press&ID=37541dfa-d3cc-40ed-be6d-f11c1c8538fd.

73. Law 88/2003.

74. Khalifa al-Dasuqi, "Al-sikhawi yatrah mashru' qanun al-zaka li-l-ra'y al-'amm"
[al-Sikhawi Presents a Draft Law on al-Zakat to Public Opinion], Nuwwab Ikhwan,
October 29, 2008, http://www.nowabikhwan.com/Index.aspx?ctrl=press&ID=
c90f6caf-c333-4fce-8f29-ae0223f36a3a; 'Abdullah Shehata, "Al-sikhawi yuqadim
mashru'a qanun li-hal mashakil misr al-iqtisadiyya" [al-Sikhawi Submits a Draft
Law to Solve Egypt's Economic Problems], Nuwwab Ikhwan, October 24, 2008,
http://www.nowabikhwan.com/Index.aspx?ctrl=press&ID=20c2ee4b-5dab-4421-
ab98-554a76c77c6b.

75. Law 12/1996.

76. Khalifa al-Dasuqi, "Radi yataqadam bi-mashru' qanun li-l-tifl" [Radi Proposes a
Draft of the Law of the Child], Nuwwab Ikhwan, May 22, 2008, http://www.
nowabikhwan.com/index.aspx?ctrl=press&ID=a6a32b23-ded6-4005-909a-
65263f52f676.

77. 'Abd al-Mu'iz Muhammad, "Al-ikhwan wa-l-dawr al-thalitha: hujum al-qawanin"
[The Muslim Brothers and the Third Session: The Offensive of Laws], Ikhwan
Online, July 16, 2009, http://www.ikhwanonline.com/Article.asp?ArtID=51615&
SecID=251.

78. In particular, the Brotherhood bloc fought the Minister of Culture's 2000 decision
to ban women TV anchors from wearing hijab and the Minister of Education's 2002
permission for universities to ban the niqab on their campuses. On the decision to
ban female TV anchors from wearing the hijab, see "12 mudhi'a misriyya . . . labasna
al-hijab fa-hurimna al-'aml" [12 Female Egyptian Television Presenters . . . They
Wore the Hijab So They Were Prohibited From Working], Ikhwan Online, http://
www.ikhwanonline.com/Article.asp?ArtID=3688&SecID=250; "Al-hijab fi misr . . .
waza'if mamnu'a 'ala al-muhajibat" [The Hijab in Egypt . . . Jobs Off Limits to
Women Who Veil], Ikhwan Online, http://www.ikhwanonline.com/Article.
asp?ArtID=11166&SecID=304; and on banning the niqab, see Mahmud Jum'a,
"Ikhwan misr yarfadun man' al-niqab" [The Egyptian Brotherhood Rejects the
Prohibition on the Niqab], al-Jazeera, October 9, 2009, http://www.aljazeera.net/
NR/EXERES/6797BDD7-59AC-48F3-9C9F-B90809743011.htm.

79. Law 126/2008.

80. Mariam Ali, "Egypt's Child Protection Law Sparks Controversy," July 24, 2008, Ikhwan Web, http://www.ikhwanweb.com/article.php?id=17432&ref=search.php.

81. Ali, "Egypt's child protection law sparks controversy."

82. Reem Leila, "Law Versus Practice," *Al-Ahram Weekly*, no. 906, July 17–23, 2008, http://weekly.ahram.org.eg/2008/906//eg7.htm.

83. Hamdi Hasan, "Hamdi hasan yaktib: kuwuta kuwuta . . . khalasat al'hadawata . . . halwa wa la?" [Hamdi Hasan writes: Quota Quota . . . End of Story . . . Good or Bad?], Nuwwab Ikhwan, June 13, 2009, http://www.nowabikhwan.com/index.aspx?ctrl=press&id=4cdef126-71de-488f-9b27-7ce0afc48bd5.

84. Article 40 of the Egyptian Constitution.

85. "Translation: Muhammad Badie's acceptance speech," Ikhwan Web, January 17, 2010, http://www.ikhwanweb.net/article.php?id=22674.

86. "Translation: Muhammad Badie's acceptance speech."

CHAPTER 3

1. Muhammad Abd Al Qadir Abu Faris, *Safahat min al-tarikh al-siyasi li-l-ikhwan al-muslimin fi al-urdun* [Pages from the Political History of the Muslim Brotherhood in Jordan] (Amman: Dar al-Qur'an, 2000).

2. The complete text of the 2003 platform can be viewed at: http://www.jabha.net/body9.asp?field=LIB&id=1.

3. "Islamists of Jordan: Prepared to Assume Authority," Islam On Line, January 29, 2006.

4. Personal interview, July 5, 2006.

5. The text of the interview can be viewed at http://www.jordanembassyus.org/hmka06192006.htm.

6. A quick review of this issue is Jillian Schwedler and Janine A. Clark, "Islamist-Leftist Cooperation in the Arab World," ISIM Review 18 (Autumn 2006), pp. 10–11, http://www.isim.nl/files/Review_18/Review_18-10.pdf.

7. Ruhayl Al Ghurayba, quoted in *Al Ghad,* September 18, 2006.

CHAPTER 4

1. For more on the arrests related to the Morocco bombings, see "Dozens Held Over Morocco Plot," al-Jazeera English, February 21, 2008, http://english.aljazeera.net/news/africa/2008/02/2008525135916835712.html; "More Arrests in Morocco Plot," al-Jazeera English, February 24, 2008, http://english.aljazeera.net/news/africa/2008/02/2008525131245169340.html.

2. For more on the Morocco arrests (in Arabic), see "Hal hizb al-badil al-hadari al-islami bil-maghrib wa hajiz asliha" [Dissolution of the Islamic Civilizational Alternative Party in Morocco and Confiscation of Weapons], al-Jazeera, February 21, 2008, http://www.aljazeera.net/News/archive/archive?ArchiveId=1084163.

3. "Hiwar ma'a sa'd al-din al-'uthmani, al-amin al-'am li-hizb al-'adala wal-tanmiya al-maghribiyya" [An Interview with Sa'd al-Din al-'Uthmani, General Secretary of the Moroccan Justice and Development Party], *Arab Reform Bulletin,* Carnegie Endowment for International Peace, December/January 2005, http://www. carnegieendowment.org/arb/?fa=show&article=21686&lang=ar.

4. "The Islamists Left Out of the Movement for All Democrats," *al-Sabah,* March 3, 2008, print edition.

5. Muhammad Ma'ruf, "Sadiq al-malik yu'asis hizban maghribiyan jadidan bi-ism al-asala wal-mu'asara" [The King's Friend Founds a New Moroccan Party by the Name "Authenticity and Modernity"], SwissInfo.ch, August 21, 2008, http:// www.swissinfo.ch/ara/index.html?cid=394836.

6. "Al-maghrib..al-'adala wal-himma fi ikhtibar intikhabi ghadan" [Morocco . . . al-'Adala and al-Himma in an Electoral Test Tomorrow], Islam Online, September 18, 20008, http://www.islamonline.net/servlet/Satellite?c= ArticleA_C&cid=1221720099320&pagename=Zone-Arabic-News/NWALayout.

7. The analysis offered in this section is based on the PJD's parliamentary activities between 1997 and 2010.

8. "U.S. Democracy Promotion Policy in the Middle East: The Islamist Dilemma," CRS Report for Congress (Washington, D.C.: Congressional Research Service, June 15, 2006), p. 11.

9. Interview with Sa'd al-Din al-'Uthmani, *al-Khalij Newspaper,* February 13, 2004, print edition.

10. 'Abdullah al-Rashidi, "Ikhwan awn layn yuhawir 'abdullah baha al-qiyadi fi hizb al-'adala al-maghribi" (Ikhwan Online Talks with 'Abdullah Baha the Leader in the Moroccan Justice Party), Ikhwan Online, July 7, 2008, http://www.ikhwanonline. com/Article.asp?ArtID=38661&SecID=341.

11. "Hiwar ma'a sa'd al-din al-'uthmani, al-amin al-'am li-hizb al-'adala wal-tanmiya al-maghribiyya" [An Interview with Sa'd al-Din al-'Uthmani, General Secretary of the Moroccan Justice and Development Party], *Arab Reform Bulletin,* Carnegie Endowment for International Peace, December/January 2005, http://www. carnegieendowment.org/arb/?fa=show&article=21686&lang=ar.

12. "Hiwar ma'a sa'd al-din al-'uthmani, al-amin al-'am li-hizb al-'adala wal-tanmiya al-maghribiyya" [An Interview with Sa'd al-Din al-'Uthmani, General Secretary of the Moroccan Justice and Development Party], *Arab Reform Bulletin,* Carnegie Endowment for International Peace, December/January 2005, http://www. carnegieendowment.org/arb/?fa=show&article=21686&lang=ar.

13. For more on this topic, see Hussam Tamam, "Separating Islam from Political Islam: The Case of Morocco," *Arab Insight,* vol. 1, no.1, Spring 2007, p. 99.

14. For a review of the book (in Arabic), see Usama 'Adnan and 'Abdulawi Likhlafah, "Al-akhta' al-sitta lil-haraka al-islamiyya bil-maghrib: 'ard li-kitab" [The Six Mistakes of the Islamist Movement in Morocco: A Book Review], Islam Online, May 8, 2007, http://www.islamonline.net/servlet/Satellite?c=ArticleA_C&cid= 1178193353442&pagename=Zone-Arabic-Daawa%2FDWALayout.

15. Sa'd al-Din al-'Uthmani, "Al-'uthmani: al-din wal-siyasa fasl la tamyiz" [al-'Uthmani: Religion and Politics a Separation Without Distinction], Islam Online, January 3, 2008, http://www.islamonline.net/servlet/Satellite?c=ArticleA_C&pagename=Zone-Arabic-Daawa%2FDWALayout&cid=1199279245400.

16. Al-Hassan al-Surat, "Nadiya yasin: al-nizam ya'is min al-tafawud ma'a al-'adl wal-ihsan" [Nadia Yasin: The Regime Gave Up on Negotiating With Justice and Charity], al-Jazeera, December 14, 2006, http://www.aljazeera.net/News/archive/archive?ArchiveId=1027025.

17. See, for example, news coverage of PJD MP Mustafa al-Ramid's statements in parliament following the elections, in al-Maghribiyyah, November 1, 2007, print edition.

18. 'Abd al-Kabir al-Minawi, "Al-maghrib: al-intikhabat al-juz'iyya tu'id al-barlamanin aladhin ubtila intikhabuhum ila majlis al-nuwab" [Morocco: The Partial Elections Return the Parliamentarians Whose Elections Were Annulled to the House of Representatives], Asharq al-Awsat, September 21, 2008, http://www.aawsat.com/details.asp?section=4&issueno=10890&article=487694.

19. Results of June 2009 municipal elections from the Moroccan Ministry of Interior, http://www.elections2009.gov.ma/res/Default.aspx.

20. "Ihsa'iyat hizb al-'adala wal-tanmiya hawl tarshihatihi wa nata'ijihi wa tahalufatihi" [The Statistics of the Party for Justice and Development on Its Candidacies, its Results, and Its Alliances], Party for Justice and Development, July 23, 2009, http://www.pjd.ma/ar/spip.php?article36;

21. Results of June 2009 municipal elections from the Moroccan Ministry of Interior, http://www.elections2009.gov.ma/res/Default.aspx.

22. 'Adil Iqli'i, "dua'at al-maghrib wal-siyasa..al-makhzan wal-sirk" [Morocco's Preachers and Politics . . . The Makhzan State and the Circus?], Islam Online, November 14, 2005, http://www.islamonline.net/servlet/Satellite?c=ArticleA_C&pagename=Zone-Arabic-Daawa%2FDWALayout&cid=1172571579499.

CHAPTER 5

1. The best source by far on various Islamic movements in Kuwait is a dissertation by Ali Fahed Al-Zumai, The Intellectual and Historical Development of the Islamic Movement in Kuwait 1950–1981, Ph.D. dissertation, Arabic and Islamic Studies, University of Exeter, 1988. Also very useful are two Arabic-language studies: Falah 'Abd Allah al-Mudayris, Jama'at al-Ikhwan al-Muslimin fi al-Kuwayt [The Society of Muslim Brothers in Kuwait] (Kuwait, 1994); and Sami Nasir al-Khalidi, Al-Ahzab al-Siyasiyya al-Islamiyya fi al-Kuwayt [Islamic Political Parties in Kuwait] (Kuwait, 1999).

2. Isa Shahin, personal interview, Kuwait, October 2006.

3. Mubarak al-Duwayla, personal interview, Kuwait, October 2006.

4. An extremely useful and rich database on Kuwaiti politics, compiled by Michael Herb, can be found at http://www2.gsu.edu/~polmfh/database/database.htm.

5. See Michael Herb, "A Nation of Bureaucrats: Political Participation and Economic Diversification in Kuwait and the United Arab Emirates," International Journal of Middle East Studies, vol. 41, issue 3, August 2009.

6. I have written of the Kuwaiti Islamist movement elsewhere in "Pushing Toward Party Politics: Kuwait's Islamic Constitutional Movement," Carnegie Paper no. 79, January 2007, http://www.carnegieendowment.org/files/cp79_brown_kuwait_final.pdf, and "Kuwait's 2008 Parliamentary Elections: A Setback for Democratic Islamism?" Carnegie Web Commentary, May 2008, http://www.carnegieendowment.org/files/brown_kuwait2.pdf.

7. There is now a fairly large body of writings on attempts to integrate *shari'a* with constitutional law. I have analyzed these efforts with Adel Omar Sherif in "Inscribing the Islamic Shari'a in Arab Constitutional Law," in Yvonne Yazbeck Haddad and Barbara Stowasser, *Islamic Law and the Challenges of Modernity* (Lanham, Md.: Alta Mira Press, 2004) and with Clark Lombardi in "Do Constitutions Requiring Adherence to Shari'a Threaten Human Rights?: How Egypt's Constitutional Court Reconciles Islamic Law with the Liberal Rule of Law," *American University International Law Review,* vol. 21, 2006, pp. 379–435.

8. See Hadas history presented by the party: *Musirat Ithna 'Ashar'Aman,* p. 42.

9. I have written of this in *The Rule of Law in the Arab World* (New York: Cambridge University Press, 1997), Chapter 6. See also Mary Ann Tetrault, *Stories of Democracy* (New York: Columbia University Press, 2000).

CHAPTER 6

1. Muhammad Muhsin al-Zahiri, "Al-mujtama' wal-dawla fil-yaman: dirasa li-'alaqat al-qabila bil-ta'addudiyya al-siyasiyya wal-hizbiyya" [*Society and State in Yemen: A Study of the Relation Between the Tribe and Political and Party Pluralism*] (Cairo: Madbuli, 2004).

2. Sarah Phillips, "Evaluating Political Reform in Yemen," Carnegie Endowment for International Peace, Carnegie Paper No. 80, February 2007, http://www.carnegieendowment.org/files/cp_80_phillips_yemen_final.pdf.

3. Live dialogue with Zayid 'Ali al-Shami, "Al-islamiyun wal-siyasa..tajribat hizb al-islah al-yamani" [Islamists and Politics . . . The Experience of the Yemeni Islah Party], Islam Online, July 6, 2000, http://www.islamonline.net/livedialogue/arabic/Browse.asp?hGuestID=Td3r93.

4. 'Adil al-Shajrabi, "Al-tajammu' al-yamani lil-islah: bayn al-barnamaj al-siyasi wa shi'ar al-islam huwa al- hal" [The Yemeni Congregation for Reform: Between the Political Platform and the Slogan Islam Is the Solution] (Sanaa: Yemeni Observatory for Human Rights, 2008).

5. Ahmad Muhammad al-Daghashi, "Al-salafiyun wal-'amal al-siyasi: jadaliyat al-'alaqa bain al-markaz wal-atraf wa surat al-mustaqbal" [Salafis and Political Activism: The Center-Periphery Dialectics and the Picture of the Future] (Sanaa: Marib Press, 2009).

6. All election results are taken from the United Nations Programme on Governance in the Arab Region, http://www.pogar.org/resources/publications.aspx?cid=22&t=3, and the Yemeni National Information Center, http://yemen-nic.info/contents/Politics/detail.php?ID=9379.

7. Jillian Schwedler, *Faith in Moderation: Islamist Parties in Jordan and Yemen* (Cambridge: Cambridge University Press, 2006), p. 103.

8. As an additional ministerial portfolio, Islah got first the Ministry for Food Security and later the Ministry for Education. See 'Abdullah al-Faqih, "Al-tatawur al-siyasi fil-jumhuriya al-yamaniyya 1990–2009" [The Political Evolution in the Yemeni Republic: 1990–2009], published on http://dralfaqih.blogspot.com/2009/03/1990-2009.html, March 25, 2009.

9. Jillian Schwedler, *Faith in Moderation: Islamist Parties in Jordan and Yemen* (Cambridge: Cambridge University Press, 2006), p. 65.

10. Muhammad 'Abd al-'Ati, "Amin al-tajammu' al-yamani: nakhud al-intikhabat wa natahamal al-hajma" [The Secretary of the Yemeni Congregation: We Contest the Elections and We Endure the Onslaught], interview with Muhammad 'Abdullah al-Yadumi, al-Jazeera, April 23, 2003, http://www.aljazeera.net/news/archive/archive?ArchiveId=52251.

11. See http://www.scer.org.ye/arabic/indexa.htm.

12. Sarah Phillips, *Yemen's Democracy Experiment in Regional Perspective: Patronage and Pluralized Authoritarianism* (New York: Palgrave Macmillan, 2008), p. 165.

13. Ahmed Abdelkareem Saif, "Strengthening Parliaments in Conflict/Post-Conflict Situations: Case Study on Yemen," United Nations Development Programme, 2005, http://www.parlcpr.undp.org/pwdocs/Yemen.pdf.

14. Phone Interview with Rajih Badi, editor-in-chief of Islah's newspaper *al-Sahwa*, conducted on February 12, 2009.

15. Sarah Phillips, *Yemen's Democracy Experiment*, p. 147.

16. Jillian Schwedler, "The Islah Party in Yemen: Political Opportunities and Coalition Building in Transnational Polity," in Quintan Wiktrowicz, ed., *Islamic Activism: A Social Movement Approach* (Bloomington, Ind.: Indiana University Press, 2004), p. 221.

17. Sheila Carapico, "How Yemen's Ruling Party Secured an Electoral Landslide," Middle East Report Online, May 2003, http://www.merip.org/mero/mero051603.html; April Longley, "The High Water of Islamist Politics—The Case of Yemen," *Middle East Journal*, Spring 2007, pp. 240–261.

18. The percentages are based on the numbers and figures of the Supreme Commission of Elections and Referendum, http://www.scer.org.ye. See also Muhammad al-Sayyid Ghanim, "Al-tajarib al-intikhabiyya fil-yaman wa marahil al-tahawul al-dimuqrati" [Electoral Experiences in Yemen and the Stages of Democratic Transformation], al-Jazeera, October 3, 2004, http://www.aljazeera.net/NR/exeres/C836F037-306D-48EA-8124-F1EA5C23B730.htm; National Democratic Institute for International Affairs (NDI), "Report on the 2006 Presidential and Local Council Elections in the Republic of Yemen," http://www.ndi.org/files/2152_ye_report_elections_042407.pdf.

19. Yemeni Congregation for Reform, "Ada' wa mawaqif al-kutla al-niyabiyya lil-tajammu' al-yamani lil-islah 2003-2009" [The Performance and Stances of the Parliamentary Bloc of The Yemeni Congregation for Reform], (Sanaa: The Yemeni Congregation for Reform, 2009).

20. Jalal Ibrahim Faqira, "Al-ada' al-siyasi lil-barlaman al-yamani 1997-2003" [The Political Performance of the Yemeni Parliament 1997-2003], al-Jazeera, April 3, 2004, http://www.aljazeera.net/NR/exeres/E1B6DECE-90C8-473B-8EE9-BE9EB-AC916A5.htm.

21. 'Abduh 'Ayash, "Mashru' intikhab al-muhafizin yujadid khilaf al-sulta wal-mu'arada bil-yaman" [Proposed Amendments to the Governors' Elections Renews the Disputes Between Regime and Opposition in Yemen], al-Jazeera, April 13, 2008, http://www.aljazeera.net/NR/exeres/20957537-DAFD-4122-977A-A440E-8DE4968.htm. See also the text of Law 4/2000 for local councils amended by law 18/2008 and ratified by the Yemeni Parliament on April 17, 2008, Supreme Commission of Elections and Referendum, http://www.scer.org.ye/arabic/authoritylawa.htm.

22. 'Abd al-Salam Tahir, "Al-hizb al-hakim fil-yaman yuwaqi' ma'a al-mu'arada itifaq mubadi' li-daman intikhabat naziha" [The Ruling Party in Yemen Signs an Agreement of Principles with the Opposition to Guarantee Fair Elections], *Asharq al-Awsat*, June 19, 2006, http://www.aawsat.com/details.asp?section=4&article=36 9003&issueno=10065.

23. "Al-lajna al-'aliya lil-intikhabat tu'akid fashalha wa 'adam ahliyatha al-dusturiyya wal-qanuniyya wal-idariyya wal-fanniyya" [The Supreme Committee for Elections Confirms Its Failure and Its Lack of Constitutional, Legal, Administrative, and Technical Capacity], al-Islah.net, September 3, 2006, http://www.al-islah.net/details.aspx?pageid=3663&pagename=gen.

24. 'Abd al-Basit al-Qa'idi, "Al-na'ib 'abd al-razaq al-hijri: man ya'taqid an al-qada' mustaqil wahim, wal-idariyun janah al-sulta al-akhir" [The Deputy 'Abd al-Razaq al-Hijri: Whoever Believes the Judiciary is Independent is Delusional, and the Administration Is the Other Wing of the Authority], *al-Ahali*, February 19, 2009, http://www.alahale.net/includes/print.asp?id=2106.

25. Phone Interview with Rajih Badi, editor-in-chief of Islah's newspaper *al-Sahwa*, conducted on September 18, 2009.

26. "Ijma' barlamani 'ala mashru' 'ashal bi-sha'n qanun al-husul 'ala al-ma'lumat" [Parliamentary Consensus on 'Ashal's Draft on the Issue of Access to Information], al-Islah Net, February 16, 2009, http://www.al-islah.net/print.aspx?pagename=gen&pageid=6946.

27. Yemeni Congregation for Reform, "Ada' wa mawaqif al-kutla al-niyabiyya lil-tajam-mu' al-yamani lil-islah 2003–2009" [The Performance and Stances of the Parliamentary Bloc of the Yemeni Congregation for Reform] (Sanaa: The Yemeni Congregation for Reform, 2009).

28. Yemeni Congregation for Reform, "Ada' wa mawaqif al-kutla al-niyabiyya lil-tajam-mu' al-yamani lil-islah 2003–2009" [The Performance and Stances of the Parliamentary Bloc of the Yemeni Congregation for Reform] (Sanaa: The Yemeni Congregation for Reform, 2009). See also *Asharq al-Awsat*, Hussein al-Jaribani, "Al-yaman: al-islah yansahib min jalsat al-taswit 'ala ta'dilat qanun daribat al-mabi'at" [Yemen: al-Islah Withdraws from the Voting Session on Amendments of the Sales Tax Law], *Asharq al-Awsat*, July 6, 2005, http://www.asharqalawsat.com/details.asp?section=4&issueno=9717&article=310202&feature; "Al-barlaman

yu'id mashru' qanun al-tamwil al-asghar ila al-lajna al-maliyya" [The Parliament Returns the Draft Law on Micro-Finance to the Finance Committee], *al-Sahwa*, March 16, 2009, http://www.alsahwa-yemen.net/view_news.asp?sub_no=1_2009_03_16_69239.

29. Yemeni Congregation for Reform, "Ada' wa mawaqif al-kutla al-niyabiyya lil-tajammu' al-yamani lil-islah 2003-2009" [The Performance and Stances of the Parliamentary Bloc of the Yemeni Congregation for Reform], (Sanaa: The Yemeni Congregation for Reform, 2009).

30. Phone Interview with Rajih Badi, editor-in-chief of Islah's newspaper *al-Sahwa*, conducted on February 12, 2009. See also "Majlis al-nuwab yastakmil munaqasha-tahu taqrir lajnat taqnin ahkam al-shari'a al-islamiyya" [The Deputies' Assembly Completes Its Discussion of the Report of the Committee for the Codification of the Judgments of Islamic Law], website of the Yemeni Parliament, February 11, 2009, http://www.yemenparliament.com/det.php?sid=725; Nabil 'Abd al-Rab, "Al-mawad al-diniyya al-shar'iyya tuthir khilafan bayn al-barlaman wal-hukuma" [The Religious Legal Material Stirs Up a Disagreement Between the Parliament and the Government], al-Motamar.net, February 26, 2005, http://www.almotamar.net/news/19594.htm.

31. Abdul-Aziz Oudah, "The Parliament Increases Age of Marriage to Seventeen," *Yemen Observer*, February 14, 2009, http://www.yobserver.com/local-news/printer-10015774.html.

32. Nabil al-Sufi, "'An hay'at al-fadila: ma'a qudsiyat al-ikhtilat wa did razilat al-riqaba wal-ghuraf al-mughlaqa" [On the Virtue Council: In Defense of Integrating the Sexes and Against the Sin of Censorship and Closed Rooms], Marib Press, August 9, 2008, http://marebpress.net/articles.php?id=4031. See also 'Abd al-Salam Muham-mad, "Bayn takhawuf siyasiyin wa da'm 'ulama kibar bil-hizb - al-amr bil-ma'ruf al-yamaniyya taqsim hizb al-islah" [Between Fears of Politicians and the Support of Prominent Ulama—The Virtue Councils' Divide in the Islah Party], Islam Online, June 14, 2008, http://www.islamonline.net/servlet/Satellite?c=ArticleA_C&pagename=Zone-Arabic-News/NWALayout&cid=1212925307466.

33. In the current parliament, the representation of Islah MPs in standing committees is as follows: 2 out of 11 in workforce and social affairs; 3 out of 17 in constitutional affairs; 2 out 13 in foreign affairs; 3 out of 12 in justice and endowments; 2 out of 11 in local governance; 2 out of 7 in Islamic codification; 2 out of 12 in defense and security; 3 out of 15 in public liberties and human rights; 1 out of 12 in trade and industry; 3 out of 14 in education; 3 out of 10 in information, culture, and tourism; 2 out of 15 in public health; 3 out of 15 in higher education; 2 out of 19 in oil and development; 1 out of 13 in water and environment; 1 out of 17 in services; 3 out of 18 in finance; 1 out of 17 in agriculture, irrigation, and fisheries.

34. Islah By-Laws, 2005.

35. Phone interview with Rajih Badi, editor-in-chief of Islah's newspaper *al-Sahwa*, conducted on March 22, 2009.

36. Mustafa Nasr, "Mu'tamar al-islah..al-ansi: al-mu'tamar waqfa taqyimiyya li-ada' al-islah..al-sufi: al-idara al-hizbiyya al-islahiyya lam tastati' al-inhiyaz lil-barnamaj al-siyasi..al-duktur al-shu'aybi wa huza' yutaliban al-islah bi-mu'arada wataniyya

fa'ila" [Islah's Conference . . . al-Ansi: The Conference Pauses in Assessment of the Performance of Islah . . . al-Sufi: Islah's Party Administration Was Not Able to Prioritize the Political Program . . . Doctor al-Shu'aybi and Huza' Demand from Islah an Effective National Opposition], Saba News, February 2, 2005, http://www.sabanews.net/ar/print87894.htm.

37. 'Abd al-Karim Salam, "Al-islah al-yamani: al-haras al-qadim yu'aziz mawaqi'ahi" [The Yemeni Islah: The Old Guard Strengthens Its Positions], Swiss Info, March 1, 2007, http://www.swissinfo.ch/ara/detail/index.html?cid=5750262.

38. 'Abd al-Qawi al-'Azani, Mansur Bil'aidi, and 'Abd al-Wasi' Rajih, "Fi intikhabat hurra wa tanafusiyya hamalat mufaja'at fil-nata'ij" [In Free and Competitive Elections That Were Characterized by Surprises in the Results], al-Sahwa.net, January 23, 2007, posted at http://www.alshibami.net/saqifa//showthread.php?t=24040.

39. Husayn al-Jaribani, "San'a': masira nisa'iyya lil-daght 'ala al-ahzab li-tazkiyat al-mara'a fil-intikhabat al-mahaliyya" [Sanaa: Female March to Pressure the Parties to Empower Women in the Local Elections], *Asharq al-Awsat,* August 20, 2006, http://www.aawsat.com/details.asp?section=4&article=378867&issueno=10127

CHAPTER 7

1. The early history of the movement is covered in Khalid Nimr Abu al-'Umrayn, *Hamas: Harakat al-Muqawima al-Islamiyya. Juzuruha-Nasha'tuha-Fikruha al-Siyasi* (Markaz al-Hadara al-'Arabiyya, 2001). A leading English-language work is Azzam Tamimi, *Hamas: A History From Within* (Northampton, Mass.: Olive Branch Press, 2008).

2. This state-building effort is analyzed in Nathan J. Brown, *Palestinian Politics After the Oslo Accords: Resuming Arab Palestine* (Berkeley: University of California Press, 2003).

3. The Arabic-language text of the charter can be found at: http://www.islamonline.net/Arabic/doc/2004/03/article11.SHTML.

4. This comes out very clearly in the various works by Khaled Hroub. See most recently *Hamas: A Beginner's Guide* (London and Ann Arbor: Pluto Press, 2006). Also of interest are Nasir al-Din al-Sha'ir, `Amaliyyat al-Salam al-Filastiniyya-al-Isra'iliyya: Wijhat Nazar Islamiyya* (Nablus: Markaz al-Buhuth wa-l-Dirasat al-Filastiniyya, 1999); Jeroen Gunning, *Hamas in Politics: Democracy, Religion, Violence* (New York: Columbia University Press, 2008); and Shaul Mishal and Avraham Sela, *The Palestinian Hamas: Vision, Violence, and Coexistence* (New York: Columbia University Press, 2006).

5. On the evolution of policies toward Hamas, see Nathan J. Brown, "Principled or Stubborn? Western Policy Toward Hamas," *International Spectator,* December 2008.

Index

Contributors

Nathan J. Brown is a non-resident senior associate at the Carnegie Endowment for International Peace and professor of political science and international affairs at the George Washington University. He is a distinguished scholar and author of four well-received books on Arab politics. Brown's most recent book, *Resuming Arab Palestine,* presents research on Palestinian society and governance after the establishment of the Palestinian Authority. His current work focuses on Islamist movements and their role in politics in the Arab world.

In 2009, Brown was named a Carnegie Scholar by the Carnegie Corporation of New York; for the 2009–2010 academic year he is a fellow at the Woodrow Wilson International Center for Scholars. In addition to his academic work Brown has served on advisory committees for Human Rights Watch and the committees drafting the Palestinian and Iraqi constitutions. He has also served as a consultant to USAID, the United Nations Development Program, and several nongovernmental organizations.

Amr Hamzawy is research director and senior associate at the Carnegie Middle East Center. He is author of *The Arab Future: Debates on Democratization, Political Islam, and Resistance,* published in 2010 in Arabic, and co-editor, with Marina Ottaway, of *Getting to Pluralism: Political Actors in the Arab World,* published in 2009. His current work focuses on the changing dynamics of political participation in the Arab world and the role of Islamist movements in Arab politics.

Hamzawy contributes a bi-monthly op-ed for the leading Arab daily *al-Hayat* and several other regional and international newspapers. He serves on the advisory committees for Human Rights Watch, the Arab Council for Social Sciences, and Crisis Action.